The Shadow World

The

Shadow
World

Life between the News
Media and Reality

JIM WILLIS

New York
Westport, Connecticut
London

Library of Congress Cataloging-in-Publication Data

Willis, William James, 1946–
    The shadow world : life between the news media and reality / Jim Willis.
        p.   cm.
    Includes bibliographical references and index.
    ISBN 0–275–93424-1 (alk. paper)   ISBN 0–275–93425–X (pbk. : alk. paper)
    1. Reporters and reporting.   2. Journalism—Objectivity.   3. Mass
media—Objectivity.   4. Reporters and reporting—United States.
5. Journalism—Objectivity—United States.   6. Mass media—
Objectivity—United States.   I. Title.
PN4797.W528   1991
070.4'3—dc20   90–40802

British Library Cataloguing in Publication Data is available.

Library of Congress Catalog Card Number: 90–40802
ISBN: 0–275–93424–1 (hb.)
        0–275–93425–X (pbk.)

First published in 1991

Praeger Publishers, One Madison Avenue, New York, NY   10010
An imprint of Greenwood Publishing Group, Inc.

The paper used in this book complies with the
Permanent Paper Standard issued by the National
Information Standards Organization (Z39.48–1984).

10 9 8 7 6 5 4 3 2 1

This book is dedicated:
Personally, to my father, who was my first writing coach,
and to my mother, who was my first teacher.
Professionally, to those like Bill Evans and John Davenport
who stayed with the *Dallas Morning News*
to bring it from shadows to substance.

Contents

Acknowledgments

This book is a mix of personal insight and of the insight from a great many others who have put much thought into the nature, role, and impact of the news media in the twentieth century. I am indebted to the keen analysis of people like Walter Lippmann, Daniel Boorstin, I. F. Stone, Marshall McLuhan, William Rivers, Ben Bagdikian, William Shirer, John Merrill, Ron Javers, Edwin and Michael Emery, Herbert J. Gans, Michael Schudson, Lewis H. Young, William Boot, Michael Massing, and all the writers and editors of this industry's incisive reviews including *Washington Journalism Review, Columbia Journalism Review*, the *Quill, Nieman Reports*, the *ASNE Bulletin*, and *Editor & Publisher*. In addition, contributors to scholarly journals such as *Journalism Quarterly, Newspaper Research Journal*, and *Public Opinion Quarterly* all have provided valuable commentary and research into the media. One television series that was especially helpful in discussing some of the lies and secrecy problems journalists face was "The Public Mind," reported by Bill Moyers for PBS in 1989. Finally, publications such as *Time* and *Newsweek* are to be commended for their weekly analysis over the years of issues involving the mews media.

I also would like to express my admiration for my colleagues in the journalism department of Ball State University and thank them for their insights over the past two years. My thanks also go to Tonya Carrick, who helped in the research for Chapter 9.

As always, I am indebted to my wife, Diane, and my son, David Min, for their patience and support throughout this year-long project.

1

The Tough Task of Reporting

To a young journalist starting out on a reporting career, the road ahead usually seems straighter than to a more experienced traveler. Fresh from journalism school, the novice still recalls those classroom reporting lectures and the journalism texts that seem to boil the reporting task down to mastering some essential skills. Observe soundly, double-check your facts, stay detached from the story, use proper style and grammar, put the piece into an inverted pyramid format, and you will have a solid piece of journalism to show for it all. If he can somehow do all these things, the young reporter feels he should be successful in portraying accurate pictures of events as they occur. Good reporting thus becomes somewhat formulaic. Do this and that, and you should have a good snapshot of reality. There even seems to be a basic formula for objectivity: Avoid becoming involved in the event, form no prejudicial friendships with actors in the event, leave your own biases at the foot of the stage, and consider yourself the impartial observer for the vast public who cannot personally attend the drama.

WINNING THE BATTLE, BUT NOT THE WAR

At the risk of appearing to minimize these important skills, I would suggest they alone will not get the traveler to the final destination—if that destination is a truthful portrayal of reality. There are still too many obstacles lying in the reporter's path, many of which the journalist has little control over. They must be recognized, and that is the purpose of this book. Since psychologists tell us that recognition of the problem is a large part of the solution itself, it should help the journalist to understand more about the extremely difficult task he or she faces in presenting reality to the public. If the reporter's destination is something less than truth, however, these skills alone *are* enough. The problem is, in too many cases, journalists settle for something less than truth—something called *accuracy*. It is important to note the two concepts are not the same. To illustrate, a journalist could set goals that are defined by the following:

1. Providing an accurate account of what a source or sources said.
2. Portraying an accurate picture of the portion of the event the reporter actually witnessed.
3. Presenting two sides of the story.
4. Presenting an accurate picture of that portion of relevant material which the reporter has uncovered.
5. Presenting an accurate account of information known at the time of the event.
6. Reporting and writing the story in such a way as to uphold the principles of an established ethical code for journalists.

Okay now, you say, what could possibly be wrong with these goals? How could a reporter be criticized for reaching these objectives which, by the way, are not that easy to achieve themselves? What more could you possibly want from a story than that it embodies these characteristics?

Plenty. Plenty, that is, if your goal is presenting reality; if it is presenting truth instead of settling for accuracy. In Journalism 101, accuracy was enough. But this study is meant for journalists who realize the importance of going beyond the basics and untying some of the *real* knots in reporting. On the other hand, maybe these objectives are enough. Maybe, for instance, the sources are telling the truth when they talk with you; maybe there *are* only two sides to this story; maybe the portion of the event you witnessed as a reporter was truly representative of other parts you didn't see; maybe the portion of the official report you uncovered is truly representative of the whole investigation; maybe there is no more information to come forth which is relevant to this investigation or event, and maybe the newsroom code of ethics is explicit and specific enough to cover all reporting situations imaginable. And, finally, maybe you have the expertise enough to understand all the technical matter you have just had to sort through and explain.

Having said all this, however, would you like to lay odds on the likelihood of all—or even a majority—of these being true for the broad spectrum of stories published daily in newspapers or aired over the evening news? How likely is it that they are all true for even *one* story?

IS THE JOB IMPOSSIBLE?

What we're talking about here is a task that some would say is impossible. Nieman Fellow and *Philadelphia Magazine* editor Ron Javers called it that once and noted, "Reporters are ordinary people who have an extraordinary mission."[1] And Walter Lippmann, the philosopher/journalist whom you will encounter several times in the following pages has cautioned that even when the editor is scrupulously fair to "the other side," fairness is not enough. There may be many other sides, unmentioned by any of the organized, financed, and active partisans.

William Rivers, a Stanford journalism professor and former Washington correspondent, has pointed out often that reporters must pursue a variety of leads, not knowing which of them is significant—or even accurate—at the moment of occurrence. Yet all must be given equal weight in the heat of battle until they are proven false—and that proof can be long in coming. The problem, of course, is that the story is being written for public consumption in the heat of the action. Truth doesn't always have time to rise to the surface that quickly. In fact, it seldom does.

The subtitle of this book, *Life between the News Media and Reality*, is not meant to connote some hinterland that is created by consciously bad or biased reporting. It simply suggests that there are a myriad of forces working against the reporter as he or she goes about trying to present a truthful portrayal of "the world outside." The best reporters are those who see these forces as challenges to be overcome through conscientious and creative reporting. But it is very, very hard to do. Reality, as mentioned earlier, is not the same thing as accuracy, as memories of Joseph Pulitzer's famous charge ("There are only three things you need to know about reporting: accuracy, accuracy, and accuracy!") and countless reporting texts would have us believe. The 1950s reporting of Joseph McCarthy's wild and untruthful accusations was accurate; the charges themselves just weren't true. Reality, instead, is built upon truth and, as the *New York Times*'s Anthony Lewis has remarked on several occasions, "Truth is something that is very, very hard to come by."[2]

ACCURACY AND TRUTH

It may well be that reporters can never understand the challenge they face until they see the distinction that can—and often does—exist between accuracy and truth. A quick primer is available in the commercial film *Absence of Malice*, wherein reporter Megan Carter reports accurately that Paul Gallagher is the target of a district attorney's probe but fails to report the truthfulness of the situation, which is unknown to her at the time. That is that he is being targeted, not because of his own complicity in organized crime, but to put pressure on him to testify about his friends who may be involved in the illegal activity. She doesn't know this because she has only seen the portion of the investigative file which the special prosecutor wanted her to see. She feels her job is done when she tries and fails to get Gallagher's side. Her newspaper's attorney advises her that, since she had such a good source for the information (the D.A.'s file), a future libel judgment against the paper is improbable because of absence of malice. Unwittingly, however, she becomes a pawn of the special prosecutor in portraying accurately the contents of his file. She also seriously damages Gallagher's reputation, and the essence of the story is untrue. He is not involved in criminal activity, nor does the prosecutor believe he is.

Going back to the six reporting goals outlined earlier, what happens if there is more to the story beyond the reporter's immediate reach? What happens if there are (as is usually the case) more than two sides to a story? What happens if the sources are misinformed about what they are saying, or if they are simply lying to further their own ends? What happens if a reporter is witnessing a relatively calm sector of an otherwise raucous street demonstration or vice versa? And what happens when the reporter realizes that all journalistic codes of ethics speak much about "fair play" and "balance" and "ethics" yet fail to provide specific, operational definitions of these abstract concepts?

ENTER THE SHADOW WORLD

What happens is that you don't develop a picture of reality. You have something less: hazy pictures of a kind of shadow world that appear all the time in the most responsible of the world's news media. They can be stories of significant events and issues, or of smaller, insignificant ones. Consider, for example, what William Rivers discovered when he studied the coverage of President John F. Kennedy's assassination in Dallas in November of 1963.[3]

Dozens of reporters were in the motorcade with the president when he was shot. Hundreds of others had descended on Dallas a few hours after the shooting. In the inevitable confusion, the accounts varied alarmingly. Some said the rifle used was by the window on the second floor of the Texas School Book Depository, yet others said it was found on the staircase near the fifth floor. Still other accounts had it hidden behind boxes on the second floor. Finally, all reports agreed it was found elsewhere—on the sixth floor.

Other reports about the rifle had it as a U.S. Army or Japanese rifle of .25 caliber, while yet others said it was a .30 caliber Enfield. Ultimately, it emerged as an Italian-made 6.5mm rifle.

In addition, the varying accounts of how many bullet wounds President Kennedy suffered and where he suffered them were in dispute for some time.

Another controversial dispute surrounded the number of stops Lee Harvey Oswald is alleged to have made in the 14 or 15 minutes between the shooting and his arrival at his rental room in Oak Cliff. If all these sightings of him were correct, he would not have had time to be all the places and done all the things attributed to him.

In addition to all of this, at least one radio report told of Vice-President Lyndon Johnson suffering a heart attack upon hearing the news of Kennedy's shooting. Obviously, that did not happen.

While this confusing array of misleading reports may be easily explained by misinformed sources at Parkland Memorial Hospital and within the ranks of the Secret Service, the fact remains that a lot of shadows were being passed on to the public as substance in the hours immediately following the president's shooting.

THE PROBLEM WITH SHADOWS

Some might say we're just talking about simple reporting inaccuracies. Why cloak them in an enigmatic phrase like "shadow world" that makes them seem more foreboding than they really are? After all, even though the above reporting was inaccurate, most of the errors were corrected later and there were good reasons for those errors in the first place. In the end, what harm came from these inaccuracies?

The problem is too many journalists don't seem to see the larger problem that inaccuracies unleash. We're not talking here about the newspaper or television station's credibility problem, although that is also a major consideration. There is an even larger problem that these inaccuracies pose for the general public. Each inaccuracy is like a single brushstroke that paints a world of shadows rather than a world of substance. And some of these shadow paintings can cause big problems for the world. Why? Because even though people may not be observing reality from the media, they nevertheless *live* in reality. And, more disturbingly, they respond to this shadow world in their real world. Walter Lippmann describes it this way:

In all these instances we must note particularly one common factor. It is the insertion between man and his environment of a pseudo-environment. To that pseudo-environment his behavior is a response. But because it is behavior, the consequences, if they are acts, operate not in the pseudo-environment where the behavior is stimulated, but in the real environment where action eventuates. . . . The analyst of public opinion must begin then, by recognizing the triangular relationship between the scene of the action, the human picture of that scene, and the human response to that picture working itself out upon the scene of the action.[4]

Take the following example. Suppose, for the sake of argument, that the 1983 Grenada operation was, in reality, not motivated by a desire to rescue U.S. medical students on the island. Suppose it was primarily an invasion by the United States designed to impose a more favorable rule in this section of the Caribbean. If a major newspaper, conservative in its editorial policy, bought the administration's rescue line and portrayed the event as saving these American students from harm, the response from the believing public would be predictable. Support the administration in its efforts to overthrow these criminals and install more humane leadership to the island. Letters would go to senators and congressmen urging more funds better targeted to helping the efforts in Grenada and similar places, and these letters and phone calls would be used to help justify this—and possible future—involvement in that and other countries.

If you don't like this scenario, take its opposite: Suppose that the operation was not an invasion but primarily a rescue mission. Either way, the point holds true: The way in which an event is portrayed to the public has more influence on how the public reacts than anything else. That was especially the case in Grenada when, not only could members of the public not attend for themselves, but the news media were even barred from the island operation. The problem is that the public's response occurs in the real world—although it is based upon the government's carefully manipulated shadow world which many media often pass on to the public as reality. Any student of Lippmann will notice immediately how this typifies his thinking about the world outside and the pictures in our heads. Since we cannot witness events in the world for ourselves in most cases, we must rely on this pseudo-world that either the media or the government—or both—has inserted between us and the event itself. If that world comes out distorted, so will our response. And, again, that response takes place in, and directly affects, actions in the real world.

MEDIA CONFORMITY AND UNIFORM SHADOWS

At this point, we might begin to see a direct relationship between media conformity (brought about by a reliance on just one or two wire services, the shrinking number of U.S. newspapers, and the similar training most reporters obtain in journalism schools) and the sameness of many shadows presented by the media in this country. Conversely, we should see an inverse relationship between grater media plurality and this uniformity of images. The point is that the more a society is able to tap into a diversity of media content, the less at risk are its people to buy into one particular version of reality and of acting in one uniformly—possibly inappropriate—way. Therefore, what at times is seen as an ideological subject (the plurality of media in a society) becomes a very practical and important one if you consider that responses to media portrayals take place in the real world. If we agree that nearly all media portrayals of reality present varying shades of shadows, then we are better off with a wide array of those portrayals instead of a few that, even collectively, don't present the truth of an issue.

What do media theorists mean when they talk about media plurality? Basically they are talking about the diversity among news organizations that serve the public. But the analysis should go beyond simply counting up the number of newspapers or television stations serving a community. John Merrill of Louisiana State University debunks the myth that there is but one concept of this plurality. Instead, he says, there are at least three types of journalistic plurality.[5] These are:

1. *Media Pluralism*. The traditional thinking among most journalists and many critics of the media is that the more media owners there are in a society, the better its people are served. The idea is that, while one media owner might be tied to a special interest or editorial viewpoint, another media owner might not or, at least, might represent a different viewpoint. Such is the basis for FCC prohibitions against one company's owning both a television station and a daily newspaper in the same market and the FCC's limitation on any one company's owning more than 12 television stations (or serving more than 25 percent of the country's viewership). These are good rules to have around if a society is concerned about the shrinking number of viewpoints coming from the media. Yet the trap we fall into, as Merrill points out, is thinking that a large quantity of media outlets or a diversity of media ownership guarantees a diversity of media content. If the first part of this were true (quantity of media), then the Soviets would be receiving a greater variety of media viewpoints and reality portrayals than any other people in the world. Why? Because the Soviet Union has many more newspapers than any other country in the world. And if the second part of this were true (concerning the diversity of ownership), we would have to assume each newspaper does its own reporting on national and international events and avoids using any cooperative reporting tool such as the Associated Press or United Press International. The news media do, however, rely heavily on these two reporting sources. Therefore, a story bannered across the country by 1,000 dailies may have originated from a single reporter. Clearly, media plurality does not guarantee a diversity of messages.

2. *Message Plurality*. Anytime a wire editor chooses to go routinely with the AP or UPI perception of the day's top stories (and such a "budget" comes across at the start of each wire service cycle), that editor is putting a dent into the breadth of message plurality. This concept rests on the belief that editors at every newspaper will choose for themselves what is newsworthy and what is not. The wire services provide an invaluable function for today's news media, but they also pose a danger. That danger is that editors will stop deciding on news value

themselves and stop taking risks that their front page might not look like every other front page in the country. And when that happens, message plurality is hurt seriously. As noted earlier, this concept has nothing to do with whether the paper is owned by a group or by an individual family. Whether it is one of a hundred newspapers in a media empire or the only paper in the family doesn't affect the decision the editor makes on what stories are newsworthy and how they should be played. To be sure, some influence is always exerted on editors for certain stories to be played either up or down. But that happens in both family-owned and group-owned situations. Many observers feel, in fact, that more influence is exerted by family owned papers, because the owners are usually local and have more interest and involvement in local issues and concerns.

In some ways it is only natural that editors are looking for a standard against which to judge newsworthiness of stories. Daily journalism is full of questions and short on answers when it comes to knowing what to cover, how to cover it, and how to play the story. Since AP and UPI have gained respect over the past several decades in covering such a broad range of stories accurately (although even the wire services have scored significant errors), many editors see them as the standards for excellence in the business. And they see no problem letting these wire services set the national and international news agenda on most days. The problem, of course, is that they may not always be right in their perception of what is big news and what isn't. Is an international terrorist incident always worthy of front-page play? Suppose an individual editor decides the media are encouraging more terrorism by giving it large play. Shouldn't the editor decide for himself or herself to take the story inside, despite the perception of the wire service that it is the major story of the day? In fact, many courageous and independent-minded editors do just that. Buy many don't. To them, if the wire service says it's big news, then it's big news for their papers, too.

I have a reporter friend who once uncovered some rather startling information about a drug operation in the St. Louis area. He had done a lot of digging on the leads he had received, and when he knew he had the story, he presented it to his city editor. What did that editor do? He read the reporter's story and then walked over to the wire editor to see what AP or UPI had on the operation it described. When he found they had nothing, he refused to run the story at all, thinking it too risky and questioning its validity. After all, he thought, why was this newspaper the only one to have such a big story? Shortly thereafter, the reporter left the newspaper and took the unpublished story with him to his new job at a local television station. That station made a five-part series out of the investigative piece, and the reporter won a great deal of acclaim for his accuracy and enterprise.

Editors used to call these exclusive enterprise pieces "scoops." You don't hear much about scoops anymore, because we live in an age that is populated by too many slaves to conformity in the news business. The paradox between conformity and journalistic independence will be discussed later. For now, the point is: Enter conformity, exit message plurality.

One of the reasons many journalists admire the *Washington Post* so much for its Watergate series is not that Bob Woodward and Carl Bernstein recognized the story when they stumbled into it. Newspeople are supposed to do that. What made the *Post* courageous—especially in the initial weeks of the story—was that it continued to run the story at all when no other news media seemed to be chasing it. On more than one occasion, *Post* managing editor Ben Bradlee must have shouted, "Why are *we* the only ones who think this is a story?" Still, the evidence uncovered by Woodward and Bernstein was sufficient to keep the series alive. And the rest, as they say, is history.

3. *Communicator Plurality.* In the end, this may be the most significant kind of plurality, if the desired goal is message plurality. Having a broad range of ethnic, socioeconomic, and geographic backgrounds—mixed among the two sexes and across a range of ages—may exert more of a positive influence on message plurality than any other factor. In addition, not only will a diversity in the reporting corps produce different kinds of stories, it will also produce different perceptions of those stories and different ways in which those stories are told.

In the area of communicator plurality, however, the U.S. news media are not doing well at all. As of 1983, only 3.5 percent of practicing U.S. journalists were black or Hispanic. Another 6.2 percent were Jewish or Asian, leaving more than 90 percent of the journalistic workforce composed of other mainstream, white reporters and editors.[6] This is despite the fact that only 78 percent of the total U.S. population was white in the same year (a percentage that is declining rapidly with the much-heralded "Latinization" of America).

Women were faring better in their media opportunities in 1983 but were still in the minority, accounting for only 34 percent of the news staffs at newspapers, and 33 percent of television news staffs.[7]

All in all, these statistics don't paint a favorable picture for communicator plurality in the United States. One positive sign, however, can be seen. That is in the acknowledged political leanings of journalists in the 1980s. Contrary to popular belief that most journalists embrace liberal politics, survey results indicate most favoring a centrist position.[8] This could be because journalists are sensitive to the charge of being seen as part of a unified, liberal force in this country and so provide survey answers saying they are more moderate than liberal. Or, hopefully, these results may just signify a more balanced political stance on the part of a professional group that is already prone toward embracing neutrality in its work.

AN UNINTENTIONAL SHADOW

The U.S. news media are never without critics, both from the Right and the Left, who charge there is a conspiracy afoot among journalists to portray a certain version of reality. Former Vice-President Spiro T. Agnew was the most vociferous of such critics in the late 1960s and early 1970s, with his tirades against the "liberal, eastern media establishment." The vice-president, speaking in Des Moines, Iowa, denounced the television networks and newspapers for having multiple media holdings and saying these media exercised too much of an influence over public opinion. Clamp limits on their growth, he warned, or they will present an even larger, more distorted view of the world. Time and again he chided the media for their failure to be impartial and fair in their reporting of the Nixon administration, and he criticized network management for using commentators with a leaning toward "eastern establishment bias" and for failing to provide a "wall of separation" between news and comment.[9] In all, this was the first time such a high-ranking government official took such direct aim at the nation's news media, although his aim rested on media he considered to be liberal and not conservative in their political leanings.

Agnew has not been without allies in his public outcry against the news media. More recently, Sen. Jesse Helms of North Carolina, Reed Irvine of Accuracy in Media, and even Ted Turner—founder of CNN—have blasted the "liberal" media for betraying the country. Joining them have been publishers such as Edward L. Gaylord of Gaylord Publishing Co. and Arnaud de Borchgrave, editor of the *Washington Times*. They all claim the media are too liberal for the country and are betraying mainstream American values.

With all due respect to these and other media critics, it is hard to believe that anyone who has ever worked in a newsroom can honestly accuse a news operation of an intentional campaign to betray mainstream American values. Working among journalists, one quickly realizes how difficult it is to get two or three reporters or editors to pool their efforts for any story, save a major disaster like the San Francisco earthquake or an East Coast hurricane. If there is one overriding trait of any experienced journalist, it is skepticism, and that skepticism is omnidirectional, doubting just as much that which takes place within the newsroom as outside of it. Add to that the individual and competitive spirit that many journalists feel—even in this age of wire service uniformity and tradition-bound editors—and a unified attempt at collusion becomes almost impossible. When was the last time you heard of two separately owned newspapers pooling their efforts to cover a story, let alone unite in an editorial campaign? The news media even shrink from the idea of a press pool to cover military engagements, preferring instead to staff the events individually. The news media are not a monolithic brotherhood or sisterhood of like-minded journalists, although certain professional traits do seem to be a common denominator. But these traits—such as independence, skepticism, competitiveness, and working to right a wrong—are not ones which underlie a unified attempt at betraying American values. Indeed, as will be shown in Chapter 2, the values that seem to keep appearing in news stories are the same ones that most Americans hold near and dear.

The fact that the news media present a shadow world to the public should be obvious to even the casual observer. In fact, it's almost inevitable. But we must remember that this world of shadows is, for the most part, an unintentionally incomplete or distorted view of reality, and if they could, journalists would make it conform even more closely to reality.

The following chapters will explore more of the reasons behind the existence of the shadow world. These reasons include everything from faulty journalistic perspectives to the overuse of stereotypes, to relying too heavily on official sources, to reporters who are not specialists in areas they cover, to the inadequate funding and leadership in newsrooms, to bad sources, to a craving for pseudo-news, and on and on the list goes. And yes, it does include shoddy reporting.

To help establish the existence of the shadow world, the following pages will look deeply into some events of the past several decades and compare media portrayals of them to the way in which they were actually played out in history. These events go back as far as the Yellow Journalism days of William Randolph Hearst, and as recently as the media's role in Sen. John Tower's fall from grace as he was denied the post of secretary of defense. These comparisons are not presented to heap coals on the media for intentionally distorting events. Rather, they are meant to show the tremendous challenge facing any journalist who tries to describe a capsule view of reality on deadline.

Finally, the book will discuss techniques and perspectives that journalists can adopt which may lead toward a more correctly focused world of reality. Some of these techniques include perceiving news stories not as single, isolated events, but rather as links in a longer chain. When this historical perspective becomes more focused, the reporter can trace the development of an event and possibly even predict (with some degree of accuracy) its eventual outcome. Obviously this type of reporting, in which the journalist draws from the research techniques of the historian as well as social scientist, takes longer to do and requires more space or airtime to present. Nevertheless, if the news media are serious about presenting more of reality and less of the shadow world, this is an acceptable trade-off. It means, however, that management must funnel more resources into the newsrooms, and that is something many media owners have been reluctant to do. This is especially true in an age where high acquisition prices of newspapers make media groups even more cost-conscious. As media analyst John Morton notes, too many publishers still see the newsroom as a non–revenue-producing center of the newspaper and refuse to make greater investments in the quality of the news product, thinking the economic pay-off will be too late in coming.[10] The paradox, of course, is that without the improved editorial quality, most quality-conscious subscribers will refuse offers of long-term subscriptions.

Another brick in the reporter's road to reality comes from realizing there is more than one way to do the job of reporting and more than one orientation to bring to the task. These various reporting perspectives will be discussed in Chapter 2, but the point is that journalism must break out of its current rut of conformity to one or two approaches to reporting and embrace more innovative techniques. In so doing, reporters can present more of what Maxwell McCombs calls a "social mosaic."

As a close reader of this text will notice, there is this paradox among journalists today: an independent, skeptical, competitive spirit versus a sense that this job of reporting should conform to norms of the past, whether those are worth continuing or not. It's as if, on a day-to-day basis, journalists would prefer to be left alone to do their own job but, in a larger sense, they will do it within the boundaries of tradition and conformity to professional norms.

Harvard management specialist Chris Argyris has long chided newspapers for being slaves to conformity and impervious to real change and innovative thinking. And his viewpoint is not one of the ivory-tower professor, either. Argyris spent over a year as a participant-observer in one of the country's largest newspapers, analyzing its organizational dynamics in the newsroom and recommending changes. Among his chief conclusions are that newsrooms are places low in professional trust and high in professional conformity.[11]

Chapter 7 will focus on the problems associated with generalist reporters who are sent to cover highly technical stories. There is an obvious need for more specialty reporters and editors in the field, and there is some indication that more specialists are being hired for these sensitive and technical stories. For instance, the managing editor of Dow Jones's financial wire service, *Professional Investor Report*, holds degrees in both journalism and economics. Other media are hiring lawyers to cover legal stories, doctors to cover medical matters, and artists/performers to cover the arts. What a better, more truthful view of the world we would have if (1) we had uniformly competent journalists doing the reporting, (2) they were also specialists in their field of coverage, and (3) they realized the historical linkage that connects seemingly isolated brushstrokes into a larger, fuller painting.

So this book is a blend of philosophy and practicality, much like journalism itself should be. It offers an insight into the practice of journalism that often shows the profession coming up short in presenting reality, but it also suggests a few ways out of the dilemma. In no case is this discussion meant to discourage potential journalists who might see an insurmountable challenge in reporting the news of the day truthfully. In fact, if there is one thing that makes journalism such an enticing career to many young people it is this challenge. Journalists are like explorers who possess only crude maps and their own wits to reach their destinations. For many journalists, it is this exploring itself that is so rewarding and enjoyable. Although it may sound cynical, few journalists believe their stories will bring about lasting change. Most realize there always will be individuals and institutions out for personal gain, at the public's expense, despite the presence of prying news media.

Still, to many journalists, just serving as signposts in a confused and frustrated world is more than enough of a reward. Indeed, many journalists feel reporting is more of a calling than a career, more—as Don Quixote might say—an impossible dream than a reachable star.

NOTES

1. Ron Javers, "Journalism: The Necessary Craft," *Nieman Reports*, Autumn 1979, p. 16.
2. Anthony Lewis, "Business and the Media: Anatomy of a Libel Case," Columbia University Graduate School of Journalism Media and Society Seminar, Palo Alto, Calif., 1984.
3. William Rivers, *Finding Facts: Interviewing, Observing, Using Reference Sources* (Englewood Cliffs, N.J.: Prentice-Hall, 1975), pp. 16–17.
4. Walter Lippmann, *Public Opinion* (New York: Macmillan, 1922), pp. 10–11.
5. John C. Merrill, *The Imperative of Freedom* (New York: Hastings House, 1974), pp. 1–20.
6. David H. Weaver and G. Cleveland Wilhoit, *The American Journalist: A Portrait of U.S. News People and Their Work* (Bloomington, Ind.: Indiana University Press, 1986), pp. 19–21.
7. Weaver and Wilhoit, p. 23.
8. Weaver and Wilhoit, pp. 25–26.
9. Edwin Emery and Michael Emery, *The Press and America: An Interpretive History of the Mass Media*, 5th ed. (Englewood Cliffs, N.J.: Prentice-Hall, 1984), pp. 594–97.
10. John Morton, "Are Newspapers Losing Their Grip?" *Washington Journalism Review*, September, 1984, p. 52.
11. Chris Argyris, *Behind the Front Page* (San Francisco: Jossey-Bass, 1975).

2

Setting the Stage for the Shadow World

To begin seeing how journalists enter the shadow world of reporting, we begin with a communication model provided by George Gerbner of the University of Pennsylvania. That model breaks the mass communication process down into phases and shows how each phase influences the message received by the news consumer. For instance, Gerbner explains, the communication process begins when "someone perceives an event and reacts in a situation through some means to make available materials in some form and context, conveying content of some consequence."[1]

If you consider the number of elements described in this communication process, you begin to see how much room there is for reality distortion and faulty communication. For within this communication process that Gerbner describes, can be found (1) a source (reporter, in our case), (2) the source's message, (3) a transmitter (news medium), (4) noise source, and (5) message received. You can even back up one step from the beginning of this model and find the source that the reporter gets his or her message from, and you can go one step past the end of the process and find a decoded message that is often different in meaning from that which was sent. A breakdown in any one of these elements can cause a distorted view of reality for the reader or viewer. This chapter will look at some of the problems that can influence the journalist and the message. It seems natural that we start at the beginning of the process and look at reporter—or message source—considerations.

INFLUENCES ON THE JOURNALIST

The Reporter's Persona

There is not, and never will be, a way to totally define the news reporter's personality. Nevertheless, a lot of researchers are trying to do just that because reporters are so vital to the communication process and the type of messages—distorted or real—that the public gets. Alas, there is no such thing as a single reporting perspective that typifies the industry, regardless of what numerous media critics would have us believe. It is simply and obviously easier for a critic to attack "the media" if he or she can lump all reporters into one category having one perspective on reporting and one common set of values. Sometimes these critics can be found *within* the news media, and it seems odd that they, too, fall into this trap of seeing a monolithic press corps. For example, on March 19, 1984, the publisher of the *Daily Oklahoman*, Edward L. Gaylord, told a group of Oklahoma City businesspeople that many of the prestigious newspapers in the country are populated by radical liberals and are dangerous to the country. "They are a disgrace to the industry," he said. "*The New York Times* and *Washington Post* are just left-wing, radical, propaganda papers. Eastern reporters don't care anything about patriotism. I would call them traitors. They want to take over the country. They think they can run government better. They are out to get Reagan."[2] Not escaping his attack were the major networks and, in particular, Dan Rather and San Donaldson as two who "run wild" with their reporting.

Even though Gaylord seemed to confine his observations to journalists working on East Coast papers and in the networks, it is still ludicrous to cast them all in the same mold—especially the mold he defines. After all, we're talking about a few thousand journalists who come from all parts of the country and all different socioeconomic backgrounds. And, as David Weaver and Cleveland Wilhoit found in their massive, 1983 nationwide study, U.S. journalists represent all five points of the political spectrum, from "pretty far to left" to "pretty far to right."[3] In fact, a nearly equal number of journalists responded to being far-right (18 percent) as those responding far-left (22 percent). Most of the responding journalists (57.5 percent) put themselves squarely in the middle of the road. Even the Lichter-Rothman-Lichter study, published in 1986 (but which used a small sample base than Weaver and Wilhoit), found almost half (46 percent) of the responding journalists to be centrist or right of center in their political leanings.[4] And two of the dominant newspapers represented in this study were the *New York Times* and the *Washington Post*. This is hardly enough documentation for indictments, like Mr. Gaylord's, condemning the press corps for being uniformly liberal.

One interesting attempt at providing an overall look at journalists' values was done by Columbia University sociologist Herbert J. Gans. Performing interviews and a content analysis of stories from CBS, NBC, *Time*, and *Newsweek* over a period of ten years, Gans came up with what he feels is a glimpse into the journalist's mind and heart. For much of that evidence, he looked at the journalists' product, their news stories,

and discovered several "enduring values" which these stories addressed. It is important to note that many news stories address the
violation of these values instead of their maintenance. Gans feels this
may be an effort by the news media to show Americans where we're
deviating from accepted values. Many critics see these violation stories
as simply "bad news" and chide the media for being so occupied with
them. However, many journalists feel this is how the self-righting process works best: by pointing out to the public how, at times, the system
is failing to work at all.

As Gans notes about this procedure in identifying these "enduring
values":

The methods by which I identified the values were impressionistic; the values
really emerged from continual scrutiny of the news over a long time. Some
became apparent . . . from the ways actors and activities are described, the tones
in which stories are written, told, or filmed, and the connotations that accrue
to commonly used nouns and adjectives, especially if neutral terms are available
but not used. When years ago the news reported that Stokely Carmichael had
"turned up" somewhere else; or when another story pointed out that a city was
"plagued by labor problems," the appropriate values were not difficult to discern.[5]

Gans also analyzed the types of people about whom stories were
written to get a feel for the journalists' sense of who is worth reporting
on and who is not. From all these indices, he identified the following
values which he feels are representative of the journalists he studied:

1. *Ethnocentrism*. Children might put this value in the form of "My
dog's better than your dog." To a nation, however, it is a feeling that
its own values and governmental system is superior to any other nation's. Gans feels this value is most recognizable in stories about foreign
countries in which these countries are invariably judged in light of American values and American standards. Therefore, a U.S. reporter in New
Delhi might describe a street scene as utterly chaotic and poverty-
stricken, not realizing these are relative terms and that New Delhi is
decades ahead of other Indian cities, like Calcutta, in its degree of so-
phistication and ability to take care of its own. Next to U.S. standards,
however, his observations hold true.

This ethnocentrism is at the base of placing prime importance on a
story like the recent emigration of thousands of East Germans into West
Germany through Hungary. After all, is not life in democratic West
Germany superior to life in Communist East Germany? It is also at the
base of turning an international story, like the opening ceremonies of
the 1984 summer Olympics, into a flag-waving American story, simply
because the event took place in Los Angeles.

In the movies, this ethnocentrism comes across in the early scenes of

The Year of Living Dangerously, when Australian journalist Guy Hamilton is dumbfounded by what he sees in the streets of Jakarta and realizes he is totally unprepared to understand it or deal with it. It is only as he begins to see Jakarta as the Indonesians see it that he can make sense of it and come close to reporting reality.

Ethnocentrism also appears to be at the base of the kind of coverage devoted by *Time* to the Soviet shootdown of Korean Air Lines Flight 007, as described in Chapter 9. Here there was no attempt at balancing views of the Soviets and the U.S. officials who, while unidentified for the most part, got most of *Time*'s play.[6] Meanwhile questions regarding the culpability of U.S. officials in the disaster got scant attention. When, a few years later, it was a U.S. warship that shot down an Iranian airliner, the magazine's treatment of the incident was decidedly different, blaming neutral high technology for the shootdown as opposed to U.S. error or intentions.

Finally, ethnocentrism is one major reason to only 5 to 10 percent of the news appearing in U.S. newspapers is foreign news. U.S. editors seem to place much more value on domestic news, possibly because this is what many readership studies show to be popular.

2. *Altruistic Democracy.* If the U.S. news media feel their values and standards are superior to other countries, then they also feel altruistic democracy (of the people, by the people, and for the people) is superior to self-interest government. Therefore, when you have a story about a senator or congressman manipulating audiences into buying his self-published book as a favor for addressing the group, you have a story addressing a possible violation of altruistic democracy. Political reporters thrive on seeking out violations of this enduring value, and too much haste in chasing such stories can possibly result in as much damage as good to society. More will be said about this in later chapters.

3. *Responsible Capitalism.* It is interesting, in light of what many media critics perceive as an anti-business posture by the media, that a 1980s study found the opposite may be true: that newspaper business editors may be more in love with capitalism than the general public.[7] Regardless, Gans found a number of stories addressing people or institutions that either upheld this enduring value or violated it. Most of the U.S. media seem to feel that the free enterprise system is the best in the world, albeit with some serious problems. However, when a company decides to take risks that endanger customers, society, or nature in general, it is big news. So when a major oil company causes an oil spill that threatens beaches and wildlife, this is seen as a violation of responsible capitalism. Or when deadly gas is leaked from a foreign plant, half-owned by a U.S. company, the same holds true and it is a solid story.

4. *Small-Town Pastoralism.* Another of Gans's enduring values suggests that the simple is preferred to the complex, that nature and small-

town life and values are superior to the seething problems plaguing the big cities. So when a story comes along about a small town in Maine which is believed to be the last town using hand-cranked telephones with an operator everyone knows, it strikes a responsive, nostalgic chord and winds up in the *New York Times*.

5. *Individualism*. This may be the strongest value represented in stories, in terms of readership. Anytime a reporter can present a story about an individual who is swimming upstream against a strong current, that is going to be a well-read story. The story doesn't even have to be about a person. I wrote a story once about a hundred-year-old grain elevator in an Oklahoma town that caused demolition experts several days worth of grief in trying to remove it so a condo could go in its place. The grain elevator seemed to personify the rugged individual's fight against progress.

6. *Moderatism*. Stories centering on this value will normally address violations of it. Most newspeople will tell you there is no story in reporting, for instance, on a mainstream group like the Humane Society conducting its everyday business. But if you can get a story about a local animal rights group that is picketing a medical research facility which experiments on animals, it will be an interesting piece. This is the same reason organized labor doesn't make much news unless it is striking a plant or other business. Some obvious groups make good subjects for stories addressing the violation of moderatism. These would be the American Nazi Party, the Ku Klux Klan, or, in the 1960s and 1970s, the radical Weathermen group.

7. *Order*. There are so many stories addressing the violation of order, it is impossible to catalogue them. Anytime there is a story about crime, there is a story about the violation of order. The Colombian drug story is a shining example of a story addressing the violation of order.

8. *Leadership*. A story extolling the achievements of a Lee Iacocca is a story about leadership. Many stories also deal with the deviation from good leadership, as in the case of an elected official who makes a wrong decision or misses the chance to make a positive impact.

We've spent some time on these enduring values because they show one way in which the reporter, as the message source, decides what messages will even be sent to the public in the first place. According to this thinking, the reporter will have certain personal values which he or she believes are worthy of maintaining. Gans feels this particular list of values does not constitute a liberal viewpoint at all, but rather a reformist position. Whether that is true or not, these values definitely influence a reporter in what to report on, and the resulting news reports are the messages that are sent to the news consumer.

Still another way of assessing the impact of the reporter on the message sent is to look at the several different perspectives, approaches, or orientations that are present in the journalistic community today. For again, there is no one single way in which journalists assess their job, regardless of what many media critics believe. Some of these orientations, as I see them, are as follows:

1. *The Joe Friday Approach.* As most television buffs remember, Joe Friday was the by-the-book, no-nonsense, quintessential Los Angeles cop, always seeking "just the facts, Ma'am." Applying this perspective to journalism, you come up with the standard J101 textbook approach to reporting which includes the following elements: strict adherence to objectivity (and a belief it can be obtained), total devotion to the facts of the story and the story itself, avoidance of personal involvement in the story, reverence for the basic newswriting format of the inverted pyramid, use of neutral language, avoidance of any subjective impressions concerning the event or people involved in it. These last guidelines go so far as to prefer the attributive verb "said" over all other comers such as "revealed," "insisted," "joked," or "admitted," because these all suggest subjective inferences by the reporter.

2. *The George Plimpton Approach.* Along with the Tom Wolfe Approach which follows, this perspective represents the opposite extreme from the Joe Friday Approach. As the name of its standard-bearer suggests, this is reporting where the journalist gets involved in the action to feel what it's like to sweat with these people, or to feel the jubilation of achievement or the frustration of defeat. It is a quest for greater realism wherein the reporter can deliver these sensations first-hand because he or she is feeling them. It's the type of reporting Plimpton has done so often and which is evidenced in his book *Paper Lion* and *Open Net*. Reporters working in this manner would probably be the first to admit that you sacrifice some objectivity by not distancing yourself from the actors in the event. But they would be quick to add that you get more than you give up, because describing what you—as one of them—are feeling is closer to reality than interviewing someone else on what it felt like to throw a touchdown pass.

3. *The Tom Wolfe Approach.* This perspective has some things in common with the Plimpton approach. For one thing, both approaches value how the story is told as much as what the story has to say. There is a strong literary tradition found in these two approaches that often gets reduced to formulaic writing in the Joe Friday Approach. Yet most of the reporters coming from the Wolfe pack do not go as far as Plimpton in becoming part of the action. Instead, they seek its greater realism through a combination of techniques including:

• The reporter sparing no effort in trying to invade the psyche of the person being interviewed. This is done to such an extent by Wolfe and his followers that it has sometimes been dubbed "imperialistic reporting" by other observers.

- A recording of the most minute mannerisms of the speaker and people listening to him or her.
- A kind of social autopsy where the reporter paints a scene-by-scene portrait of events relating to the story.
- The use of much dialogue, some of which is based on the reporter's impressions of what the individual *would* say, given his or her personality and similar reactions to stimuli.
- Adapting techniques of fiction writing, such as starting with details that lead to mounting action and climax, followed by a neat—and often surprising—ending. Incidentally, this technique is often found in stories not of the Wolfe genre, as in much of the reporting on television news programs like "60 Minutes" or "20/20".

4. *The Scientific Approach.* If one is thinking in terms of story documentation, this would be on the pole opposite the Tom Wolfe Approach. Championed by such people as Philip Meyer, in his book *Precision Journalism*, this approach insists that reporters must have better documentation if their stories are going to mirror reality. And, say these journalists, some of the best documentation is found in quantitative research techniques such as those used by social scientists and including the random sample survey, content analysis, and controlled experiments. By understanding and adapting these research methods to reporting, the journalist is better able to explain—and predict—trends and events happening in society. These social-science journalists explain that many of these statistics are already being kept by the institutions reporters cover. Therefore, it is easy for reporters to obtain this information as they go about covering their beats. Back in the newsroom, if these reporters would apply some statistical analysis to this trend data, they at least would have a solid springboard from which to interview officials about these problems or societal improvements.

An elaboration of this precision journalism was formally introduced in 1976 by Maxwell McCombs, Donald Shaw, and David Grey. Termed "Social Indicator Reporting," this perspective calls upon journalists to avoid traditional "iceberg journalism" which only gives readers the tip of the story and instead to pull together the historical and contextual strands—hopefully using some of Meyer's methodology as well—into a more complete "social mosaic." The researchers cite Raymond A. Bauer's Definition of social indicators when they note:

Social indicators include all forms of evidence that enable us to assess where we stand and are going with respect to our values and goals, and to evaluate specific programs and determine their impact. . . . A small number of observers can monitor vast segments of the community from such vantage points. . . . The traditional use of the news beat is steeped in the event-orientation of the press. . . . This new viewpoint calls for a broader, more systematic look at the data compiled by public agencies. It looks beyond the single obtruding event to see the mosaic, to see how all the pieces fit together.[8]

5. *The Woodstein Approach.* Popularized in the 1970s by Bob Woodward and Carl Bernstein of Watergate fame, this is the investigative approach to journalism. While some observers believe it is characteristic of all reporting, I do not. There are some unique aspects of investigative reporting that the everyday beat reporter does not have the luxury to use. For one thing, investigative reporting takes a great deal of time, even though much of that time may be spent on researching just one story or one aspect of it. It takes reporters out of the daily production of copy and allows them to devote weeks or months to the production of one story or a short series of stories. A St. Louis television news director, for instance, told his two "I-Team" reporters when he formed the team that he didn't expect to see them around the newsroom much. Often these two journalists were gone for a month at a time but, when they returned, they generally had some excellent enterprise pieces. So it is expensive reporting for the news medium, and that is why fewer newspapers—and very few television stations—still have identifiable investigative reporting teams.

A second aspect of the Woodstein Approach also makes it somewhat unique. As it is practiced by so many investigative reporters, dating back to *McClure's* Lincoln Steffens, this is a somewhat cynical viewpoint of the world. For example, Steffens was fond of saying he would go into reporting situations assuming corruption was present. It was simply his job to ferret it out and bring the perpetrators to light. It is a perspective that often leaves the reporter with a feeling that people are more wrong than right with regards to morality and contributions to society. Possibly this is because investigative reporters are in the business of making public something which someone else is trying to keep secret. Or possibly it is because these reporters have been lied to one too many times for them to trust people very much.

Because of the utter devotion to the story, investigative reporters will often evidence another characteristic: a belief that, in most cases, the ends justify the means of getting the story. Even a casual reading of Woodward and Bernstein's *All the President's Men* will reveal the number of schemes these two journalists used just to get sources to be candid and honest with them. At times, the methodology behind this and other stories they did seemed to bother Woodward. Speaking at the Defense Information School at the Army's Fort Benjamin Harrison, for example, Woodward cited the infamous Janet Cooke story which he, as metro editor, was responsible for releasing to the public. In that story, to be discussed in detail in Chapter 9, the reporter manufactured an eight-year-old heroin addict which she passed off as a real child in the story.

The piece won a Pulitzer Prize, and then the hoax was revealed. The *Washington Post* handed back its prize, made a public apology, and fired Cooke. In reflecting on that story, Woodward said he should have acted more humanely and thought first about helping the addicted child. Instead, he said, he thought about what a great story it was and published it without checking enough on its validity or on who this child was or how he could be helped. Had he taken that perspective, he not only would have displayed more humanity but might also have prevented the *Post* from its most embarrassing moment to date.

6. *The Friendly Eye Approach*. This is the approach that characterizes such journalists as former literary great William Dean Howells. An editor of *Harper's* magazine, Howells was a product of the Realism Movement, but he defined realism as seeing life steadily and wholly and not letting crises or momentary reactions play a bigger part in characterizing a person than they should. When a reporter does his or her homework on their subject, Howells would say, they will often find the kindlier view of man is apt to be the truer view. Because of this view, the Friendly Eye Approach could be placed on the opposite extreme of the Woodstein Approach, at least as regards the inevitable cynicism that makes up much of investigative journalism.

7. *The Who–Shot–J. R. Approach*. The August 11, 1980, cover of *Time* featured an artist's rendering of television bad guy J. R. Ewing of "Dallas" fame. The single-word headline above the picture was, "WHO-DUNIT?" As even casual viewers knew during the summer of 1980, that was the big question to be answered come September and the renewal of the series. So it may not be surprising to some that newspapers like the *St. Louis Post-Dispatch* featured front-page stories on Saturday, September 20 (the morning after the attacker's identity was revealed), letting their readers know the culprit was Kristin Shepard. The magnitude of this story was amazing.

All this is fascinating, but what does it have to do with journalism? Just this: The J. R. Ewing saga is a classic example of shadow passing itself off as substance to millions of Americans. And it is doing it with the help of the U.S. *news* media. I even remember reading about a southern church congregation getting so carried away with the drama that it actually prayed for the soul of J. R., should he die. Now *that* is news, even though it is bizarre behavior generated by so many news media stories about the J. R. mystery.

Daniel J. Boorstin, librarian-emeritus of Congress, refers to this type of sensation-seeking reporting as *pseudo-journalism*.[9] It comes from the knowledge reporters have that America is yearning for the image: for something more bizarre, more exciting than people think they can experience with reality. The problem, Boorstin notes, is that the news media (in their race to get readers and viewers) are serving up that image by reporting on a wide range of pseudo-events. What is a pseudo-event? Briefly, it is an event that is designed to be dramatic and, therefore, features much more flash than substance. It is planned, as opposed to spontaneous, and it has little—if any—significance on the life of readers or viewers. In fact, the only impact many of these events have on the public is to titillate them, make them laugh, or utter a gee whiz! The problem is this is a manipulated gee whiz and outside the arena of real news and into the arena of public relations and/or sales.

This critique is not meant to discount the importance of the media's entertainment function. It is simply a plea for an understanding that this *is* entertainment and shouldn't be interpreted as news.

Where reporters fall prey most often to pseudo-journalism, however, is not in chasing the J. R. Ewing stories but in chasing subtler events and lower-profile personalities who try to disguise their press conferences or staged events as newsworthy. On more than one occasion, reporters have been made to look foolish by their over-reliance on the press conference, in fact. Several years ago, for instance, a New York journalism professor claimed to be a medical researcher who had found a cure for infertility in a giant cockroach pill. He assembled some fake documentation and, with his disguised identity, called a press conference in New York City that was attended by several reporters, including those from the wire services. These reporters wrote their story and dispatched it, with the result that many dailies picked it up around the country. Finally, the professor came forward and announced that he had successfully—and rather easily—hoodwinked a gullible press with his fake identity, fake documentation, fake story, and fake press conference. The lesson for the media was clear: Just because an event may be easy to cover doesn't mean you're getting a clear picture of reality. A sobering picture of how much the media rely on routine channels of information was portrayed in a recent study that found over half the stories in researched editions of the *New York Times* and the *Washington Post* (and over two-thirds of all wire stories) came through routine channels of information like press conferences, press releases, and official proceedings.[10]

8. *The Libertarian Approach.* Most of the earlier approaches—with the possible exception of pseudo-journalism—evidence a kind of group social consciousness on the part of reporters. Journalists who would follow the Joe Friday or Woodstein or Friendly Eye or other perspectives would say they must keep their social obligation in the forefront of their thinking as they attack their work. Libertarian journalists, on the other hand, see a threat in this social responsibility theory of the media. To them it represents just one more attempt at censoring the individual journalist, at returning a society to its authoritarian roots. It isn't that libertarian journalists don't believe in being responsible to society. Generally they

do. It's just that these reporters want the freedom to determine that responsibility for themselves. It is this personal freedom to report and write the way they see the story that LSU's John C. Merrill calls the imperative of freedom.[11] And, Merrill feels, this personal freedom should serve to keep even editors at bay from dictating to reporters what to cover and how to cover it. He resents any conformity to professional codes that robs journalists of their selfhoods by forcing a mass-mindedness upon them. The journalist must be free, and the press must be autonomous, no matter how it performs its function. In other words, freedom is an end in itself. It is not just to be used to secure a worthy end. The social responsibility theory carries with it an implication that someone else will judge for the individual reporter what is right and fair and ethical. To the libertarian, that is dangerously close to authoritarianism.

The reason for taking so much time in outlining these various reporting perspectives is that each will influence how a story—the story the public sees—is molded and fashioned. Thus, they and the factors that follow are influential on the message source who is always a very human link in the chain of communication. Often these very human reporters get caught up in a type of thinking that seems to make conditions even more favorable for the shadow world. This thinking is known as two-valued logic.

Two-Valued Orientations

In the years preceding the Revolutionary War, Boston radical Samuel Adams worried the colonists might not want to endure a prolonged battle for independence. To help cement their determination, he organized the Committees of Correspondence to spread inflammatory messages about the British occupational troops in the colonies. The messages from these patriots' pens were phrased in a carefully crafted manner, formalized by Adams, who once called himself the anonymous manipulator of man, events, and nations. Edwin and Michael Emery wrote of this patriot, "Sam Adams was not only the propagandist of the revolution, but he was the greatest of them all. He was truly the 'master of puppets' and 'assassin of reputations' as his enemies dubbed him."[12]

Adams's form of presentation was based on several guidelines including:

1. Advertising the eventual rewards of victory while minimizing the risks of defeat.
2. Neutralizing any opposition, no matter how logical.
3. Phrasing all issues concerning separation in black and white, right and wrong,

patriot and British. There would be no room for common ground nor gradations of viewpoints to distract prospective converts to the patriot cause.

Among other legacies, this technique left an irony in U.S. history: Those who would cry the loudest for independence and human rights would be the same ones to deny others the same rights. Since there were only two ways to view the issue of separation, and since only one (the patriots') view was correct, the Tory viewpoint was evil and dangerous. So Tory publishers like James Rivington saw their newspapers torched by zealous purveyors of freedom like Sam Adams. Ironic indeed.

An even more lasting legacy of this propaganda technique, however, is the narrow and confining vantage point it places on issues. Semanticists like S. I. Hayakawa refer to such a two-sided presentation as two-valued logic or two-valued orientations to language and issues.[13] Used consciously, it represents an intentional method of simplifying issues, even though the simplification causes distortion, as later discussion on the embedding process will point out. A writer does not have to advocate one of the two viewpoints to use the two-valued logic. Indeed, all good reporters avoid any such endorsement in their stories. However, anytime a complex issue (and most are complex) is boiled down to only two sides, two-valued logic is at work. This technique did not originate with Adams. Nor did it end with him. Poet John Milton had opposed the two-valued thinking of Oliver Cromwell in 1644 when he penned his *Areopagitica*. In the treatise, Milton argued for allowing a multitude of opinions to have their day in the public arena. The truest of them would survive; the weaker and untrue viewpoints would perish in combat.[14] Later in America, the framers of the Constitution borrowed from Milton's reasoning when they drafted the First Amendment and called for many voices to be heard on issues and opinions.

Two-valued thinking also has been used by some of the world's worst criminals. Hitler, for example, used two-valued logic throughout his propaganda blitz engineered by Joseph Goebbels. Together, they classified almost everything and everyone into one of two competing groups: Aryan (good) and non-Aryan (evil). The lion, for example, was said to be an Aryan animal because of its strength and power; the lamb was obviously non-Aryan.[15] There was simply no other way of seeing anything.

Today, the Soviet Union and United States use many of Adams's techniques. Thought patterns are divided into Eastern and Western; the entire world seems a dialectic of good and evil, depending on one's political perspective. There are few, if any, gradations of viewpoints presented by national leaders. Such refusal to admit the existence of common ground impedes progress in many arenas of negotiations the world over.

The British adopted two-valued logic in minimizing or concealing the losses in the Falklands War; the United States took the example further in denying the press the right even to cover the Grenada operation. The nation was told by President Reagan—following the invasion—that there were only two perspectives from which to view the operation: his own and the Communists'. There was no middle ground.

It is difficult to justify a democratic leader's use of this two-valued logic, although all presidents have used it. When the institution charged with being the independent, detached observer for the American public—the Fourth Estate—starts using the logic, justification is harder still. Nevertheless the media do use two-valued thinking in so many of their stories. Part of this is due to the nature of news. Two of the most universally accepted notions of news are that (1) news is an event or person or issue that deviates from the norm and (2) a news event is one that includes conflict, either overt or covert. In each case, two poles get the media's attention. In the former, it is the norm and the deviation; in the latter, it is the two people, emotions, or ideas in conflict. The stronger the polarity, the stronger the news story. The weaker the polarity, the weaker the story and the poorer the play.

What contributes to such weakness? The existence of mitigating circumstances, tertiary viewpoints, or common ground. Recently I overheard a newsroom conversation between an editor and his reporter who had discovered that an elected official was under pressure to resign for his poor attendance at recent meetings. The editor considered this a potential front-page story because the norm of responsible public service (leadership as Gans would see it) was being violated. The reporter then said he had not been able to reach the official to question him about his absences. Should he continue trying or present the story without the reasons? "Well," the editor pondered, "we could let it go as is without the reasons and have a pretty strong story of an irresponsible town board member. Or you could call him and see if his reasons are good. But if they are, we probably have a weaker story." To his credit, the editor ordered the reporter to continue calling, and the reporter finally made contact. He found the reasons for the absences were due to a continuing illness in the official's immediate family, and he verified this to be true. The story went deep inside in the next issue.

As a former editor, I have fallen victim to this two-valued logic many times. Indeed, my best memories of strong stories were when a reporter would bring in a clear-cut conflict; my worst memories were when the reporter would lay out the conflict but added, "Although, it's really not such a conflict because . . . " I felt at times like yelling, "Hey! Don't tell me that!"

At times, the news media's portrayal of reality seems perilously close to a television soap opera where good and evil are etched ever so obviously in characters. And, like a soap opera, the stronger the conflict between these characters, the better the show and the greater the audience pull. The great press barons have all realized the marketability of a good conflict.

So the very nature of news gives reason for editors to honor Adams's two-sided way of telling a good story.

If this all seems like an ivory-tower attack against an institution that can really do no better, that may be. The news media, after all, operate on something called deadlines, and only so much can be done between editions. That doesn't help, however, in giving the public a daily dose of reality if other viewpoints go unreported. In a recent talk, Bob Woodward addressed this issue and said if reporters had to chase down every possible viewpoint to a story, few stories would ever get into print. The best the press can do, he said, is to present what is documented at the time, then add to the story in later editions. After all, that was the scenario of the Watergate stories. Still, even Woodward would agree that the best reporters are those that use the time they have to exhaust as many possible viewpoints to a story as possible.

Hayakawa notes that some of the reason behind the two-valued logic is the need for ascribing people, ideas, or issues to one classification or another. Picture a postal clerk sorting mail into different post office boxes, and you have this idea personified. It is easier to find a document when it is pigeon-holed; it is easier to grasp an issue if there are only two sides to it, and each is clearly marked right or wrong. One is either a liberal or conservative; one is either a materialist or an idealist. There is little common ground, few (if any) gradations of viewpoint. Because of this, meaning is distorted; subtleties lost. Yet to news media restricted by time, space, and audience attention span, such labels are seen as vital to attracting the modern, busy news consumer, presenting the polarization as quickly as possible to grab the attention of readers or viewers.

INFLUENCES ON THE MESSAGE

In addition to the journalist, there are several other influences on the message that appears in print or over the air. Included in these are the story's structure, the depth of reporting, the marketing orientation, the tendency to stereotype, good and bad story sources, organizational requirements, and quality of newsroom leadership.

The Inverted Pyramid: Useful, Troublesome

The story structure most helpful in presenting a conflict quickly is the inverted pyramid, known to every student of journalism from high school days forward. In one sense it is simply a way of arranging facts in a story; in another sense it actually does things to the meaning of that story and the portrayal of reality it contains.

In its basic form, the inverted pyramid calls for a summary lead of one to two brief paragraphs in which most of the major questions posed by the story are answered. Typically these have been known as the "five W's and H," although more astute journalists have recently been tacking on the "SW" or the So What. The origin of the inverted pyramid in this country seems to have arisen from Civil War days when Northern correspondents, writing behind enemy lines, saw the need to pack as much into their opening paragraphs before sending them over telegraph lines which could be cut by Southern troops at any moment.

What is not detailed in most reporting textbooks, however, is another aspect of the summary lead which most editors want. That is a clear statement of the conflict, without which there would probably be no story at all. Therefore, the inverted pyramid—functional as it is—poses a problem in that it shoves the conflict to the fore. Coincidentally, the journalist is taught to keep his lead paragraphs short (generally no longer than 40 words each), and this leaves little room for the revelation of any middle ground existing in the conflict. That usually comes later in the story where it does not dilute the punch of the lead's statement of conflict. Memories still ring clear in my mind of a state editor at the *Daily Oklahoman* who constantly insisted that we reporters "punch up" our leads. I recall one particular story about a jail escape in which I described a lone prisoner scrambling over a hospital wall and into the night. When the story appeared, however, the prisoner was "scaling a wall amid a hail of gunfire," which in reality amounted to one or two misdirected shots at most.

It's not that I don't understand the need for crisp, punchy leads. But it's always nice when they conform to reality and don't distort it too much just for the sake of readership.

Marketing's Influence on the Story

The media's penchant for classifying people and ideas into polarized groups is partially based on the impact of market orientation. Recently a top newspaper consultant called the media's increasing interest in marketing the most important and most favorable thing to happen to newspapers in decades. Yet what have marketing studies shown? Taking the product of such research, *USA Today*, one finds much of the public asking for shorter stories, simplified issues, stories of obvious conflicts and little interpretive or investigative reporting. Most editors don't believe readers of local newspapers want any of this in large measure, but obviously much of the reading public does, or *USA Today* would not be the second leading U.S. daily in circulation. And to have this format, editors must have ready-to-use classification systems; they must adopt a two-valued orientation for many stories that punches up the conflict and makes it as obvious to the reader as possible.

In the interest of fairness, a reporter does toss the same tough questions at a Democratic president that he or she would aim at a Republican president. In the process, though, the reporter is ever seeking out the conflict. No answer is the "right" answer; it only leads to another question that seeks to perpetuate the conflict. Consider the presidential press conference wherein a chief aim is to get the president to say something quotable and, hopefully, significant. When President Reagan was first questioned about the rumors of a Libyan hit squad on the prowl for him, he at first ducked the issue despite persistent reporters' questions. When he did relent and confirm the rumors to be true, however, at least one reporter demanded, "Sir, don't you feel it is unwise to make such an admission?" Small wonder some public officials feel badgered by the press at times, but such gyrations are necessary if the two-valued orientation—and the conflict it represents—are to be kept alive.

Exceptions to the Rule

Despite all this, there are still many opportunities for journalists to desert this two-valued orientation and engage in some serious *interpretive* journalism that ropes in several alternative viewpoints to stories. Journals of interpretive reporting still exist with papers such as the *New York Times, Washington Post, Los Angeles Times, Christian Science Monitor*, and the weekly newsmagazines. And on television, there are shows like "This Week With David Brinkley" and "The MacNeil-Lehrer News Hour." Still, one has only to look at the time slots for these programs and others like "Nightline" to see they are not the prime-time shows that the conflict-oriented network newscasts are. Yet it's good to see them on the air. May their number increase.

Iceberg Reporting and Reality

McCombs has called the traditional focus of the media the "iceberg theory" of reporting. He describes it this way:

Just as radar scans sea lanes for the tips of icebergs portending danger, the news media daily scan the local community and the nation for signs of imminent disruption and danger. That, of course, is part of the job of the press but the unaided human observer unfortunately can describe only the tip of the iceberg. The major portion . . . remains invisible and undescribed beneath the surface. The analogy holds. Public affairs reporting, with its emphasis on discrete news events, typically describes only the tips of our social icebergs and usually only when they are close to being major disruptive forces in our communities. But the capability is available for the profession to render much more valuable service.[16]

Ways in which reporters can tap these capabilities will be covered in the last chapter of this book. For now, we are describing pathways—indeed sometimes highways—into the journalist's shadow world. This event-orientation in reporting is one such road. For even if the events described or the statements published are accurate in and of themselves, that does not mean they accurately represent the larger truth of the situation. In Chapter 1, reference was made to the "straitjacket reporting" surrounding coverage of Sen. Joseph McCarthy in the early 1950s. Yes, his quoted statements were accurate. No, they were not true. So a restrictive perspective on objectivity cased the media to become an unwitting aide to McCarthyism.

Several examples in coming chapters will show how inadequate this iceberg reporting, which focuses on individual events as if they are somehow disconnected from the string of history or other events, really is. After all, we *are* talking about truthful portrayals of reality. Because of so much attention to individual conflict-laden events, it is no wonder that every year the wire services' list of top-ten stories is laden with event-oriented stories, while the list of top-ten most underreported stories is laden with issue-oriented stories.

The Tendency to Stereotype

Journalists are no different than anyone else in several regards. One similarity, for instance, is the tendency of all journalists to stereotype people, issues, and situations. Possibly some journalists do it less than nonjournalists because they make a living looking at facts, but the tendency is still there, especially when the facts are not fully known or the deadline is pressing too quickly for a more accurate description. What is stereotyping exactly? In one sense it is a simple admission that journalists—like every other human being—do not bring a blank slate of experiences, values, and attitudes into their job. And these experiences serve as a guide for what the journalist selects out of his or her surroundings and how they should view those things. Walter Lippmann, who wrote so often about the impact of stereotyping, described it this way:

For the most part we do not first see, and then define. We define first and then we see. In the great blooming, buzzing confusion of the outer world we pick out what our culture has already defined for us, and we tend to perceive that which we have picked out in the form stereotyped for us by our culture. . . . In untrained observation we pick recognizable signs out of the environment. The signs stand for ideas, and these ideas we fill out with our stock of images. We do not so much *see* this man and that sunset; rather we notice that the thing is man or sunset, and then see chiefly what our mind is already full of on this subjects.[17]

The problem is that a stereotype is a generality, and all generalizations leave something to be desired in the interest of accuracy. A Democratic presidential candidate may be a liberal, but he may also be a conservative on several issues. But stereotypes don't deliver these subtleties. As Lippmann notes, there is neither time nor chance for intimate acquaintance. Instead, we perceive a trait that signals a familiar type, and we fill in the rest of the picture with our own stereotypes. We may be told a man is a labor leader and scroll up a particular image; we may be told someone is a Harvard man and scroll up another instant image. And, if believing these stereotypes to be true isn't bad enough, often we believe everyone else shares our same image of these people. In other words, we chalk them up to "common sense," only to find what is common sense to someone else, may not be to us. For instance, a professor in graduate school one day asked us each to write out on a sheet of paper where the "West" begins in America. I recall my surprise when, after I chose Arkansas, someone else had chosen Indiana, and another person had even chosen western Pennsylvania. It is interesting, and possibly not so surprising, that I grew up in Oklahoma, while the other two grew up in Pennsylvania and New York respectively. Our backgrounds had colored our "common sense."

Certainly there is some value in stereotypes and also some truth. Most members of the ACLU probably are card-carrying (whatever that means) liberals. Most, if not all, members of the Ku Klux Klan, believe in white superiority and the inferiority of blacks, Jews, and Catholics. Stereotypes provide easy baskets to drop all these traits into without taking up lines of copy explaining them. Still, they often are inappropriately used, and sometimes are flat-out inaccurate. When they are, the story's portrayal of reality is distorted. Lippmann notes that if our philosophy informs us that each person is only a small part of the world, that his or her intelligence catches only phases or aspects in a course net of ideas, then, when we use our stereotypes, we tend to know that they are only generalities, to hold them lightly, to revise them happily.[18]

Good and Bad Story Sources

In Chapter 1, we saw how many different statements masquerading as facts came out of one event: the assassination of President John F. Kennedy in 1963. One reason for so many inaccuracies early on in that story was that some sources were good and some were bad. Some were relating what they saw, others were relating what they had been told or what they had assumed. Still other sources embellished their accounts a great deal. That tends to happen in the moments after being a part of a tragedy like that. Adrenaline flows in the veins of witnesses as well as reporters on deadline.

There was a time when reporters felt like they were let off the hook if an inaccuracy in their story could be attributed to a bad source. After all, it was reasoned, that was *his* fault, not mine. I did my job in accurately quoting him. If he was wrong about what he told me, that is his problem. While some reporters may still feel vindicated in this manner, most don't. Today the notion of accuracy goes beyond simply recording what a source said and parroting it back to the public. The idea of accuracy today allows for—and in most cases demands—that statements be verified as truthful. The best reporters are those who do try to verify information before they use it. The mediocre ones don't. Either way, verification is not an easy process.

Sources can feel even more temptation to embellish or slant comments for personal gain if they know they won't be held accountable for what they say. And anonymous sources don't have to be accountable, because no one knows who they are. They can say whatever they want to, accuse anyone of anything. The only safeguard is the reporter who must somehow detect if the source is lying or embellishing. If he or she thinks the source is straight, then—in granting anonymity—the reporter is really vouching for the credibility (or at least the appropriateness) of the source. This is something many reporters don't understand. A journalist wouldn't use a named source whom he didn't think credible or knowledgeable to speak on an issue. But, with a named source, the reader or viewer can judge for themselves the source's credibility and/or expertise. The use of anonymous sources takes that ability to judge from the hands of the news consumer and puts it in the hands of the reporter. And, with all the other problems reporters have to worry about, that is a weighty responsibility.

Few, if any, reporters believe they can avoid using anonymous sources entirely. I agree. Especially in the realm of investigative reporting, the use of anonymous sources is almost a requirement. Political reporters in Washington say the same thing. And, they counsel, they have dealt with anonymous sources so long they have become adept at discerning various motives and embellishments. That is undoubtedly true. And if these reporters adopt the technique of triangulation (getting three sources for key story elements), they are probably on safe ground. Not enough reporting goes that far, however, and the anonymous source becomes a too-convenient method of getting *someone* to say *something*. The problem is exacerbated if the story is a one-source piece.

Columnist James J. Kilpatrick decried this practice of "trust-me journalism"[19] in a 1988 article for *Washington Journalism Review*. In the piece, Kilpatrick recalled the fall of Douglas Ginsburg and the rise of Anthony Kennedy as nominees to the U.S. Supreme Court. He noted the large number of published, anonymous sources that were critical of Ginsburg. These sources were described only as a Harvard law professor, a member of the ABA screening committee, a White House faction, a Republican politician, a senior White House official, a former federal ethics official, an administration source, a Democratic aide, and so on. All these were critical of Ginsburg and, by November 8, the candidate's chances for the Supreme Court were history. But the anonymous sources were still there. In fact, the page-one lead in the *Washington Post* on November 8 read, " 'My God this is embarrassing,' a well-connected Republican groaned yesterday afternoon."[20] And the parade of anonymous sources continued with the confirmation proceedings of Kennedy. Only this time, the candidate outlasted his anonymous accusers.

After surveying numerous uses of anonymous sources in a myriad of other stories, Kilpatrick concluded:

Enough! More than enough! I look at trust-me journalism and, like the little girl in the *New Yorker*, I say it's spinach, and I say the hell with it. The reporter who constantly relies upon unattributed sources is engaged in an act of colossal arrogance. "Trust me," he says to his readers. "Trust me that these sources truly exist, that I have not created them out of whole cloth, and that I have quoted them accurately." But if a reader dares to ask, "Who are they? the reporter is coy. "I won't tell," says the reporter, "because I don't trust you to keep a secret."[21]

The prevalence of anonymous sources was revealed in a recent study which showed 80 percent of all national and international stories in researched editions *Time* and *Newsweek* magazines contain anonymous attribution, that 33 percent of the stories in the *New York Times* and *Washington Post* uses them, and that more than 50 percent of all network newscasts use them as well. In fact, the study found, 30 percent of all Washington interviews are conducted off the record.[22]

Sometimes journalists put more stock in particular sources than they should, or generalize from their comments too much. This is especially true of sources who have axes to grind or who have vested interest in the subject of the story. Nieman Fellow Michael Kirkhorn discussed this phenomenon recently and cited the household radon gas story as an example. Hundreds of stories have been written about its dangers to homeowners in recent years, but Kirkhorn notes that the source of the anxiety is four epidemilogical studies of underground miners who have been exposed over time to large doses of radon. Reporters, he points out, rarely say that the analogy between household radon and mining

is speculative and controversial at best.[23] He adds that many scientists
doubt the connection at all and notes:

When public health officials, scientists, and journalists get together . . . to discuss
radon, the unmobilized voice of dissent is overwhelmed by the official consensus, concern for the public welfare, and by the willing complicity of journalists,
who are eager to play their part in the vigorous business called "risk communication."[24]

   Risk communication is defined as alerting the public to dangers, generally in the environment or the foods we eat that may cause cancer.
It's not that journalists shouldn't do this; it's just that often they sound
alarms that are premature at best. Too many generalizations come from
narrow studies, or too many leaps are made from data as in the case of
the radon story. As Kirkhorn says, journalists may be too willing to
sound the Klaxon without analyzing the fact that their traditional role
has been to wait and assess the alarmers before going into print—or on
the air—with their story. This is a special problem with television, due
to the extreme shortness of time to devote to what generally are
"readers," or 20-second blurbs read by the anchor with no video. It is
impossible to accurately condense a study in the *New England Journal of
Medicine* in 20 seconds. What gets aired is a general statement of a
finding; what gets omitted are the important qualifiers to this finding.
The whole world is looking for causes of cancer, and it seems the media
are too quick to interpret narrow medical studies as finding such causes.
   Much of this problem comes from the sources themselves. Politicians
try to paint environmental studies in their districts in ways favorable to
them, or at least in ways that minimize the damage to them caused by
their avoidance of the problem in the first place. Scientists, who must
realize most reporters have higher verbal than quantitative skills, still
speak in research jargon that is obfuscating and misleading to the lay-
person. And, even if the story is told in the scientist's own language,
the audience will either tune it out or misinterpret it for themselves for
the same reasons many reporters do.
   But part of the problem lies with the journalists who, as cited earlier,
have a strong preference for the clearcut and easily categorized findings.
As recently stated in the booklet *Health Risk Reporting*, journalists "have
a low tolerance for ambiguity, which they often treat as if it were synonymous with vagueness and therefore the obverse of one of their car-
dinal virtues, clarity. On occasion their writing is contrived to conceal
what they do not know."[25]
   Add to these problems the fact that many journalists feel the only
solid medical story sources are those with an M.D. or Ph.D. behind their

name, that they stand in awe of these people when they interview them, that they take their comments to be gospel, and you have the potential for some really distorted stories on the risks the public faces.

A final observation on sources seems needed before concluding this section. This deals with the *paid* source: the public relations practitioner. With this individual the reporter encounters a person hired to present his or her company's image in the best possible light. The government itself probably hires more "public affairs" people than the entirety of private industry, and they also are paid to paint their bosses or agencies in glowing colors. Public relations practitioners are the chief purveyors of pseudo-journalism, discussed earlier. They stage press conferences, grand openings, celebrations, anniversaries, and numerous other subtler events to maximize their company's image. They pull out all stops to make these events visual for television. They hire celebrities to speak for environmental issues contained in PBS shows their companies underwrite. Tobacco company spokespeople offer themselves up in ads as expert sources for stories dealing with the dangers of smoking. They work behind the scenes, encouraging op-ed writers to publish favorable editorials; they work in front of the scene, hammering away at reporters to cover a particular event. In short, they do what they are paid to do. It's not unethical in most cases—no more than most reporting is unethical. But journalists must recognize the vested interest PR people have in these issues, and their comments and urgings must be judged in that light and in the light of the public's need to have a candid appraisal of an event or issue or person. Several cases will be presented in later chapters that clarify the influence public relations practitioners have on actual stories, and on how some reporters have responded to them.

Another area of journalist/source problems that can affect truthful reality portrayals is the actual relationship between the two individuals. A scathing attack on how journalists treat these relationships was delivered in the March 13 and March 20, 1989, editions of the *New Yorker* by writer Janet Malcolm. Her series, "Reflections: The Journalist and the Murderer," focused on the relationship between author Joe McGinniss (*Fatal Vision*) and his source, subject, and business partner, Jeffrey MacDonald. MacDonald was the former Green Beret who was convicted of murdering his wife and two daughters, and the book was about him and the incident. Among other things, Malcolm charges McGinnis with deceiving MacDonald into thinking he was going to write a book sympathetic to MacDonald when, all along, McGinnis had a different plan in mind. Regardless of what critics might think of McGinnis's tactics, one has to wonder if the kind of responses he got from MacDonald were not colored by the imaginary, sympathetic kind of book that the source anticipated. Would his responses have been as candid if he felt the book were going to be a more objective—even highly devastating—account? And did the fact that McGinnis seemed to have a preconceived focus in mind distort the picture he portrayed of MacDonald? We'll never know.

Nevertheless, Malcolm telescoped out from this rather narrow focus on the McGinnis/MacDonald relationship and unleashed a blast at all journalists. In her explosive lead, she wrote:

Every journalist who is not too stupid or too full of himself to notice what is going on knows that what he does is morally indefensible. He is a kind of confidence man, preying on people's vanity, ignorance, or loneliness, gaining their trust and betraying them without remorse.[26]

Malcolm's attack, in turn, unleashed a barrage of reactions from some respected journalists. Most of them criticized the sweep of her accusations yet also agreed reporter/source relationships pose a lot of problems. In a recent *Columbia Journalism Review* for instance, the following reactions surfaced:[27]

As a journalist you do some role playing. You don't turn all your cards face up. . . . [But] in a sense it's pointless to try to make distinctions between seduction and persuasion or urging or whatever. In each case what you're trying to do is to get cooperation.

Mike Wallace ("60 Minutes")

There can scarcely be a reporter, a writer, an editor . . . who is not arrested by Malcolm's startling opening sentence. I must say, however, that the beginning seems to me a profoundly silly one. I am certainly not denying that reporters do their share of manipulation. Of course they do. But the relationship is *mutually* manipulative.

J. Anthony Lukas, author of *Common Ground*

Those ivory-tower arguments of Malcolm's were just so much crap to me. That opening sentence just blew me away. If anything, I think many of the people I have interviewed as a policeman and as a journalist were trying to con *me* all the time. I never felt that I was conning anybody.

Joseph Wambaugh, author of *The Blue Knight*

The way I read her, Malcolm was finally airing the dirty little secrets of journalism. . . . Everyone has a different style of setting their subjects at ease, so that they will then tell you what, as Tom Wolfe said, in their own best interest they should never tell you.

Sara Davidson, author of *Loose Change*

Every reporter who has done even a few interviews knows the problems that reporter/source relationships can pose to objectivity and a detached portrayal of reality. A trap many novice reporters fall into, especially with sources they admire, is to write the story for that person rather than for the reader. Conversely, a trap many veteran (and more cynical) journalists land in, according to Sara Davidson, is to write more sarcastically, evoking a sense that they are somehow superior to the subject.[28] Either trap produces a distorted view of reality.

Organizational Needs as an Influence

A great deal of influence on the story comes from requirements that the news organization itself has. Among these internal factors to consider are the fact that (1) there is a daily newspaper or several newscasts to fill with news and advertising, (2) these must be filled within a specified budget, (3) they must be filled on deadline, and (4) they must be filled with stories acceptable to editorial management.

The first of these organizational requirements seems quite obvious: There is a daily news product that needs filling. What may be less obvious, however, is that while a newspaper and evening newscasts come out daily, there is not always a great deal of significant, breaking news occurring each day. Despite that, the 60 percent of the newspaper devoted to news may translate into 50 or more pages of newshole for a metro daily. Actually, the larger daily has an easier time of filling that newshole than smaller papers do. The reason is its news staff covers a larger geographical area and therefore reports on a great deal more breaking news than would occur in a smaller city or town. Larger dailies also can justify the use of more national and international wire copy and syndicated feature material than smaller, more community-oriented newspapers.

This brings us to one contrast between editing a larger and a smaller daily. On the larger daily the editor is usually having to cut stories to get all the desired news in, while the editor at the smaller paper often finds he or she must ask the reporter to write longer to fill empty space. This is especially true at weeklies and smaller dailies. It is the reason more press releases find their way into smaller papers than larger ones. It is also the reason for marathon-length coverage of local government meetings in smaller papers and scantier mention of them in larger dailies.

On the television front, show producers have an even bigger problem. Each day a station in a metro market may be looking to fill from 1 to 2 1/2 hours of newscasts every evening—not to mention a noon newscast. Even without commercials that amounts to 44 to 110 minutes of news, weather, and sports, all of which must be originated new each day. Add to that the fact that large television stations operate with only a fraction of a metro newspaper's staff and the fact that they must produce news that is visual, and you begin to see how organizational requirements can very definitely affect television news stories and the reality they portray.

The visual requirement alone cuts many legitimate news stories out of a television newscast or, at minimum, relegates them to becoming 15- or 20-second readers down in the body of the newscast. It is the reason we often see what we would consider to be soft news at the top of a newscast: It was just more visual than anything else in the array of news for the day. One day a St. Louis television reporter was covering an on-campus seminar on financial aid to university students. It was an important story, because the Reagan administration had just cut back on the amount of aid students could qualify for. That was to be one of the lead stories on the newscast that night, and I admired the station for choosing it to be, since it was not all that visual. During the seminar, however, a student on the other side of campus decided to end his state of depression by pulling a gun from his pocket and shooting himself in the head. When the TV crew heard of it, they rushed from the seminar to the suicide scene. The 6 o'clock producer was notified back at the station, and there was to be a reshuffling of lead stories for the evening newscast. The seminar piece could wait. The example is not finished, however, because by the time the crew got to the shooting scene, the body had been taken away. All that was left on the sidewalk was a small pool of blood. Again the producer was notified, and what was to be a lead story was turned into a 20-second reader to be run later in the newscast. This situation is normal for most television stations, and it was not an unusual day in the life of a TV crew. Television news, by its very nature, lives for the most immediate happening—unless it isn't visual.

To a public who responds in surveys that it gets most of its news from television (and indeed gets its own news agenda from newscasts and believes television more than newspapers), relying on the medium too much poses problems. The above, chaotic example is one reason why.

Also, by its nature, television looks for stories to be told in a dramatic way. Just as the inverted pyramid poses problems for print reporters, so the television narrative poses problems for its portrayal of reality. Consider this staff memorandum from Reuven Frank, then producer of the "NBC Evening News": "Every news story should have structure and conflict, problem and denouement, rising action and falling action, a beginning, a middle, and an end."[29]

The problem, of course, is that not all selected news events have such a neat outline. For instance, the story may be an ongoing one and may simply be another link in a very long chain whose end is still unseen. Therefore, providing an ending may lead viewers to think the story— or at least this part of it—has ended when, in fact, it may still be ongoing. Another problem is that this type of structure tends to take events out of their larger historical context. Isolating a story from its context can produce some real distortion. As far as focus on conflict goes, television's most popular weekly newsmagazine, "60 Minutes," has drawn plenty of criticism for that and for its novelistic (some say manipulative) form of telling stories.

In another memo, Frank wrote of the difference between the appeal of stories run on television and in newspapers: "A newspaper . . . can easily afford to print an item of conceivable interest to only a small percentage of its readers. A television news program must be put together with the assumption that each item will be of some interest to everyone that watches."[30]

Frank explained the reason is that, while a newspaper may add a little to its circulation by printing limited-interest items, a television station will only detract from its overall audience.

Still another example of how a media manager's concept of news stories affects the portrayal of reality can be found in Van Gordon Sauter's perceptions turned into law at CBS during his tenure. Commenting on his boss's principles, managing editor Karl Fleming explains, "For a story to work, there must be something in it that touches your heart, that gets across some kind of emotion—anger, joy, fear. Don't just give me the facts; tell me a story. Unless there's human drama, the facts get lost."[31] So reporters and producers at CBS began going for these emotional "moments." It's not that they lost sight of the facts; it's just they felt the human drama would convey those facts better. Analyzing CBS's new style under Van Gordon Sauter, writer Michael Massing noted the following: CBS loves the weather, seven-second soundbites, regards viewers as restless children in constant need of sweets (so drab news items are offered up in rhymes, alliteration, and cliché), is mesmerized by joy, pain and hope, chases a lot of superficial stories, and operates on the "why care" factor in covering foreign news.[32]

This all brings us to the second organizational requirement: budgets. There isn't a news director or producer in television or an editor in newspapers who wouldn't like to spend more money on the news product. Many cannot understand why they don't have more money to work with. Nevertheless, to top management, the newsroom is just one of several departments in the organization vying for money. What many journalists don't realize is that it gets the lion's share of the company's payroll. It even gets more than the advertising department.[33] What makes newsroom salaries seem so small in comparison to advertising, however, is there are many more reporters and editors on a newspaper's staff than advertising salespeople. Still, it is the newsroom budget that often dictates how many—and what kind of—news stories can and can't be covered. It is the reason some newspapers can afford to take more wire services than others; it is the reason some newspapers cannot staff out-of-town athletic events; it is the reason some copy is edited by more editors than other copy. And it is the reason for the waning interest on the part of many newspapers to do real investigative reporting. A panel on investigative reporting at a 1984 American Bar Association convention declared that investigative reporting is dead or dying. The reasons, the panelists said: an arrogant government, timid editors, and an uninterested public. Pam Zekman, a former *Chicago Sun-Times* investigative reporter/turned television reporter said, "Chicago used to have two papers and three TV stations doing thorough investigative reporting. Now one TV station has disbanded its investigative unit entirely. One of the newspapers has, I think, entirely abandoned investigative reporting, while the other does short shots."[34]

Budgets are also the reason that, in television, some stories wind up on the air when even the show's producers don't think they should. Because an average metro network affiliate may have only 20 reporters on staff, because some of those will be off on any given day, because a camera person must be assigned to each story, and because an average television story assignment may require at least a couple hours of field work alone, each outing represents an expenditure that is not taken lightly. So when a reporter comes back to the station after two hours saying, "Gee, this story didn't pan out like I thought it would," the producer is not so inclined to junk the story. Especially in the afternoon, when the 5 o'clock newscast is only an hour or two away and the assignment board says this 90-second package is targeted for that show. What else is going to go in that hole? It's not like this is a large daily newspaper with ten other stories standing in line to take its place. Most television stories are produced the day they are aired, and there just aren't that many extra stories sitting around on cassettes.

Organizational need number three is a real headache: the deadline. It is also one of the most dominant distorting influences on reality portrayals. The deadline is a constant companion of television reporters, and it is only a little less friendly to the newspaper reporter. Television deals in immediacy, and the larger the crisis event, the more immediately the story must be told. A St. Louis television reporter was preparing for her 6 p.m. newscast when, at 5:30, word came over the police scanner that an explosion several blocks away had blown most of an apartment, together with its resident, out into the street. "This is going to be a live shot at the top of the show," she was told by the 6 p.m. producer. "Get moving!" At this point, the reporter knew absolutely nothing about what kind of explosion it was, who was hurt or killed, or how she was going to get even that scant information within another 25 minutes and be ready to go on the air with at least some semblance of credibility. Yet that was her task, and, after the 5- minute ride to the scene, there was only 20 minutes left before going live. Miraculously, and it seemed so even to the initiated, she managed to grab a lower-ranking police official at the scene and hold him long enough to get the sketchy outline of what had occurred—or at least what he *thought* had occurred. And that perception was all that could pass for fact on that particular newscast. Update later at 11. Meanwhile, the newspaper reporters at the scene had another six hours to get the story straighter and in more depth. If more people understood the nature of such news coverage, it seems unlikely they would be saying (as they do in almost all surveys on the subject) they trust television news more than they do newspaper stories.

As difficult as it is to write accurately under deadline pressure, some reporters feel the deadline somehow causes them to write better. They claim it is like the adrenaline athletes feel when they are working against the ubiquitous clock. That adrenaline enables them to do what they couldn't if they had more time.

This feeling notwithstanding, even if it is possible to portray an event accurately under intense deadline pressure, there is absolutely no time to put that event into context. So we keep adding to our storehouse of bits-and-pieces stories, keeping the advocates of iceberg reporting happy but infuriating those who seek to know how a particular event stands in relation to related events and actions. One thinks again of Lippmann's point that "News is a signalization of an event, but *truth* is revealing the hidden items and presenting the story in context."[35] The deadline is not usually conducive to the unfolding of truth. At least not on the day a newscast is aired or the newspaper is published.

Still another organizational requirement—informal and ironic though it may be—is the desire by news executives to present roughly the same lineup of lead stories that other media are presenting. This is not a requirement that many news executives talk about, let alone boast of. After all, this is supposed to be a highly competitive business. Nevertheless, many television news directors will walk away second-guessing their producer's news judgment if a competitor station leads with a story different from their own. As far as newspapers are concerned, there may be even more uniformity in lead stories of metro dailies across the country, if that story is national or international in nature. One reason is the uncanny ability many editors have of attaching importance to the same story. It must be said, however, that this ability is enhanced by the "budget" that both the Associated Press and United Press International send across to the nation's wire editors at the top of their cycles. These budgets give the wire services' version of the most important stories due to come over the next few hours. Because of the continuing nature of many stories, and the difficulty in missing the value in a big, breaking story, many editors select the same national or international stories to lead with each day. Everyone uses AP and/or UPI, so everyone gets the same budgets and the same stories.

Because of the ambiguity present in almost every area of the gate-keeping process, and because no editor wants his news judgment to be seriously questioned by his peers, there is a sort of daily, personal search under way for a standard; for a high priest of wisdom that will reveal whether a story is legitimate or not. Since there is no such guru, AP and UPI usually suffice in the minds of editors. If a story is on the wire, the editor generally will feel it is legitimate. If not on the wire, it's legitimacy is questioned and it may not make the paper until it is legitimatized. Timothy Crouse wrote of this process in his book *The Boys on the Bus*. While covering the 1972 presidential race, Crouse found more than one political reporter who had their stories spiked by doubting editors who could not find a similar story or angle on the wires. The fact that the pleading reporter would try to explain that that was what constituted a scoop often did no good.

Good and Bad Newsroom Leadership

More damage to reality portrayals has probably been done by bad newsroom leadership than by any other single cause. Take a look at some of the areas in which editors have—and continue to—err:

- Arbitrary editing of news copy in which the reporter is not consulted.
- Failure to communicate to the reporter what the editor would like to see covered in a story.
- Reshaping a news story to fit an editor's preconceived story line, even if the facts don't seem to support that stereotype (Anyone who has done much reporting has seen this happen more than once.)
- Hyping a lead for drama and putting a more intense color on the action than actually occurred.
- Failing to treat reporters as professionals and doubting their judgment too often.
- Being too much a slave to newsroom style and policies that may be outdated and even obsolete.
- Lacking the courage to go with a story their reporter has, despite the fact no other news media has it.
- Failing to obtain and use reporters' input into solving problems reporters deal with every day.
- Trying to be some kind of senior, hands-on writer instead of being an effective people-manager.
- Lacking sufficient reporting background themselves to coach their own reporters on the best ways to do the job.
- Hiring on the quick, "warm-body" principle too often and being stuck with reporters who fulfill the editor's prediction of being untrustworthy.

- Failing to conduct adequate reference checks on job candidates and winding up with a Janet Cooke.
- Failing to participate in newsroom leadership seminars of the American Press Institute, American Newspaper Publishers Association, and/or the Poynter Institute.
- Refusing to heed the results of readership surveys and instead isolating themselves from the readers they serve and communities they cover. (It is difficult to present a truthful account of reality if you don't really know what is happening in town.)
- Continuing to believe that management styles which work in other types of businesses cannot work in the newsroom because of the daily deadlines.

All of these problems—and many more—can be found in a lot of newsrooms across the country. This despite the fact that, as a manager, it is the editor's job to grease the wheels and not throw sand in the gears. It is also the editor's job to understand that, to a great extent, the quality of work produced by the staff is dependent on the quality of leadership their editors exhibit. Trite as that may sound, it has not sunk in to the thinking of many editors and probably fewer television news directors. An article in *Washington Journalism Review*, for instance, portrayed management in TV newsrooms this way:

Most [news directors] adopt or inherit obsolete management styles that invariably lead to much of the stress found in the news business. Sadly, few TV news directors realize that the high-anxiety staff, the seemingly fickle viewers and the news director's own vagabond lifestyle are all problems *they* have sown. There can't be a better example of self-destructive management than the "modern" newsroom. Little has changed from the classic newspaper newsrooms of the 19th century.[36]

The situation is not much better in some newspaper newsrooms, either. After an exhaustive study that took more than a year to complete, Harvard management specialist Chris Argyris had this conclusion about the management of a large, metropolitan daily newspaper:

It is doubtful that a newspaper or any organization can develop effective self-examination processes if its personnel hold such pessimistic attitudes about change. However, unlike most organizations, newspapers are protected by law. This protection can be healthy to the extent that newspapers can manage themselves effectively to produce news and editorial products of the highest quality. [But] . . . the leaders of a newspaper have a difficult job. They are faced with systems that resist change, and with people who condemn the system but would be threatened by change, and they are monitored by craft unions and an increasingly disgruntled citizenry.[37]

For the most part, the style of leadership that results in newsroom environments like those described above is an authoritarian style which is often malevolent in nature. It is top-down, heavy on directives, control, and swift discipline. It is often a slave to conformity and traditions, running the gamut from a strict reliance on Associated Press style to how a particular story gets covered in the first place. Phrases often uttered by the editor might include "This is the way we've always done it around here," "We tried that once, and it didn't work," and "It's my way or the highway." As part of this style of leadership, the editor might set up some intramural competition in the newsroom hoping to have reporters compete against each other as well as rival media. Fear becomes a strong motivator among the staff—fear of being ridiculed in public by an overwrought editor and even fear of losing the job.

It's not just that an authoritarian leadership style creates an uncomfortable working atmosphere or makes job security ambiguous. That would be bad enough, because studies have shown it results in low morale and high turnover. The real problem is the same studies have shown that production quality suffers under such leadership and that employees don't strive for (or put their heart into) the work; they simply labor at it. And that means stories don't get told in the best way, and the reality portrayals suffer.

It might help, at this time, to visualize the four main manager types which researchers have identified over time. They are the following:[38]

1. *The Official* relies on rules and directives, preferably in writing, uses an impersonal style of management, and knows the "right way" to get things done. This is also the punitive authoritarian manager who places a strong emphasis on control and discipline.

2. *The Expert* operates out of personal experience and usually has the skills needed to perform the work he or she is asking their staff to do. This manager tends to give directions based on "what I say," and acts directly to get results under pressure, tending to keep a hand in the business, even when not needed. This manager, while authoritarian, is more benevolent in his or her approach than the Official manager. To some extent, this editor would be typified by television's Lou Grant: gruff on the exterior, softer on the inside.

3. *The Counselor* maintains personal relationships with reporters, tries to build trust, and sets mutual goals with each worker. He or she encourages the reporter, but also expresses disappointment when goals and standards are not met.

4. *The Team-Builder* has the same high standards as other managers but stresses openness and consensus in decision making. This consensus is not always defined as unanimous decisions, but it is defined by letting everyone in the group (often a "quality circle") have their say and then letting the group vote on the decision. This manager tries to achieve balance between group choices and organizational goals and is obviously ready to take a personal risk in sharing decision-making powers. There

is a manager who uses the work group itself as a source of both motivation and discipline, realizing that staff members care about what their peers think of them.

Management studies by scholars such as Rensis Likert, Frederick Herzberg and Abraham Maslow conclude that the more a manager moves from the Official end of the spectrum to the Team-Builder, the more positive the work environment will be and the better the quality of work produced. Argyris would agree with that as well, because a more open, consensual style of management allows for greater experimentation and assumes that reporters are professionals who have valuable information and ideas to contribute that will result in a higher quality of editorial product. Even though most everyday newsroom decisions are made on deadline and don't lend themselves to decision by consensus, there are many ongoing newsroom problems that can be studied by quality circles and resolved by them. One such problem area that receives scant attention in many newsrooms is just how that particular newspaper defines news in the first place, where it should put its emphasis, and why. If these decisions are made by top management who have been removed from the streets for several years, they may not be as relevant to reality as if some current street reporters were consulted and made a part of the decision-making process.

Some editors have found that Team-Building principles work well in the newsroom. Scott Bosley, managing editor of the *Detroit Free Press*, for instance, says, "Some news people think they are different from people at IBM or Ford. I don't think they are. People in every industry have deadlines. We are people like everyone else."[39] And other executives of Knight-Ridder newspapers began installing quality circles in their newsrooms in 1981. Today they have 90 such circles in operation.[40] These are made up of workers in each department, including the newsroom, who meet regularly on company time to address ongoing departmental problems and offer solutions to them. The *Philadelphia Inquirer* is one paper taking advantage of quality circles and has one in its newsroom. In fact, during a strike at that newspaper in the mid–1980s, the newsroom's quality circle kept meeting on a weekly basis.[41]

In sum, if a correct reality portrayal is to be achieved by a news operation, it is as much the responsibility of the editor (and a function of leadership style) as the reporter.

The Embedding Process as an Influence

A direct influence on the reporter's portrayal of reality comes about as a result of something called the "embedding process." This is the phenomenon outlined by media researchers G. W. Allport and L. Postman in which a lot of information gets squeezed out of the story from the time of original reporter observation to the time the story is written. The embedding process is actually made up of three distinct phases:

1. *Leveling*, when the description becomes shorter, more concise, more easily grasped and told.
2. *Sharpening*—the selective perception, retention, and reporting of a limited number of details from a much larger context.
3. *Assimilation*, when a reporter absorbs new information in a way that will not disturb the habits, interests, and sentiments in the subject's mind. In a way, then, this is a kind of individual interpretation—or spin—that a reporter will give to a story.

Commenting on this process, William Rivers notes, "These three processes occur simultaneously and represent an effort to reduce a large amount of information to a simple and meaningful structure."[42]

And, as most reporters know, this process can take place a second time on the same story when the editor starts working on the piece and trying to make it conform to a small newshole.

The Effect of Priming on News Selection

A study reported in 1989 by James Roche of the University of Maryland concluded that many journalists:

1. Assign a higher news rating to an event or issue if they have been primed for it by reading or seeing something about it recently.
2. Assign a story a news rating that is consistent with their own personal level of interest in a story.
3. Assign a higher news value to a story if they believe more in an active press (or a press that is in business to alarm the public about societal problems) as opposed to a passive one (or one that simply informs the public about events).[43]

Therefore, if this study's conclusions are valid, journalists' personal values and interests come into play at a critical part of the gatekeeping process. It should be kept in mind that research shows these personal influences to be part of a triad of influences, with the others being traditional news criteria, such as timeliness, proximity, prominence, etc., and professional influences, such as publisher pressure, reprimands from superiors, or peer pressure. But personal influences have been found to come very heavily into the news selection process. These influences include things like a journalist's beliefs, opinions, attitudes, interests, and perceptions.

So Roche's study found that a journalist's priming (or the idea that recently or frequently activated thoughts are more likely to be at the forefront of one's thinking than less active ideas) has an important role in the news selection process. Along with priming seems to come false consensus, where a journalist tends to think his or her attitudes are typical of others, whether or not they represent society's interests. So the journalist may assume that others would make similar decisions in similar circumstances.

Roche asserts, "At the least, it's likely that subtle forms of personal influence take place practically every time a journalist makes a news judgment. These influences could result in a damaging long-term effect on the news consumer."[44]

For example, the researcher argues, uses and gratifications theory suggests that people use news to aid them in creating personal identities, to help them integrate themselves socially, to interact with others, and to help them establish their self-worth. This is, of course, in addition to the use of news stories for straight information and entertainment purposes.

So it stands to reason that, if the journalist is being led by personal influences not common to his or her readers, the reporter may be giving them a false view of the world—and of themselves.

The Chilling Effect of Libel

Although the phrase "chilling effect" has been used so much that it sounds trite, it does represent accurately the powerful effect that libel threats have had on many stories—some of which have never seen the light of day because of the fear of libel suits. The statistics are not encouraging for journalists: At any one time there are 2,500 libel suits working their way through the legal system, with an average of 500 new libel suits being filed each year. Some 83 percent of these suits are lost by the media at the trial level, and judgments of $1 million or more are becoming increasingly more common. The one bright ray of hope for the media is that appellate judges are reversing—or reducing the amount of awarded damages in—71 percent of these libel suits.[45] The problem is, however, that even where news media win libel suits they still may put hundreds of thousands or even millions of dollars defending themselves as CBS did in the William Westmoreland libel case. Add to those large legal fees the time taken away from business in depositions and court appearances, and the toll is too heavy for some news media to get involved very deeply in doing investigative stories at all. So because of this chilling effect, some messages are not even getting through in the first place.

Shoddy Reporting and Editing

Most of the earlier influences on the message don't speak ill of the actual reporter doing the story. Some of these influences are unconscious and are simply an evidence that reporters, like everyone else, are only human. Some of the influences are market-based, and it is hard to fault the news media for wanting to survive against the competition and in the face of declining readership. Even the influence of bad newsroom leadership addresses more a lack of management training among people who didn't plan on becoming managers when they entered reporting. Bad sources are an influence that reporters have only minimal control over. Without anonymous-source reporting, a lot of Washington reporting like Watergate would not get done. So most of these influences that shape and sometimes distort reality are not the fault of the reporter. That is not so with the next influence: shoddy reporting.

In most cases, the reporter who commits this act does it knowingly. In the interest of expediency, or laziness, or whatever, the second or third sources are not consulted. The reporter maybe puts in one telephone call to get a person's denial of an accusation. Quotes are doctored or made up out of whole cloth. An article in a recent *Columbia Journalism Review* should send chills up the spine of a lot of sources and should anger the journalistic community. "Did He Really Say That?" describes how frequently reporters commit the sin of doctoring quotes. The writer even finds some reporters willing to admit they have concocted quotes on more than one occasion.

Many in the journalistic community also take their colleagues to task for shoddy reporting. In a 1983 workshop for members of Investigative Reporters and Editors (IRE), journalists indicted many reporters for sins ranging from ego trips to sloppy writing. IRE president Tom Renner wondered

if we're not succumbing to our own sirens, glamour and greed. . . . We stand on the battlements, practice confrontation journalism, lose valuable resources, deal with public relations hacks from federal and local law enforcement, and never really gets inside and deal with those who can do us the most good—the field investigators, intelligence agents, homicide dicks, corruption probers and terrorist-radical watchers.[46]

No matter what its form—and it takes many—shoddy reporting is indefensible and the journalistic community knows it. That is one reason for the myriad of professional programs in writing and reporting put on by groups like the Society of Professional Journalists, American Society of Newspaper Editors, Associated Press Managing Editors, and Investigative Reporters and Editors. Shoddy reporting leads to lost credibility and lost libel suits. The news media can withstand neither in an age when they are fighting for readers and viewers. And the news consumer, so in need of a talented intermediary that can give him or her an accurate and comprehensive portrayal of reality, deserves better.

But shoddy reporting is only half of the newspaper's problem. Often it is bad editing that takes what was a good story and turns it into a bad one. Or, in some cases, takes a non-story and turns it into a story. Gene Grabowski, former AP and *Washington Times* writer, said he became upset because an editor committed this latter sin, then left Grabowski's name on the piece. The editor, Grabowski said, had been trying to find a story that established his belief that Democratic presidential candidate Michael Dukakis had been treated by a psychiatrist for severe depression. When Grabowski came up with the fact that "the chatty, ingenuous sister of Kitty Dukakis had conceded a remote possibility that her brother-in-law might have informally discussed an emotional letdown with a psychiatrist friend in 1978, [although] she never knew of his being treated for depression or any other mental illness," the editor indeed thought he had his story.[47] Grabowski disagreed vehemently, citing the phrase as an unguarded one, made in an ambiguous moment, in a very tentative way. Nevertheless, he said, it became the foundation for the next day's story which featured the headline "Dukakis kin hints at sessions," and, according to Grabowski, "had a twisted lead suggesting that Dukakis was hiding counseling that his family members knew about. . . . It wasn't until the fifth paragraph that the story revealed the entire quote in which Peters firmly rejected the notion that private counseling took place." Concluding, Grabowski wrote that "the 'smoking gun' [the editor] thought he had seen in his excitement was in reality a smoldering ethical fire that periodically flares into public view when [this newspaper's] flinty conservative bias strikes hard against the instincts of its reporters."[48]

If Grabowski is correct in his interpretation of these events, it only points up what many reporters have sometimes found to be true: that editors are human as well, with their own priorities, value sets, and beliefs, just like reporters. The problem arises when reporters are dispatched to seek facts that confirm preconceived beliefs, return without the goods, are sent out again on another fact-finding mission, return again without the evidence, and the story is fashioned to meet the editor's preconception anyway. In theoretical terms, this would constitute the assimilation phase of the embedding process discussed earlier.

While this is a more conscious form of shoddy editing, an unconscious form takes place more often when editors fail to consult with reporters before changing important parts of the story. This changing is done either to make the story read better or to clarify the meaning. The problem is, without the reporter's input, the new meaning may be different from that which was originally intended. A 1982 study of what reporters find most frustrating about their job, in fact, concluded that too much arbitrary editing was one of the chief demotivators.[49]

The next several chapters will discuss specific examples of reporting that has missed the mark for many of the reasons discussed in this chapter. Contained in each of these examples is at least one dominant factor causing the reality distortion. The final chapter will discuss some ways in which reporters might present a more clearly focused version of reality.

NOTES

1. Werner J. Severin with James W. Tankard, Jr., *Communication Theories*, 2d ed. (New York: Longman, 1988), p. 40.

2. Glen Bayless, "Gaylord Calls 'Left-Wing' Eastern Media a Disgrace," *Daily Oklahoman/Times*, March 20, 1984, p. 23.

3. David H. Weaver and Cleveland Wilhoit, *The American Journalist* (Bloomington, Ind.: Indiana University Press, 1986), p. 26.

4. Ibid.

5. Herbert J. Gans, *Deciding What's News* (New York: Vintage Books, 1980), p. 41.

6. "Atrocity in the Skies," *Time*, September 12, 1983, pp. 10–17.

7. Robert A. Peterson, Gerald Albaum, George Kozmetsky, and Isabella C. M. Cunningham, "Attitudes of Newspaper Business Editors and General Public Toward Capitalism," *Journalism Quarterly* 61(1): p. 56 (1984).

8. Maxwell McCombs, Donald L. Shaw, and David Grey, *Handbook of Reporting Methods* (Boston: Houghton Mifflin, 1976), pp. 20–21.

9. Daniel J. Boorstin, *The Image: A Guide to Pseudo-Events in America* (New York: Atheneum, 1985), pp. 9–12.

10. Jane Delano Brown, Carl R. Bybee, Stanley T. Wearden, and Dulcie Murdock Straughan, "Invisible Power: Newspaper News Sources and the Limits of Diversity," *Journalism Quarterly* 64(1): p. 45 (1987).

11. John C. Merrill, *The Imperative of Freedom* (New York: Hastings House, 1974), pp. 1ff.

12. Edwin Emery and Michael Emery, *The Press and America*, 5th ed. (Englewood Cliffs, N.J. Prentice-Hall, 1984), p. 69.

13. S. I. Hayakawa, *Language in Thought and Action*, 4th ed. (New York: Harcourt, Brace, Jovanovich, 1978).

14. Rufus Wilmont Griswold, ed., *The Prose Works of John Milton*, Vol. 1 (Philadelphia: J. W. Moore, 1856).

15. Hayakawa.

16. McCombs, Shaw, and Grey, p. 6.

17. Walter Lippmann, *Public Opinion* (New York: Macmillan, 1922), pp. 54–55.

18. Lippman, p. 60.

19. James J. Kilpatrick, "Trust-Me Journalism: An Identifiable Source is Fed Up," *Washington Journalism Review*, January/February 1988, p. 45.

20. Ibid.

21. Ibid.

22. K. Tim Wulfemyer, "How and Why Anonymous Attribution is Used by *Time* and *Newsweek*," *Journalism Quarterly* 62(1): p. 81 (1985).

23. Michael Kirkhorn, "The Media and Risk Communications," *Nieman Reports*, Summer 1988, p. 27.

24. Ibid.

25. Kirkhorn, p. 33.

26. Martin Gottlieb, "Dangerous Liaisons: Journalists and Their Sources," *Columbia Journalism Review*, July/August 1989, p. 21, quoting Janet Malcolm, "Reflections: The Journalist and The Murderer," *New Yorker*, March 13, 1989, p. 31.

27. Gottlieb, pp. 23, 24, 29.

28. Gottlieb, p. 30.

29. Edward Jay Epstein, *News From Nowhere: Television and the News* (New York: Vintage Books, 1974), p. 153.

30. Epstein, p. 40.

31. Michael Massing, "CBS: Sauterizing the News," *Columbia Journalism Review*, March/April 1986, p. 30.

32. Massing, pp. 36–38.

33. Jim Willis, *Surviving in the Newspaper Business: Newspaper Management in Turbulent Times* (New York: Praeger, 1988), p. 26, quoting *1986 Inland Cost and Revenue Study* (Park Ridge, Ill.: Inland Daily Press Association), p. 13.

34. "Is Investigative Reporting Dead?" *Editor & Publisher*, August 25, 1984, p. 14.

35. Lippmann, p. 60.

36. Ted Dracos, "News Directors are Lousy Managers," *Washington Journalism Review*, September 1989, p. 40.

37. Chris Argyris, *Behind the Front Page: Organizational Self-Renewal in a Metropolitan Newspaper* (San Francisco: Jossey Bass, 1974).

38. Fred Pearson, description of four leadership styles contained in training literature developed at the University of Chicago Human Resources Center, Chicago.

39. Kathleen Newton, "In Search of Excellence," *Editor & Publisher*, November 23, 1985, p. 9.

40. Ibid.

41. Ibid.

42. William Rivers, *Finding Facts: Interviewing, Observing, Using Reference Sources* (Englewood Cliffs, N.J.: Prentice-Hall, 1975), p. 60.

43. James Roche, "The Effects of Priming, False Consensus, and Role of the Press on News Selection," paper presented to the Newspaper Division of the Association for Education in Journalism and Mass Communication, Washington, D.C., August 1989, pp. 1–5.

44. Ibid.

45. Jay Black and Frederick C. Whitney, *Introduction to Mass Communications* (Dubuque, Iowa: William C. Brown, 1988), p. 174.

46. M. L. Stein, "Gloss Is Taken Off Investigative Reporting," *Editor & Publisher*, October 22, 1983, p. 10.

47. Gene Grabowski, "A Reporter's Problem: Conservative Editors," *Washington Journalism Review*, December 1988, p. 34.

48. Ibid.

49. Jim Willis, "The Editor as a People Manager," unpublished doctoral dissertation, University of Missouri School of Journalism, June 1982.

3

Objectivity from the Yellow Kid to John Tower

One of the hallmarks of traditional journalism is the concept of objectivity. The idea is that the more objective the story is, the closer it will come to representing reality accurately. From the first day of Reporting 101, college students are taught the absolute necessity of remaining detached from the action and of treating people fairly. To many journalism students, that is objectivity in a nutshell. Not so to editors, however. It is fairly easy to get editors to agree on what certain attributes are contained in objectivity, but it is very hard to find two who will emphasize the same attributes at the same time. For instance, in 1981, researcher John Boyer studied how editors feel about objectivity and came up with some interesting findings.[1] Wire editors at 50 daily newspapers agreed to participate in the study and were allowed to develop their own definitions of objectivity. After similar definitions were combined, a total of 26 different definitions was found. Even though there were so many, however, they differed mainly in what aspects of objectivity editors emphasize the most with their staffs.

A factor analysis was performed on the 26 definitions, and three different emphases were discovered. They were:

Type 1: Eighteen of the 50 editors fell into this category, which values the aspects of balance and believes there are two sides to each question and the reporter's job is to represent both accurately. Those in this group believe objectivity is completely attainable by journalists.

Type 2: Seventeen editors belonged to this group, which sees objectivity as an unattainable goal. Nevertheless, these editors see the ideal as a way of minimizing reporter opinions while optimizing reporter experience in achieving balance.

Type 3: Fifteen editors followed this emphasis, which is close to Type 1 in seeing a primary need for balance. The difference here is that this balance is more relativistic or situational than in Type 1, and seems to equate balance with a lack of bias on the reporter's part.

The clearest predictor of what type editors will fall into is the number of years they have in their current editing job. Type 1 editors, for instance, have more experience at their jobs than Types 2 or 3. They are also the most traditional in their outlook and generally come from dailies of over 100,000 circulation.

What difference does all this make to the shadow world? Well, if traditional journalism tells us this world of shadows can be pierced with objectivity, yet objectivity is such an ambiguous goal (indeed one which many editors feel can't be reached), then there is a problem.

Adding to this definitional problem of objectivity is that the concept has undergone some major changes in the past 100 years, and some really radical changes in the past 40 years. An analysis of some journalism history helps to clarify these changes, and that is the purpose of this chapter.

OBJECTIVITY AND FABLES

The 1890s, some would say, began the modern era of journalism. So it seems right to start our look at objectivity at this point. As William Randolph Hearst moved into New York in 1893 to do battle with Joseph Pulitzer, the so-called era of yellow journalism was under way. The era gets its name from the chief character in Richard F. Outcault's color comic strip, "The Yellow Kid." The toothless, michievous grin on the kid's face became an appropriate symbol of this age when *any* pretext of objectivity was trampled upon in the name of newspaper competition between Pulitzer's *New York World* and Hearst's *New York Journal*. The newsholes at both dailies were turned into receptacles for some of the most outlandish, sensationalized reporting in history. Typical of the headlines and the stories that were to follow them were:[2]

- "Real American Monsters and Dragons"—over a story of the discovery of fossil remains by an archaeological expedition.
- "A Marvellous New Way of Giving Medicine: Wonderful Results from Merely Holding Tubes of Drugs Near Entranced Patients."
- "Henry James' New Novel of Immorality and Crime."
- "The Surprising Plunge of the Great Novelist in the Field of Sensational Fiction"—the *Journal*'s way of announcing publication of *The Other House*.
- "The Mysterious Murder of Bessie Little."
- "One Mad Blow Kills Child."

- "Startling Confession of a Wholesale Murderer Who Begs to Be Hanged."
- "Strange Things Women Do for Love."

Actually, they are the same kinds of headlines one would expect to find on supermarket tabloids in the 1990s or a New York or Chicago daily tabloid. Some things never change—or do they? For part of yellow journalism, a la Pulitzer and Hearst, was the actual manufacturing of news that went beyond stretching the facts of a story to make it a better yarn. This type of yellow journalism was more serious, in that it was having serious ramifications in the real world. A prime example of this brand of journalism was the role Hearst and Pulitzer took in actually starting the Spanish-American War.

In the 1930s, systematically documented studies by Marcus M. Wilkerson and Joseph E. Wisan provided strong evidence that these yellow journalists reported the events leading up to the climactic sinking of the battleship Maine in such a way that a war psychosis was created.[3] Despite the fact that the newspapers were cultivating public opinion in the era of "manifest destiny," the fact remains they passed a lot of shadows off as substance in the days and weeks leading up to this event. The United States, in turn, responded to this pseudo-world that the newspapers—chief among them the *Journal*—created. A full account of how these two publishers created the war fever that propelled America into the Cuban conflict with Spain is found in Chapter 9.

This type of active-agent reporting is sometimes seen today in the mainstream press. Examples are the pressure the media applied on NASA to keep launches on schedule and the role the media played in President Reagan's near-selection of former president Gerald Ford as a vice-presidential running mate in 1980. Both of these stories will be discussed in more detail in later chapters.

Yet, even as the *World* and the *Journal* were turning objectivity into storytelling and setting the pace for much of daily journalism in the 1890s, another movement was mounting steam in another part of New York. That movement, headed by the rejuvenated *New York Times*, was to take journalistic objectivity into its next stage.

THE FACTUAL SIDE OF OBJECTIVITY

By 1896 the *New York Times* was facing bankruptcy. It had fought against the yellow journalism of the period and had come up the loser until Adolph S. Ochs, a former printer from Tennessee, rescued it from financial turmoil and began the modern-day version of the "Gray Lady." Ochs's plan to save the *Times* was relatively simple. He did not plan on matching the sensationalism of Pulitzer and Hearst, and he didn't intend to popularize the *Times* stories in a half-hearted effort to stay abreast of the circulation leaders in the New York market. Rather, he intended to publish a newspaper of record with solid news coverage and editorial stances designed for readers tired of overemphasis on features, entertainment, and celebrities. Ochs himself declared the operating principles and goals of the *Times* when he wrote:

It will be my earnest aim that *The New York Times* give the news, all the news, in concise and attractive form, in language that is parliamentary in good society, and give it as early, if not earlier, than it can be learned through any other reliable medium; to give the news impartially, without fear or favor, regardless of any party, sect or interest involved; to make the columns of *The New York Times* a forum for the consideration of all questions of public importance, and to that end to invite intelligent discussion from all shades of opinion.[4]

Historians Edwin and Michael Emery note that Ochs began succeeding almost from the start.[5] The *Times*'s comprehensive, no-nonsense journalism scored well with the educated classes of New York City. Ochs refused to run "stunt" stories, banned comics from the pages, downplayed pictures, and chided his fellow yellow journalists. He even advertised the *Times* under the slogan "It Does Not Soil the Breakfast Cloth" prior to dropping that and going with the famed "All the News That's Fit to Print."

And so, under Ochs and the *New York Times*, objectivity began taking a turn away from the storytelling of Hearst and Pulitzer to a kind of no-nonsense fact-telling. Interpretation was kept to a minimum, and sensationalism was nonexistent in the pages of the *Times*. Pure, unadorned facts were strung together in an attempt to make a comprehensive newspaper that focused as much on national and international events as local events and issues. Many times a reporter's would-be novelistic style would be sacrificed at the altar of the *New York Times* copy desk, which has gained the reputation over the century as being one of the toughest and most tradition-bound in the newspapering business.

OBJECTIVITY AS SKEPTICISM

To a great extent, the history of journalism in the twentieth century has been the history of a conflict between these two strains of reporting which came out of the late nineteenth century. Yet neither form of journalism seemed prepared for the attack on innocence and naiveté the early twentieth century presented. Three major developments during the first quarter of this century resulted in a press that became much more skeptical of society's institutions, and that skepticism was to grow into an important part of twentieth-century objectivity. These three developments were the Age of Realism, World War I, and the rise of public relations.

In both fiction and nonfiction, the first few years of the twentieth-century were characterized as less glamorous than ever before. Scandals in companies like the Standard Oil Co. and institutions like the meatpacking industry provided great inspiration for crusading writers like Lincoln Steffens and Ida M. Tarbell. Steffens became known for his cynical viewpoint on city politics. His orientation to journalism was that, in any given city, there is evil present; his job as a journalist was simply to ferret it out and report it. He believed every major city was run on the surface by an official government but in reality by an unofficial government, which was generally hidden from public view and which was almost always corrupt. This philosophy took him from New York to St. Louis, Chicago, and other cities writing his "Shame of the Cities" series for *McClure's* magazine. *McClure's* was also responsible for publishing Tarbell's 1903 series, "History of the Standard Oil Company," which set about methodically exposing the Rockefeller oil monopoly in the United States. This new age found journalists using solid documentation for their increasingly accurate portraits of life in some of the heretofore most respected U.S. institutions: government and business. This was the dawning of the age of mass skepticism in the press, and it was assisted by the Wilson administration's successful propaganda campaign prior to, and during, World War I.

As Robert Karl Manoff noted in a New York University Conference, "War, Peace, and the News Media," popular wars presented neither serious political nor journalistic problems for democratic states until 1914.[6] That first world war, however, proved to be the first of several exceptions. This was the Great War that proved to be a great divide between different factions of American society. For the Wilson administration, which had promised to keep the United States out of war, it required the war-long mobilization of civilian populations in the belligerent states for the first time. Anti-war sentiment was running rampant in the United States. Indeed, Manoff notes, "Democratic politics, which had introduced mass war in the eighteenth century was, in the twentieth, threatening to deprive the state of the means with which to wage it."[7] In other words, public opinion, so necessary to get the country into wars in the past, was now threatening to keep America out of the European conflict altogether.

To counter this popular opposition, Wilson created the Committee on Public Information (CPI), headed by muckraking editor George Creel, to flood the country with war propaganda. Journalists even of the stature of Walter Lippmann required little arm-twisting to play the role Wilson asked of the American press. As Manoff explains, "The press not only supported the war . . . but did so on the terms established by the state."[8] Reflecting on this mobilization effort, Lippmann called it the single most effective effort in history at creating one unified public opinion.[9] And Frank Cobb of the *New York World* wrote, "For five years there has been no free play of public opinion in the world. Confronted by the inexorable necessities of war, governments conscripted public opinion. . . . They goose-stepped it. They taught it to stand at attention and salute."[10]

The after-shock of this all-out, successful propaganda campaign was a press that began becoming more skeptical of its government. After all, if journalists had been led en masse one time for one cause, couldn't they be led at other times, for other causes which might not be so virtuous? Nor were the lessons of Creel's campaign lost on private business and industry, either. If the government could be successful in propagandizing Americans, why couldn't the private sector? This led to the second major development, the rise of public relations.

One of the writers joining Creel's CPI campaign was Edward L. Bernays, who most observers see as the father of public relations in the United States. The CPI offered Bernays and others a chance to conduct programs that would influence public opinion and to experiment in methods of publicity campaigns. The lessons were soon adapted to promoting everything from corporate images, to political candidates, to nonprofit organizations. Bernays published a book entitled *Crystallizing Public Opinion* which, along with Lippmann's *Public Opinion*, laid out the way in which such opinions are formed and the techniques used to manipulate public opinion.

Now, with both the government and business making use of public relations counselors and with writers like Steffens and Tarbell showing what really was going on in the halls of power, the press had real reason to adopt a more skeptical approach to statements coming from both quarters.

Lippmann began making the point over and over again in this writings that subjectivity is a reality in daily reporting. He said all thought is a mix of reason and passion and, if reporters want to insure a separation of fact and values in their stories, they might want to apply some of the scientific method to their reporting. This sterilization procedure was one way, Lippmann felt, that reporting could be purified. Newspapers responded to Lippmann and the other recent influences by acknowledging that subjectivity is a factor in reporting, hiring reporters more specialized in the fields they cover, publishing the work of more syndicated columnists to put ideas and events into perspective, and discussing the value of interpretive reporting.

INTERPRETIVE JOURNALISM

Now the idea of objectivity came to include more skepticism of official sources and institutions, but reporting still fell short of the mark in many cases because the norm was to trot out fact after fact with no real attempt at stringing them together and interpreting them or predicting what they might mean. To a large degree, for instance, Americans found themselves caught unaware by the Great Depression because there had been little interpretive reporting leading up to the Crash. Once again, many people blamed the media for this state of unpreparedness, and journalists began asking themselves if something wasn't missing from their perspective on reporting.

Later we will see how the U.S. media chose, to a large extent, to look the other way during the rise of Adolph Hitler, not realizing his threat to world peace. That was partly because there was little interpretive reporting being done on the events in Europe at this time.

This criticism of the messenger can only go so far, however. After all, the U.S. media then—as they do now—were taking many of their cues from the readers. If editors sensed the American public was too depressed and turned off by accounts of a German dictator or the downturn of the national economy, then those stories would likely receive little play. And they did.

Still, during the 1940s an idea started growing in the media that more interpretation in news stories might be needed. Curtis MacDougall was partly responsible for this new trend line with his popular reporting textbook, *Interpretive Reporting*. It became a standard in journalism schools around the country, and he advocated going beyond the simple facts to linking those facts together to form a larger picture. MacDougall pointed out that interpretation is analysis, not editorializing or opinionating, and reporters therefore should not be afraid of using this technique. Preceding MacDougall's call for more interpretation was Lippmann's idea regarding scientific journalism, of somehow sterilizing the reporting process so that stories would rest on harder, more systematic documentation and would therefore reflect more of the reality of the situation. Both themes were picked up later in the 1960s.

One newspaper that came to be known as the newspaper of interpretation was the *Christian Science Monitor*, established in 1908 by Mary Baker Eddy, who founded the Christian Science church. It was to go beyond the church, however, in that it was to be a national, general-interest newspaper that countered the sensationalism of other dailies and their emphasis on crime, disasters, and stunt stories. It did well in developing Washington and foreign news, published significant regional stories from around the United States, and did a lot of serious features related to subjects like music, art, and literature.

Its chief hallmark, however, became its proficiency in interpreting developments at home and around the world—to sort out the facts, link related ones, and come up with a larger picture of what was going on. The paper has suffered from lost circulation and an aging readership over the past several years, but still is regarded as a top-notch journal of interpretation.

STRAITJACKET JOURNALISM

It would seem now that reporters had it right: that objectivity was to include a strict adherence to facts, a healthy skepticism of institutions, and a need to link facts together to form a larger picture of the event or issue under study. So how did the media become chief publicists during the early 1950s for one of the most frightening figures in U.S. political history, Sen. Joseph McCarthy? Possibly because one chief component of latter-day objectivity was missing at the time: verification. Possibly, also, because the type of "stenographic" reporting that characterized the McCarthy period was a natural outgrowth of Lippmann's attempts to "sterilize" reporting and take the reporter out of the picture as much as possible. The McCarthy era also showed how effectively the news media could be manipulated by a man who made so many daily accusations that there was little time to investigate whether the individual charges were true or not.

The McCarthy era began with a lie and lived on lies for four years until the senator was finally exposed by Edward R. Morrow. On February 9, 1950, Joseph McCarthy, Wisconsin's Republican junior senator, delivered a speech in Wheeling, West Virginia, in which he claimed to have in his hand a list of 205 State Department employees who were Communists. From that day forward, scarcely a day went by that McCarthy was not "revealing" new lists, never mentioning any specific names and always changing the numbers of "Communists" on the list. James Boylan recently noted of the McCarthy era:

As yea-sayer to power, journalism had proved a fine vehicle for negotiating the tricky ice floes of the Cold War, when former enemies swiftly became staunch friends and vice versa. But it had not proved that it could move upstream against a political current, and the tide in the 1950s was running with the new Red Scare, personified in Sen. Joe McCarthy. Journalism's one recognized elite, the Washington press corps, failed to meet the test, in the basic journalistic sense of offering an account that could stand even rough historical scrutiny. Rather than challenging McCarthy, for four years the capital's chief news supplier, the [then] three wire services feasted from McCarthy's abattoir.[11]

To a great extent, McCarthy was able to accomplish his manipulative mission because he fed off the journalist's unwritten creed of using the official source and going with what you've got. The idea of trying to certify what the official was telling you was somehow outside the bounds of objective, arms-length journalism. Possibly because it was seen as reporters casting too much personal doubt on the statements given them, reporters as a group did not spend much time trying to verify official statements. The idea was to act as neutral as possible, somewhat like a stenographer or a court reporter who is charged with simply taking down what is said and attributing it correctly. It is not surprising, then, that this brand of journalism came to be known, over time, as straitjacket journalism.

As a result, the press aided McCarthy as he went about ruining reputable characters and bringing powerful (and often innocent) people to their knees. McCarthy seemed to have the reckless abandon of a mischievous child. The press catapulted McCarthy to power, maintained him, and—in the end—took the net away and brought the lies crashing down.

It was not that the press actually believed all (or even most) of McCarthy's accusations. It was simply that this U.S. senator made good copy, especially in an era where fear of Communism was at its height. The press couldn't ignore him because the State Department and the Senate were taking such an interest in him, and his charges were so hard to verify. Reporters would no more than think about verifying one batch of accusations than McCarthy would be at it again the next day, delivering a new round of charges.

The point was that the country needed some Communist scapegoats in the early 1950s, Joe McCarthy delivered his version of them, and the press delivered McCarthy to the public. The ironic thing is that many editors condemned McCarthy's tactics in their editorial columns, but allowed the news columns to continue giving venue to his newest allegations. Once such editorial voice against McCarthy was *Boston Herald-Traveler* columnist Drew Pearson. For his troubles, Pearson was cited by McCarthy as having "an important place in the Reds' plans," and was called "the voice of international Communism." Pearson challenged him to make these statements off the Senate floor and without protection of senate libel immunity law, but McCarthy never did. To the public, it didn't seem to make any difference. Many believed McCarthy.

So the stories and headlines continued. Columnist Richard Mason said it was a situation like "a circus, with Sen. McCarthy swinging trapeze style from one charge to another to the blare of big, black, beautiful headlines. It was a strange sort of circus, however, with unfunny clowns and jokes without laughter, played under a bigtop of senatorial immunity. It was a Roman style circus with reporters clawed apart and slain daily for the crowd."

In 1954, when McCarthy was nearing the end of his run, the *Herald-Traveler* ran a series "Hero or Zero" every day for a week. Reporter Sandra Starr cast McCarthy as the hero, with Richard Mason taking the counterview. The verdict was left up to the readers.

The beginning of the end of McCarthy came on March 9, 1954, on a fateful episode of Edward R. Murrow's controversial but popular "See It Now." Murrow was, by now, totally disgusted with McCarthy and decided to state his thoughts on the air. After showing films of the senator in action, Murrow said:

As a nation we have come into our full inheritance at a tender age. We proclaim ourselves . . . the defenders of freedom abroad . . . but we cannot defend freedom abroad by deserting it at home. The actions of the junior senator from Wisconsin have caused alarm and dismay amongst our allies abroad and given considerable comfort to our enemies, and whose fault is that? Not really his. He didn't create this situation of fear; he merely exploited it, and rather successfully. Cassius was right: "The fault, dear Brutus, is not in our stars, but in ourselves."[12]

The final days of Joe McCarthy came during the 35-day Army-McCarthy hearings in 1954. Television was now delivering McCarthy on a daily basis for 187 hours to 20 million Americans. The senator did not play well on the home screen. Now the senator, who sounded so great in print, looked like a buffoon on television. Television is a tremendous vehicle for solidifying or changing impressions and perceptions, and the public perception of McCarthy was changing fast. People started to laugh at him; he became a joke. Then he became a bore. When he stopped becoming good copy, the press deserted him. His popularity sank to a 36 percent favorable reading from the public, he was censured by the senate, and died in 1957.

Commenting on the way the news media played the McCarthy story over most of the four-year period from 1950 to 1954, James Boylan notes:

The serious challenges to McCarthy—the Edward R. Murrow broadcast of March 9, 1954, is the one that has entered memory—came late, only when McCarthy's exit chute . . . was clearly visible. Such an experience is, for an institution, a little like a serious illness. There may be recurrences. But after recovery there may be a kind of immunity. The failure to respond more actively to McCarthyism, or more accurately the embarrassment rising from failure, remained ever after a reference point invoked in other contexts: the Bay of Pigs, Vietnam, the Pentagon Papers, Watergate. The great surprise, in retrospect, is the speed with which the bedraggled, victimized press of the 1950s came to see itself as an apparently potent, apparently adversary press in the 1960s.[13]

The truly ironic thing about the McCarthy era was the role investigative television reporting played in bringing him down. Criticized so much today for pandering to superficial stories, foisting off false images of political candidates, and taking its lead from the print media, television may have seen its finest hour in 1954, with Edward R. Murrow as its champion and model for reality-based reporting.

VIETNAM, WATERGATE, AND VERIFICATION

Partly because of the way the media had handled Joe McCarthy in the 1950s and partly because the media—especially television—were becoming such a high-profile industry complete with budding celebrities and stories of corporate goings-on, objectivity became a term of abuse in the 1960s. This was the decade of the "critical culture" in America, and many were upset that the media had been providing only "the official story" about this country's slide into the Vietnam conflict without questioning the assumptions on which U.S. entry was made. So, to many observers, the U.S. news media became the media of the establishment, representing its viewpoint and refusing to challenge its assumptions or actions. Many felt so-called objective journalists had turned their back on the question of whether the country's power structures or policies were legitimate at all, or even rested on legitimate assumptions.

As a result, this was the decade of the underground press with advocacy newspapers springing up in nearly every major city of the country. Papers like *Harry*, the *Realist*, the *Los Angeles Free Press*, the *Aquarian Age*, and the *Berkeley Barb* became regular reading for persons associated with anti-war and counterculture leanings. The journalism appearing in these publications came to be known as advocacy reporting and participative journalism. The underground press questioned, altered, and sought to radically change the status quo of the 1960s. Abe Peck notes these "faded flowers" could be "arrogant, shrill, unskilled, adventuristic. Many also possessed the movement's strengths of dedication, cooperation, experimentation, playfulness. Radical in the best sense of the word, they examined the roots of society, acted on their findings, helped shape . . . a flowering of idealism and hope."[14]

This was also the decade that "new journalists" like Tom Wolfe and Hunter S. Thompson came to public attention. Their brand of reporting grew in favor because, as sociologist Michael Schudson said, many felt "objective" reporting only reproduced a vision of social reality that refused to examine some basic premises concerning power and privilege.[15]

Helping to underscore this awareness of manipulation by government of the media was Daniel Boorstin's *The Image: A Guide to Pseudo-Events in America*, which was published in 1961. Through Boorstin's writings, it became apparent that some government officials were doing their best to promote an image of what they were doing rather than saying honestly what they were doing. Thus, they became adept at *managing* the news.

Add in the growing U.S. involvement in Vietnam and Watergate of the early 1970s, and you had the basis for a successful counterculture movement in the United States.

In large measure, it seemed the counterculturalists were right about the news media. Growing manipulation of the news *did* contribute to the reporting of shadows over substance and to lies over truth in many cases. Schudson says the adversary culture came to see more and more problems with traditional objective journalism for the following reasons:[16]

1. The *content* of news stories seemed to rest on a set of substantive political assumptions whose validity was never challenged by the reporter. What you had was an item that looked like a news story, was structured in the right way, and seemed to have appropriate sources. But this all was concealing content that, while accurate, fell short of truthfulness. So you had a Marguerite Higgins or a Keyes Beech or a Joseph Alsop reporting the administration's officially accurate line about the Vietnam War, yet never challenging the validity of the U.S. involvement there in the first place. Schudson says it was a case of *form concealing content*.

2. The *form* of the news stories seemed to incorporate its own bias. Newspapers' copy desks seemed to insist on neutral verbiage as a way of ensuring traditional objectivity, even though more precise verbiage might have been needed to reflect the subtleties and/or passion of the situations. And yet even this rule of neutral verbiage was seemingly used as an editorial tool, according to Ron Javers.[17] Voicing some concerns of nontraditional journalists in the 1970s, Javers questioned whether U.S. journalism was the progressive influence it claimed to be. He used the play of words in stories as an example. Why is it, he asked, that if Secretary of State Henry Kissinger was a surprise visitor at an event most reporters would still say he "put in an appearance," while if some counterculture type such as Stokely Carmichael was a surprise visitor the same reporters would also say he "turned up?" Why is it that labor unions always do the "demanding" and management always does the "asking?" Why is it that an Abbie Hoffman can "scream" at a judge, but the judge "admonishes" him back (even though he may be doing so at the top of his vocal range)?

As discussed in Chapter 2, Columbia sociologist Herbert J. Gans used this verbiage pattern as a criterion for a content analysis in which he probed the "hidden values" contained in news stories.[18]

Form also can constitute bias because the inverted pyramid format always calls for a focus on the conflict and events as opposed to the processes or issues. This form also seems to favor institutions and their sources as being somehow more credible and knowledgeable than other sources. Therefore, Schudson says, we have *form constituting content*. For example, if a newspaper in the 1960s needed a conservative opinion on almost any subject they would go with a high-profile conservative politician like Barry Goldwater, even though no one elected Goldwater as their conservative spokesman on this issue that he may not even feel passionate about in the first place. Need a liberal viewpoint? Call George

McGovern. Need a preacher? Call Billy Graham. Never mind that the fragmented publics involved don't consider these individuals as their champions. You see one liberal, you've seen them all. Besides, we're on deadline. Just pull out the stereotype, dust it off, and use it.

3. The *process* of newsgathering itself constructs an image of reality which reinforces official viewpoints. Journalists become mere stenographers for the official transcript. Manipulation, a la McCarthyism, is easy. Also, like correspondent Guy Hamilton in *The Year of Living Dangerously*, the first impulse is always to seek out the highly placed official source, despite the fact that he or she may be just the one who has the most to achieve by manipulating the journalist.

In fairness, there was too much generalization taking place among counterculture, anti-media groups in the 1960s. There were many exceptions to shallow reporting among some leading dailies. One also must keep in mind that, if liberals were blasting the media for being too conservative, conservatives also were attacking it for being too liberal. The most vociferous of these critics was, as noted earlier, Vice-President Spiro T. Agnew. He took special care to zero in on the *Washington Post* and *New York Times* as being anti-war papers. Yet these were some of the very papers that came under attack from the Left during the same era for voicing the doctrine of mainstream U.S. politicians. There is a school of thought that says if *both* sides are attacking you, then you must be doing a fair job. There is some truth to that, although relying on that thinking too much can be distortive. It could just be both sides have a point.

Although it often takes the news media a while to adapt to criticism and change their behavior, the system has usually attempted to right itself. This was true in the mid- to late 1960s and 1970s when competent journalists began reacting to these attacks in at least two key ways. Schudson says these are two traditions that were always there, but became submerged for several years. They were the *literary* tradition and the new *muckraking* tradition.

Through journalists such as Tom Wolfe and Truman Capote, many reporters began fighting back against the tide of manipulation and imagery in the country's institutions with finely crafted writing which was forceful in its emotional impact. This "new journalism" allowed impressions and feelings to be brought into the journalist's work. In fact, Wolfe argued for bringing *all* the senses into the reporting process. Don't be afraid, he said, to use descriptive verbiage in place of neutral verbiage if it is more precise in describing the atmosphere and the emotional tone of the situation. Don't be afraid to invade the psyche of the person you are interviewing and to discover how he or she feels or felt at the time of the action. Don't be afraid to use profuse dialogue or to describe the most minute mannerisms of the source and other people involved in the story. Don't be afraid to actually construct a social mosaic of the scene. In short, don't be afraid to break the artificial glass between the reader and the world he or she lives in.

This literary tradition became controversial among more traditional journalists who seemed to preach against every technique Wolfe was advocating. It seemed to be on the opposite pole of Lippmann's scientific reporting. And yet it was aimed at the same goal: producing a portrait of reality instead of fantasy. It simply applied some of the tools of the fiction writer to the task. In some cases, as were typified by George Plimpton's romp as a "rookie quarterback" with the Detroit Lions, it allowed the reporter to become a part of the fabric of the story and to describe the smell of the sweat and the thrill of the action. Or, with Wolfe, it allowed you to take certain liberties in reconstructing direct quotes to approximate what a U.S. astronaut *would have said* if he were asked to describe his feelings in the space capsule as he orbited the earth.

This type of impressionistic journalism has persisted and is with us still in magazines like *Rolling Stone* and *Esquire* and in some of the best newspaper feature sections in the country. It may not be the best way at getting at the reality every time (indeed some critics say you can't get at reality with fictional techniques), but it is one way that has worked in many cases. Few would quibble over liberties taken by Capote in his impressionistic narrative *In Cold Blood* or by Wolfe in *The Right Stuff*. Nevertheless, any technique can be overused. When Wolfe spends three pages describing how the nation's first space-traveling chimpanzee felt while circling the earth, it may be stretching belief too much to feel that is really the way that chimp felt.

Certainly the muckraking tradition is one that has been with us for quite some time. Even in the nineteenth-century heyday of James Gordon Bennett and the *New York Herald*, there was some good investigative work being done in the midst of an era of circus, stunt-filled journalism. And Steffens resurrected it in the early twentieth century. But, somehow during the war years and the McCarthy era, this tradition definitely went underground and didn't really surface again until the 1960s.

Bringing it out of the mothballs were journalists like David Halberstam, Neil Sheehan, Bob Woodward, Carl Bernstein, and *Newsday*'s Bob Greene. Some of these went beyond the standard war reporting in Vietnam to discover the underbelly of U.S. involvement in Southeast Asia; some probed deep enough (while others turned away) to bring out the illegalities occurring in the Nixon administration; and still others simply probed into U.S. institutions and found several improprieties. Greene, for instance, led reporters who looked into the murder of *Arizona Republic* reporter Don Bolles in 1976 and produced a series of investigative reports that advanced the story Bolles was reporting when he was killed.

Greene, was one of those responsible for the formation of Investigative Reporters and Editors, Inc. (IRE), which acts as a support and development group for investigative reporters across the United States and around the world.

Although some still insist that all reporters are investigative reporters, journalists like these and others have gone beyond the traditional, day-to-day reporting in "triangulating" for key statements and facts in their stories and in using nontraditional methods to obtain stories. One such approach to reporting came in Chicago in 1979 when a team of undercover reporters for the *Chicago Sun-Times* set up—and staffed—a trap (boldly called the "Mirage" tavern) for unsuspecting municipal building inspectors. Into this lair, reporters posed as building owners bribing plumbing and wiring inspectors into approving of their substandard edifice. In many cases the bribes were taken, all under the gaze of newspaper photographers in a concealed loft. The result was a 25-part series of articles, the suspension of several municipal building inspectors, and a citywide investigation of the building inspection system. Although the series drew praise from some media critics, the *Sun-Times* was denied a Pulitzer Prize, largely on the basis of resorting to undercover tactics to get the story. Going undercover is seen by many editors as a last resort, because of the problem associated with using lies to obtain the truth.

OBJECTIVITY IN THE 1990s

Where is objectivity headed in the 1990s? Indications are that both the literary tradition and the muckraking tradition of the 1960s and 1970s will have rough going. Several newsrooms have cut back on their investigative reporting or "I teams." Few local television stations will field their equivalent "spotlight teams" because of budget considerations. And some editors fear a "new puritanism" is taking hold.

At an IRE conference in the mid–1980s, Frank McCulloch, executive editor of the McClatchy Newspapers, said many newspapers have already been struck by this new puritanism, which he likened to Cotton Mather and the Salem witch trials. McCulloch attributed this puritanism to a "growing crankiness of a society that lost confidence in most institutions, most certainly including the free press."[19] He also cited the growing number of libel suits which give off a chilling effect on investigative reporting, the influence on newspapers from pressure groups, and an orientation toward too much marketing and bottom-line thinking in the newsroom. He also criticized what he called "agenda journalism, which is strong on the who's, what's, when's, and where's, but very weak on the why's and how's."[20]

One of McCulloch's critiques—that of market-oriented journalism—

may definitely have an adverse affect on the growth of investigative reporting. If, by way of readership studies, readers don't rate investigative reporting high on their agenda, many newspapers will not rate it high on theirs. The influence of market-based journalism is most clearly evidence in the rise of USA Today, the nation's second largest daily newspaper which also features only one in-depth story in each of its four sections. The rest is a mix of "print soundbites" and consumer-oriented "news you can use" that market studies say "readers on the go" want. This paper is, in fact, the product of tons of market research, and that is why some observers point to it as a mirror of society's tastes and values and call it a daily sociological portrait of the American people.

Investigative reporting is also in trouble because it is expensive reporting in a number of ways. First, taking reporters out of the mainstream, daily production of news stories increases the cost-per-story factor that many business managers focus on in their bottom-line orientation. Secondly, and possibly more importantly, investigative reporting is expensive in that it seems to draw more lawsuits for libel and invasion of privacy that standard, everyday journalism. These suits, even if without merit, are expensive for newspapers to fight and they tie up editors and reporters in preliminary procedures of discovery for quite some time.

There is, however, hope that investigative reporting will continue to prosper and, in the process, satisfy some of Lippmann's criteria for separating reporter value from facts. This hope lies in the adaptation of social-science tools to the methodology reporters use in newsgathering. Philip Meyer has championed this type of "precision journalism" for more than a decade and has authored a textbook on how to apply these techniques.[21] Maxwell McCombs, Donald Shaw, and David Grey added their own version later in the 1970s.[22] These manuals, plus the new option of *database* journalism, makes it possible to put harder documentation to stories than ever before and, in the process, deliver trends and show where the problem may be headed in the future. Database journalism is an especially encouraging phenomenon. Databases are collections of information stored on computers in almost every governmental department at almost every level, and on thousands of computers in the private sector. Many daily newspapers have stored their daily product on such databases. At last count, there were more than 3,000 databases available to journalists in the United States alone. By subscribing to one or more database services such as Nexis or Lexis, Compuserve, VuText, or DataTimes, reporters can have instant background at their fingertips by simply typing in the name of the person, aircraft engine, event, or issue they want to cover.

Still, investigative reporting remains expensive and some large newspapers spend as much as $250,000 annually just to access and obtain information over one or more of these database services. For that reason alone, the future of investigative reporting is in doubt at many newspapers and television stations. It may not be until the public decides it needs more probing information about its institutions and people running them that more investigative reporting will be done.

One of the fears some observers have about the future of investigative reporting is that the goals will be sought without applying the necessary hard work, time, and independent investigative skills required to achieve those goals. This may have been what McCulloch was saying when he spoke of the pursuit of the goals becoming an end unto itself. It is also possible that former investigative reporters who become media aides working for their own political employers and against opposition candidates might understand this investigative mindset enough to turn it against the reporters. Some wonder if this wasn't the case in the 1989 Senate confirmation hearings of John Tower, who was President Bush's first choice for Secretary of Defense. Many feel the press, possibly in a fit of paranoia or fear of missing a corruption story, came down too hard on Tower and based most of their reporting on secondhand anecdotes from sources even the reporters were unclear about. For instance, even though reporters cited FBI reports about Tower on more than one occasion, these reports often repeat the unverified claims of anonymous informants.[23] In the case of Tower, his fate hinged on an FBI report which was several thousand pages long, replete with anonymous sources' unverified claims that they had seen him drunk and/or womanizing.[24] Despite the fact that this was a confidential document and kept under lock and key, many of its more serious charges found their way into the newspapers and on the air despite the dubious nature of these allegations. Sen. William Cohen called these stories "double hearsay" and claimed they were spread by Tower's enemies. In describing the media's role in the Tower rejection for secretary of defense, William Boot noted in *Columbia Journalism Review*:

Reporters helped carry out the death sentence with lethal injections of venomous claims . . . there was the assertion, reported on Page one of the February 4 *Washington Post*, that Tower could have jeopardized the national security by having " 'a protracted relationship' with a Russian ballerina, although the bureau has not yet confirmed any details." The phrase "not yet" implied that the bureau was about to do so. It never did. Then there was the claim that Tower had become a liability due to unspecified behavior involving drink and sex in Geneva—an allegation made by *The New York Times* (February 10). . . . The FBI failed to find any reliable evidence to substantiate the claims.[25]

In this one story alone evidence is seen that the media wanted the results of investigative reporting without doing the homework required to produce it. The result was a question mark as to whether Tower should or should not have been confirmed as secretary of defense. Some media observers call this type of rumor-based reporting "cheap-shot journalism." Dan Thomasson, editor of the Scripps Howard News Service, says it sometimes seems every young reporter today is, on his initial day at work, issued a detailed set of instructions on "how to make a mountain out of a molehill."[26] He charges that Watergate unleashed on America a pack of young fire-breathing reporters who are trying to turn every story—no matter how shaky—into an investigative masterpiece. Examples he gives include the *Washington Post* story claiming that the head of the National Security Council had sexually harrassed another female reporter and that a picture existed to document it. The story was run, Thomasson said, without the *Post* reporter's having seen the photo or even contacting the other reporter allegedly involved in the incident. In fact, he said, the other reporter wound up denying the whole thing.

There may be something to the notion that too many journalists are taking the idea of adversarial journalism too far. Every journalist should remain skeptical about the people he or she is covering, but that doesn't translate to taking cheap shots, writing on the basis of rumor or unverified statements, or simply assuming that every politician is corrupt. J. Russell Wiggins, former editor of the *Washington Post*, says journalists are too often "suckers for manufactured episodes. Six scholars may propound in their lecture halls a view of the universe without breaking into print. But if they were to mount their central theme on a placard and throw a rock through a store window, they will make the front page or the six o'clock news."[27]

The problem, of course, is that in tending to magnify every incident (by way of innuendo, anonymous sources, and unsubstantiated statements) into something momentous, reporters fall into the arena of the boy who cried wolf. What happens when a significant story does come along? Will it receive any more attention by the public or be believed any more than the insignificant ones? Reporters should heed the advice of Daniel Boorstin who warns them against trying to salve the public's desire for something more bizarre and sensational than they have seen before. That may sell newspapers, but it sends reality spinning off into space.

As for the future of the literary tradition, it is in doubt in the news sections of many newspapers. It is a truism in newspapers that there is little agreement or uniformity on any trend. For instance, reporters following the muckraking tradition don't generally think much of those following the literary tradition. Partly because of this lack of uniformity regarding means in reaching ends, trends become blunted in the news industry. In feature sections and in many magazines, the literary tradition of Tom Wolfe, Truman Capote, and George Plimpton still flourishes. In mainstream journalism, the clock may be ticking backward instead of forward when it comes to the literary tradition.

The real question is where television will be headed in the 1990s and beyond. The days of happy-talk newscasts seem to be fading, with the exception of the early-morning "news" shows. But there are some disturbing trends at both the network and local levels. One problem which transcends both local and network television news is the disjointed nature of news stories airing nightly. Neil Postman, in his book *Amusing Ourselves to Death*, refers to TV news as vaudeville. Under this analogy, news stories are like the one-liners that vaudevillians were so famous for. These anecdotes were never fully developed, and the humor came as much from their brevity and frequency as from the content of the stories themselves. Such is the case with television news. Although the stories are, for the most part, not meant to evoke laughter from the audience, they are meant to attract attention, and the brevity and frequency of them is meant to keep that attention. Postman says two words heard on almost every newscast at one time or another, offer quick evidence of this detached nature of television news. Those two words are, "now . . . this." Postman says, "The phrase . . . adds to our grammar a new part of speech, a conjunction that does not connect anything to anything but does the opposite: separates everything from everything."[28] It is as if television news is telling us that, when the 90 seconds is over, the event or issue itself is over. There may be another story coming on this, but we can't tell if it will be tomorrow, next week, next month, or next year. And when it does come, it will appear as disconnected from this story as this story appears disconnected from the previous one. In a sense, it is news as entertainment where viewers receive fragmented news that has no context, consequences, value, or even seriousness.

Followers of Marshall McLuhan will see a familiar refrain here: While we expect books and newspapers to follow some logical, sequential reasoning pattern that puts a story into a larger frame of reference, we have no such expectation of television news in most cases. We are not only content with a bombardment of "now . . . this" stories that may jump from a story about Indianapolis getting a Super Bowl to a story of Khaddafi threatening assassination of the president, but we seem to expect it and demand it, according to audience research reports. It is the video version of *USA Today*, with each eight-minute news segment seeming complete in and of itself. Postman says we are not even required to carry over any thoughts from one segment to the next, because we won't need them. Television, as McLuhan says, is all-at-onceness. It is not sequential; it is not always logical, and it doesn't require much audience participation.

Robert MacNeil, executive editor and co-anchor of the "MacNeil/Lehrer News Hour," says of this phenomenon that the idea is to

keep everything brief, not to strain the attention of anyone but instead to provide constant stimulation through variety, novelty, action, and movement. You are required . . . to pay attention to no concept, no character, and no problem for more than a few seconds at a time.[29]

If that observation is not bothersome enough, there is some indication that the networks may be considering cutting off their nose to spite their face. Some observers are predicting the demise of network newscasts altogether and say the job will be taken over by independent news producers who will supply national and international stories to the local stations which will take over the role of both local and network news messenger. That prediction seems depressing, because local television journalism, as always, is built around the base of ratings.

Another disturbing trend in network and syndicated television is the mixing of fact with fiction and the mixing of reality with drama. When network, prime-time news shows start recreating events for the camera and when shows like "A Current Affair," "The Reporters," "Inside Edition," and "Hard Copy" draw such large audiences and take the networks by storm, the future looks dim. Perhaps it is just a phase television is going through like newspapers did under Bennett, Pulitzer, and Hearst in the nineteenth century. Or perhaps there will always be a market for alternative television news just as there is for alternative daily newspapers by way of the tabloid press. But, with the increasing focus on market-based journalism, this type of television reporting may be the wave of the future.

In local television, the future doesn't look much better. Local television newscasts are the biggest moneymakers their stations have. Local television news departments don't lose money like their network counterparts do; they make a lot of it for television stations used to raking in profits ranging from 25 to 40 percent of gross revenues in good economic times.

To a great extent, then, news at the local level is defined by what viewers say they want. This market orientation has always been stronger in television than newspapers, and will probably continue to be so. Recently a consultant prepared a week's worth of newscast critiques for a large midwestern television station. When presented with the results of the content analysis (which, among other things, showed too much one-sided reporting and anonymous, one-source stories) the general manager turned from his Caesar salad to the consultant and said, "Yes, but you have to *link* this to audience likes and dislikes before it will interest us. You have to tell us which of this stuff, if any, causes viewers to turn us on or turn us off. That's where television is at."

That is the reality of local television, and that makes the future of quality television journalism suspect.

NOTES

1. John H. Boyer, "How Editors View Objectivity," *Journalism Quarterly* 58(1): p. 24 (1981).

2. Edwin Emery and Michael Emery, *The Press and America*, 5th ed. (Englewood Cliffs, N.J.: Prentice-Hall, 1984), p. 286.

3. Marcus M. Wilkerson, *Public Opinion and the Spanish-American War* (Baton Rouge: Louisiana State University Press, 1932); Joseph E. Wisan, *The Cuban Crisis as Reflected in the New York Press* (New York: Columbia University Press, 1934).

4. Emery and Emery, p. 328.

5. Ibid.

6. Robert Karl Manoff, comments made at the seminar "War, Peace, and the News Media," sponsored by the Gannett Foundation and New York University, New York City, March 19, 1983.

7. Ibid.

8. Ibid.

9. Walter Lippmann, *Public Opinion* (New York: Macmillan, 1922), p. 27.

10. Manoff.

11. James Boylan, "Declarations of Independence," *Columbia Journalism Review*, November/December 1986, p. 31.

12. "See It Now: Senator Joseph R. McCarthy," CBS, March 9, 1954.

13. Boylan, p. 31.

14. Abe Peck, "Faded Flowers: The Legacy of the Underground Press," *Quill*, June 1985, p. 36.

15. Michael Schudson, *Discovering the News: A Social History of American Newspapers* (New York: Basic Books, 1978), pp. 176–82.

16. Ibid.

17. Ron Javers, "Journalism: The Necessary Craft," *Nieman Reports*, Autumn 1979, p. 16.

18. Herbert J. Gans, *Deciding What's News* (New York: Vintage Books, 1980), pp. 39–72.

19. M. L. Stein, "Gloss Is Taken Off Investigative Reporting," *Editor & Publisher*, October 22, 1983, p. 11.

20. Ibid.

21. Philip Meyer, *Precision Journalism* (Bloomington, Ind.: Indiana University Press, 1973).

22. Maxwell McCombs, Donald Shaw, and David Grey, *Handbook of Reporting Methods* (Boston: Houghton-Mifflin, 1976).

23. William Boot, "Getting High on Tower," *Columbia Journalism Review*, May/June 1989, p. 18.

24. Ibid.

25. Ibid.

26. Dan Thomasson, "Cheap-Shot Journalism," *Quill*, January 1986, p. 18.

27. Thomasson, p. 21.

28. Neil Postman, "TV News as Vaudeville," *Quill*, April 1986, p. 18.

29. Postman, p. 21.

4

From Hitler to Gorbachev: Questions of Alertness

We begin, in this chapter, analyzing specific events in history and the type of contemporary media coverage each received. The purpose is not simply to study the coverage per se but to see how close it came to portraying a truthful view of reality and why that view may have come up short. Although this and upcoming chapter titles each focus on a narrow range of stories, each chapter will treat those stories as types in which certain unique factors influenced the way in which they were portrayed to the public. Chapter discussion will move from the focal story to other similar stories whose depictions were influenced by similar distorting factors. In the final chapter, we will discuss ways in which some of these distorting influences might be overcome in future news stories.

ADOLF HITLER STEPS INTO HISTORY

Although to many Americans Adolf Hitler did not become a household name until 1938 when Germany attacked Austria, the German dictator actually burst onto the scene in Western Europe January 30, 1933. The fact that more Americans were not aware of the menace Hitler posed several years before the U.S. entry into World War II is largely attributable to the news media's avoidance of him during the 1930s. To be fair, not all the U.S. news media chose to look the other way during the first several years of his regime, and other media felt they were just responding to low American interest in a rather obscure German official. After all, in 1933, the United States had been freed from the devastation of World War I for only 15 years. The unwanted memories of fighting Germans and losing sons were still too fresh to worry anew about what that country was up to. And among many Americans, there were few feelings of sympathy for Germans who might, in fact, be living under a malevolent dictator. To many who fought in the war or who saw friends and relatives die, all of Germany was still an enemy.

So it was that most of this country's media were looking the other way when Hitler came to power in 1933. The news for most newspapers at the time was more interesting and more enjoyable. There were the everyday stories of Franklin Delano Roosevelt and the economic hopes he brought to a nation reeling from recession and depression. There was the volatile story of prohibition and the antics of bootleggers and congressmen pressing for beer legislation. There were the bank robberies and the colorful Bonnie and Clyde. And there was Al Capone and the mob killings in Chicago, New York, and Detroit. There was always baseball, now in its heyday, from spring training through the World Series. In short, there was plenty to think about and write about from 1933 to 1939 other than a German politician named Adolf Hitler. And the news media knew it.

With this as a backdrop, it is not too surprising to hear accounts from journalists like William L. Shirer, probably the best-known reporter of World War II and author of *Berlin Diary* and *The Rise and Fall of the Third Reich*. Recalling the coverage of Hitler for *Boston Globe* writer M. R. Montgomery in 1983, Shirer stated, "I had the feeling the newspapers didn't want the news."[1] Continuing, however, he said maybe they did want the news, but they—like the rest of the country—just handled it with kid gloves out of fear of Communism and a growing tolerance for fascism. After all, the U.S. government seemed to be assuming the posture of tolerating right-wing governments over left-wing threats around the world, and the news media have distinguished themselves on many occasions for following the lead of the U.S. government's foreign policy.

So, in the 1930s, with the memories of the Russian Revolution clearly in their minds, along with some frightening statements from Lenin, Americans were clearly worried about Communism approaching their shores. So given the choice between a seemingly irrelevant Adolf Hitler and the "Reds," the American government, the American people, and the American news media seemed to prefer Hitler. As Montgomery notes, Americans have always thought the Bolsheviks were a threat to their wallets, and "there wasn't much in those wallets in 1933."

Keep in mind, when thinking of the ties between the U.S. government and media in the 1930s, that the ground rules were a little different then for reporting. Objectivity in the 1930s had not yet come to include the emphasis on verification that it did in the 1960s and 1970s during Vietnam and Watergate. The adversarial relationship between press and government that to a large extent exists today existed much less then. Journalistic naiveté and unchallenged patriotism were more the norm then, especially when dealing with high-level government officials. The great unifying effort by the Wilson administration that had conscripted public opinion—by using the news media—during World War I was strong evidence that the media could still be manipulated by a White House determined to do so.

With World War I over—and history as far as the news media were concerned—foreign news was being cut back. There were no CBS correspondents at all in Europe when Hitler became chancellor, Shirer recalls, adding that Edward R. Murrow would organize the system of correspondents later in 1937. Even later, when events were much more ominous for Western powers, NBC and the Mutual Broadcasting Co. withdrew their European correspondents in 1940 because they didn't want to show favoritism either way in their coverage of the European war.[2] Therefore, it was the newspapers that carried the burden of reporting Hitler's rise to power, but only a few had bureaus in Berlin in 1933, along with the wire services, of course. Still, even the wire services seemed bewildered about Hitler in the early years. The Associated Press, for instance, wrote in 1933 that Hitler had reached the "ambition of a picturesque political career" as if he were some sort of celebrity to be applauded. And, according to Shirer, the wire services developed a disturbing pattern of reporting the news of Nazis that worsened the gap between truth and knowledge among Americans. For instance, they would put any atrocities into sidebars of main stories about Nazi activities. Editors back home would usually axe these sidebars, and that was especially the case with smaller papers who were even less concerned about foreign news.[3] Since this pattern remained intact from 1933 to 1938, most Americans knew next to nothing about German atrocities for almost six years and remained intrigued by what Shirer called "the little upstart." The *Houston Post*, for example, editorializing on the basis of these wire reports, opined, "Let Hitler try his hand."

Deborah E. Lipstadt, in *Beyond Belief: The American Press and the Coming of the Holocaust*, echoes this belief that U.S. journalists buried news of the Holocaust, even as Germany was burying Jews.[4] She states that, from the beginning of Hitler's reign in 1933 to his end in 1945, the U.S. press all but missed the story of the Final Solution. A casual reader of U.S. newspapers would have been uninformed about the death camps and the extermination of millions of Jews, she says. She compares the atrocity stories to Third World bus wrecks (there are so many of them, U.S. editors felt they lost their news value after a while). She asserts the atrocities were nearly never front-page news, and they were seldom reported as uncontroverted fact. Instead, they came off as rumors, if they were written about at all. In her critique of U.S. journalism of the era, she points an especially critical finger at the *New York Times* saying, possibly because it was owned by Jews, it bent over backwards to seem detached from Jewish problems. Shirer agrees.

Two other factors seemed to influence the lax coverage of the Holocaust, Lipstadt says: anti-Semitism, which was running strong in the United States in the 1930s and 1940s, and the fact that the Roosevelt administration also was downplaying the atrocity stories. In short, since it wasn't on the president's agenda, it wasn't on the media's agenda. This theme will be addressed in more detail later.

She also posits that U.S. journalism was hampered by its own restrictive codes that required eyewitnesses and attribution and disdained crusading of any kind.[5]

Even the reporters in Berlin were taken in by Hitler's insistence that he wanted peace. Shirer recalls Frederick T. Birchall, chief of the *New York Times*'s five-man bureau in Berlin, reporting that the Nazis had no desire to go to war. Again, as Lipstadt asserts, Shirer said that possibly because the *Times* was owned and managed by a Jewish family itself, it tried to bend over backwards to be fair to non-Jews. So, even after the Jewish population in New York started calling for action to stop the atrocities in Berlin, the *Times* wrote in an editorial of a "week of evil passions and insensate folly directed against so-called dangerous minorities."[6] Still the word "Jew" was not on the editorial page of the *New York Times*. And, on January 30, 1933, the *Times* headlined another editorial "The Tamed Hitler," and said the more violent parts of his alleged program had been softened or abandoned altogether. Finally, in March of that year, the *Times* thought the time was right to start calling Hitler's program "anti-Semitism," Shirer says.

The *New York Times* was not alone in its naiveté concerning Hitler in those early years. For instance, the *Los Angeles Times* wrote, "His antisemitism is mainly rhetorical."[7] Shirer recalls that many administration powers in Washington agreed with these editorial writers, saying, "Here is a man of dynamic force."[8] Shirer also recalls how pro-fascist his old paper, the *Chicago Tribune*, was under Col. Robert McCormick. Shirer said it had a Russian bureau led by Donald Day, who would actually invent revolutions to show how threatening the Communist system was. Day even volunteered with the Finnish Army to fight Russia and was making pro-Nazi statements as late as 1944 and 1945.[9]

To be sure, not all reporters were taken in by Hitler's propagandists. Sigrid Schultz, another Berlin correspondent for McCormick, put the atrocities high up in her stories of Nazi activities. Sometimes, however, they were lowered by more cautious editors. She also wrote a book in the early 1930s called *Germany Will Try It Again*. No one would publish it until 1944, however. Once it realized the gravity of what was happening in Germany, the *New York Times* began delivering a more levelheaded assessment of Hitler's program. So did the *Boston Globe* and *Christian Science Monitor*. The following examples show how quickly these three newspapers caught on to Hitler in 1933:

- The *Boston Globe* was correct in assessing Hitler when it wrote on March 2 that he would ask for the broadest possible powers that day at the opening of the Reichstag. In an editorial that day, the *Globe* asked about the German people, "Will They Go En Masse to Armageddon?" The following day the newspaper answered its own question in a story which was headed, "All Germany Ablaze with National Spirit; Hindenburg and Hitler Sound Call for Unity as Reichstag Meets to Abolish Democracy."
- The *New York Times* published nine stories about the events of April 1 and following when Hitler ordered the national boycott of all Jewish shops and professions. A few days before that, in a March 29 editorial, the *Times* called for the German papers to print the true facts about the abuse of the Jews. "Concealment is no remedy," it said. On March 30 the *Times* editorialized that the Nazi scheme of wholesale oppression was "unbelievable." As early as a week after the April 1 boycott, the *Times* was exposing the fact of Nazi enemies being sent to prison camps. As a headline on a page-one story that day announced, "Nazis Herd Enemies Behind Barbed Wire in Big Prison Camps."
- The *Globe* wrote on April 1 that cries of "hang them" were directed against Jews at a Berlin meeting of Nazis and, looking at the propaganda being spewed out by the German press and government, asked, "Is everything [in Germany] a big lie?"
- As early as March 3 the *Globe* warned that Germany was rearming itself and warning its people of an impending war.
- On March 4, the *Christian Science Monitor* was editorializing that Germans had developed a big hatred of the Jews and advised that such hatred be curbed.

Still, a study of the coverage these three papers gave 18 significant Nazi advances during 1933 showed the *Globe* publishing only 33 stories over the six-month period or an average of just over one story per week. Most of these were AP stories. The *Monitor* did a little better, publishing 42 stories, while the *Times*—for all the criticism that Shirer laid to it—published 117. Editorially, the papers did worse, averaging only a dozen editorials each over the six-month period, or one editorial every other week. Not all of these were critical of Hitler, either.[10]

In sum, these were the three papers reputed to be among the best for international news. Despite what some might see as a paltry number of stories and editorials by at least two of them, these three papers by far supplied the most information about Nazi activities. From them, the coverage in other U.S. papers dropped off considerably.

So it was not until 1938 that most Americans became aware of Jewish persecutions and almost 94 percent disapproved of them.[11] And still many papers failed to see the real danger of the Nazis. Among these newspapers apparently was the *Detroit News* which ran a story following Hitler's May 1938 invasion of Austria under the headline "Torchlight Parade Gives Vienna a Gay Air." The story said Austria was now on the high road to financial health and that, after all, it had been under a dictatorship before anyway. And Shirer feels the *Los Angeles Times* was another. "People like [Otis] Chandler never believed us about the persecution of Catholics and Jews," he said.[12] And, when the *Times* did defend the Jews against persecution in 1940, it did so with an air of elitism as witness this editorial which read, in part, "Even if we owed them no debt of gratitude, we so-called Christians can scarcely justify any persecution of the Jews. There is always noblesse oblige—Rank Imposes Obligation."[13]

For most of the media, including the *Chicago Tribune*, the year 1938 proved to be a turning point in their thinking. The evidence of Hitler's grand design was just too strong. Still, for some editors who had tolerated him, a new theory seemed to have evolved: that he had lost control of his Nazis to a group of radical Nazis or "super Nazis" like Eichmann and Goering. But when general war broke out, the bubble burst and all U.S. papers became patriotic and united against Hitler. Still, the concept of the "good Nazi" remained throughout the war and tempered U.S. dealings with war criminals and businesses who made and sold the Nazis the gas.

In summary, the evidence indicates that most of the American media did not see the threat Hitler posed until it was almost too late for the United States. Still, there were a few of this country's best newspapers who were reporting and editorializing accurately from 1933 to 1939, and serious news consumers could have gotten word of Hitler's probable menacing design if they had taken the time to do it. Therefore, the blame must be shared by a news media that were looking for the silver lining and a public that was tired of war and rumors of war.

Even had there been more media voicing the intent and atrocities of the Nazis to the American people, it is doubtful many Americans would have paid attention. So one comes again to John Merrill's idea that, even though there is an abundance of media and message plurality, no one may be listening or reading. Think of the modern-day example of community public-access cable channels. There is generally one assigned for each cable market and over it you can get live proceedings of the city council, school board, or other governmental bodies. But does that mean the people are well informed? Not unless the people tune in that channel. It's no secret that the vast majority of viewers don't. So they remain uninformed, just as so many did during the 1930s about the Nazis' grand design.

To a great extent, this was an achievement by the Nazis' minister of propaganda, Joseph Goebbels. A master at disinformation tactics, Goebbels managed to keep much of the foreign press—as well as his own people—convinced that war was not in Hitler's thinking. As Shirer describes, many of the U.S. correspondents in Europe bought Goebbels's story, hook, line and sinker. The following passage describes the power that Goebbels's work had on the German public:

Coming generations will ask themselves how it was possible that millions of people, victims of an artificially induced enthusiasm, could be moved to do the very things which led to their own ruin. The answer could be given in hundreds of thousands of words, but, if it were expressed in one word alone, that word would be: Goebbels. Without the growth of an amoral nihilism . . . of which Goebbels was the most outstanding exponent, Hitler would never have achieved world notoriety. Without Goebbels's propaganda magic, Hitler certainly would not have become a world menace. . . . Goebbels created a new reality woven entirely out of lies. . . . Goebbels hypnotized the world.[14]

And, along with the world, he seemed to hypnotize a large portion of the U.S. press reporting from Germany.

COVERING THE SOVIET UNION

To hear Arnaud de Borchgrave, former *Newsweek* correspondent and current editor of the *Washington Times*, tell it, the U.S. media are painting a similar distorted picture of Mikhail Gorbachev, his lieutenants, and their own grand design. This time, however, according to de Borchgrave and his allies like Reed Irvine, head of Accuracy in Media, the media are distorting the picture more consciously than they did with Hitler and the Nazis. Speaking to a conservative political action group in Washington, de Borchgrave and Irvine chided the media for "not taking America's side" in confrontations with Eastern bloc countries.[15] Irvine saw no problem in defining America's side as Ronald Reagan's side when pressed by ABC's Sam Donaldson. But when Donaldson asked the audience if they also would see America's side as being Jimmy Carter's side, he was greeted with a resounding "No!" De Borchgrave attacked U.S. coverage of Gorbachev as being naive and evidencing what he called "the plague of self-hatred." This is the tendency, he said, of journalists to bash their own government while, at the same time, painting the Soviet government as growing more humane. In giving such favorable treatment to Gorbachev, de Borchgrave feels, the U.S. media is playing into the hands of Soviet disinformation specialists who know how to work U.S. reporters and editors.

In response, Donaldson echoed John Milton's refrain for truth and lies to have their day in the arena and for the public to decide which is right and which is wrong. Challenging Irvine, Donaldson asked, "Why is it that *you* can tell the difference between right and wrong, but the reading and viewing public can't?" Donaldson said the more important thing people ought to be seeking from the media is coverage of all sides of an issue, whether internationally or domestically. If a reader or viewer doesn't want such coverage, then he doesn't need the news media. All he needs is a subscription to their own party's newsletter or whatever special-interest publication trumpets their views. Donaldson concluded, "I am *not* a propagandist."

Whichever side one takes in that debate, and there are points worth pondering from both sides, we are left with the very real challenge posed today in trying to figure out just exactly what the Soviets are up to. There is no doubt that things are changing in the Soviet Union. The question is how far they are changing, why, and how long-lasting and far-reaching those changes will be. Few would argue that the Soviet propaganda system is still in high gear, just as is the U.S. system. L. John Martin and Anju Grover Chaudhary, in their book *Comparative Mass Media Systems*, reinforce that point and note somewhat ironically, 'Peaceful coexistence' and 'detente' provide excellent environments for the dissemination of pro-Soviet and anti-Western propaganda."[16] And the $3 billion Soviet dissemination system is very comprehensive. Communist countries use both print and electronic news media to disseminate its reports. For instance, TASS has exchange contracts with other large news services and national news agencies. It sends out materials, including photographs, of nearly 300 reports on domestic and foreign subjects daily to more than 400 news and press agencies, ministries of information, newspaper editorial boards, and TV and radio broadcasting companies in more than 90 countries. Soviet policies and doctrine are clearly reflected.[17] Through it all, the Soviets see their press as a partner to the Communist party, voicing its doctrine and upholding its value system. The Soviets call it a free press because it is allegedly freed from the elitists to support the value and beliefs of the working classes.

In 1961 the Soviet Union began a second news agency called Novosti or APN (The News Press Agency). Ostensibly non–government-controlled, it is a party-inspired and controlled public information service designed officially "to aid the development and strengthening of mutual understanding, confidence, and friendship among peoples."[18] An additional purpose was to disseminate favorable Soviet materials to counter "hostile capitalist propaganda." Novosti is a huge propaganda network that is operating in more than a hundred countries, including the United States.[19] So any attempt at interpreting Soviet policy, at least through Soviet information systems, must be met with some healthy skepticism.

Nevertheless, one of the strongest indications that there is a quiet revolution under way is the fact that more newspapers in the Soviet Union are starting to cover events heretofore forbidden by party officials. For instance, Soviet media policy has long dictated that most domestic disasters, whether natural or man-made, get scant coverage if any at all. One example is airplane crashes. Tradition has dictated that the Soviet news media are prohibited from covering them unless they involved a heroic, last-minute attempt by pilots or ground crew members to save the aircraft. Heroism, after all, is seen as a Soviet value worth nurturing in the people. It is worthy of coverage; senseless air tragedies are not. Never mind that hundreds of people may die. In the past, they have drawn back-page blurb coverage if at all. Irina Kirilova, one-time head of Pravda's Information Department, said "the reader must know something new and good. If there is a connection with heroism, courage or overcoming a great risk then we write about it. What's the point of writing about every plane crash? It happens that accidents occur for technical reasons—that doesn't interest us very much."[20]

The same can be said of larger disasters such as the nuclear accident at Chernobyl. How long was it before the Soviet media were even permitted to reveal that there had been an accident involving such large numbers of deaths? The normal method of telling the public what happened in such cases, if a total blackout is not feasible, is to announce the event itself, always with one additional sentence, that the "competent authorities have started an investigation." If the report mentions that officials express their sympathies to the families, this is generally an indication that there were several fatalities and injuries.[21] In his 1976 book *The Russians*, Hedrick Smith wrote, "It takes a great leap of imagination for Westerners, especially Americans who are literally blitzed by information, to picture the poverty of information in Russia."[22]

In addition, former Moscow correspondent Whitman Bassow notes that, in the Soviet Union, foreign correspondents achieve access to government sources only on a quid pro quo basis. One of many examples he cites occurred in 1933 between Konstantin Oumansky, chairman of the Soviet press department, and several foreign journalists. Oumansky exerted pressure on the correspondents to denounce a story a fellow journalist had written about widespread hunger in the Ukraine. In turn, the correspondents received credentials to cover a kangaroo court trial of a half-dozen British engineers who were charged by the Soviets with sabotage. Oumansky and the correspondents sealed their pact with Russian vodka.[23]

But today some of this seems to be changing as glasnost and perestroika are gaining more of a foothold. The Soviet system has enlarged the parameters of permissible criticism and of covering events that heretofore had not been allowed. Journalist Rick Ackermann noted recently:

Readers are writing in to ask things like how come they have to stand in all those long Russian lines when party officials don't. Recently Pravda went after some Uzbek officials who they claim live in "palatial country homes" that are much different from a Palace of Labor.[24]

Paul McMasters, deputy editorial director of *USA Today*, noted recently, "The [Soviet] press is both leading and reflecting a general loosening of tongues and minds in the Soviet Union."[25] And Reese Cleghorn, dean of the College of Journalism at the University of Maryland says, "In the great drama of recent events in the Communist world, nothing has been more arresting than the sound of shackles being broken by the totalitarian press."[26]

Even so, keeping in mind the traps U.S. reporters fell into with other totalitarian regimes like Adolf Hitler's, how do we go about covering the Soviet Union today? As Richard O'Mara, foreign editor of the *Baltimore Sun* asks, "So what happened to the worldwide class struggle, the epic contest that was supposed to end with the victory of socialism on every side? Was peaceful coexistence in place again?"[27] And, in contrast to de Borchgrave's warnings to the media about letting themselves be puppets of *Soviet* disinformation specialists, what do you do with the thinking of Stephen Cohen, Princeton historian and sovietologist? In *Rethinking the Soviet Experience: Politics and History Since 1917*, Cohen attacked many of his colleagues for their lack of objectivity and for allowing their work to be used as an instrument of *U.S.* foreign policy.[28]

So it seems the media face a steep challenge in trying to navigate between U.S. government disinformation specialists and Soviet disinformation specialists. Through it all, the press must resist its urge to be so conformist. It must guard against being manipulated by either side. If it is, its news stories will present that all-too-familiar distortion of reality. Speaking of the media's conformity, O'Mara notes:

We are trapped into pack journalism by the competitive nature of our business. It is hard to be enterprising in such a milieu, to send your only regional correspondent to Panama, say, in the hope he may uncover a major drug scandal, when every other newspaper has its man in Nicaragua because the president of the United States is waving the bloody shirt over that country. That takes a large measure of self-confidence, and a determination to be different.[29]

It also takes, once again, a historical perspective. The notion that those who ignore history are certain to repeat its mistakes is an appropriate one when it comes to covering the Soviet Union or any other totalitarian society. As always, journalists must assume the role of skeptics, hoping for the best but staying prepared for the worst, and print all of it that seems newsworthy when it happens. O'Mara seems to agree when he says, "As an editor . . . I am not preparing to recommend that we close our Moscow bureau. I do have a nagging feeling that I may have been here before."[30]

ARE THE MEDIA ADEPT AT FOREIGN NEWS?

Have the media failed us in times of rising political storms? Have they been, and do they continue to be, asleep at the switch at key times in history or too naive? Why did so few newspapers attempt to fulfill their mission of giving a truthful picture of reality during the 1930s, the 1950s with Sen. Joseph McCarthy, the early 1960s with Vietnam, and—some would say—today with the Soviet Union?

To begin with, we should realize that hindsight lets us see events much clearer than they were seen at the time of occurrence. To be sure, if the news media had realized the gravity of the Nazi question to Americans, there would have been something approaching saturation coverage of the event. But that is the challenge that reporters face daily: to judge contemporary events for both short-term and long-term significance. It is not easy, but experienced journalists who know history should be able to do a good job of it. It is one big reason university journalism schools stress the value of a liberal arts background that is deep in U.S. and European history. The accrediting agency for journalism schools requires that three-fourths of the classes taken by a journalism major be taken outside of journalism from the field of liberal arts. Journalists must have some historical sense about the world in order to effectively and accurately judge contemporary events. The sad fact is that, often, it seems the media are guilty of presenting events as if they had no context and are devoid of any relationship to previous events. Often it seems journalists themselves see events as being disconnected: a series of isolated events, hard to measure for significance because there is no appropriate context or comparative event to use as a baseline or standard.

In addition, journalists are often guilty of letting the White House or Congress set the news media's agenda. Many times in history the news media have waited until the president or some congressional committee elevates an issue to importance before they themselves do. This is in spite of the evidence that may have existed all along that trouble is afoot in a given area and is a danger to Americans. That occurred in 1933 and, in fact, occurred as recently as the Noriega controversy in Panama. In this latest instance, despite the fact that evidence abounded that Gen. Manuel Noriega had been in bed with drug smugglers for years prior to 1985, the U.S. news media waited for the Reagan administration to finally decide that he was a big enough threat to the United States to speak out publicly against him. Prior to that, the Reagan administration seemed to tolerate Noriega as an ally to prodemocracy forces in this hemisphere. When Reagan shifted his position, however, the media picked Noriega up as a major story of the day and have stayed with it ever since. Journalist Ken Silverstein wrote of this phenomenon:

Recently—and only recently—has coverage focused on General Manuel Antonio Noriega, who has been portrayed as a thug presiding over a corrupt regime. Any reporter with even a minimum of initiative—or with the encouragement of an alert editor—could have written this story years ago. Panamanian opposition figures have long tried to interest American reporters in Noriega's extracurricular activities. They had no support until late in 1985, when the U.S. government began openly criticizing the Panamanian strongman.[31]

Silverstein notes that, in analyzing editorials of six leading dailies including the *New York Times* and *Washington Post*, he found no criticism of the 1984 Panamanian presidential election. That election was won by Nicolas Ardito Barletta, a handpicked minion of Noriega. The papers' silence ended, however, in September of 1985 when the Reagan administration turned on Noriega, withholding a $5 million grant. Within a few weeks most of those same six newspapers that were earlier silent on Noriega ran stiff criticisms accusing him and his men of antidemocratic tendencies.[32]

"From this point on, Panama and Noriega received a growing amount of negative publicity both from the Reagan administration and in news stories," Silverstein says.[33]

Some might say this is all okay—that the news media themselves should not be setting the country's agenda, that the media should mirror society's agenda. But what happens when politicians, whether in office or out, are allowed to set that agenda? Ronald Reagan may be in an entirely different moral category to most than Richard Nixon, but what if Nixon's people had been allowed to set the media agenda during the Watergate era? Certainly they tried, and, with many of the country's media, they succeeded for a long time. A presidency does not always operate for the altruistic good of the people, nor do many individual congressmen and senators. That is the basis for the adversarial relationship between the press and the government. That is the reason the press is called the Fourth Estate. Yet what happens to that adversarial relationship when the press follows the administration's agenda?

In part that is easy to do, especially for reporters, editors, and producers with only a limited world view themselves. Then they become even easier to string along. The public, with even a more limited view of the world, is then obliged to follow in step. For one thing, for most people, the political map of the world is drawn by reporters and editors; not cartographers. Presumably, how editors perceive the world would affect the way they sketch the world map. And their perception, of course, helps present—or distort—reality for the rest of society.[34]

Another problem with foreign news, however, is that often American editors or television producers don't really see it as news unless and until if affects Americans themselves. In part, this is because of some

traditional criteria of news value such as proximity and local impact. But
do those values hold up when one is looking at events in Germany
under Hitler or in looking at other tragedies—natural and man-made—
in other parts of the world?

We might ask ourselves, could the media be so naive about an Adolf
Hitler today? After all, we live in an electronic age where information
abounds on a global scale. It's there for the taking, and we can retrieve
it instantaneously from services like Nexis, DataTimes, VuText, and a
myriad of other electronic information providers. We could never be
taken in by modern-day demagogues or misinterpret events in foreign
countries. Right? Wrong. It is ironic that in the current age of information, as Meg Greenfield says, "we get the impression that we know
more than we do."[35]

There are all these names and all these political tags and odd bits of information
that we string together and talk about without any more insight than you can
put on graffiti: Rafsanjani is a moderate. . . . Zhao Ziyang is a reformer. . . . Our
heads are stuffed full of snippets of lore that give us the false impression that
we know something when we don't. . . . Again and again in recent times America
has been flabbergasted by developments in places that we thought we understood. Iran and Indochina are prime examples. In both places we mistook a
mountain of data for actual understanding and superimposed on it a political
template that distorted the truth. . . . We are misled by our own information,
knowing much more than we understand.[36]

Part of the problem of knowing a lot and understanding only a little
springs from the American love of ethnocentrism. This can take several
forms, and one was alluded to earlier: a feeling that foreign news isn't
really news until it affects Americans. Take the coverage of the 1984
Union Carbide tragedy in Bhopal. Many top Indian journalists feel U.S.
reporters missed the focus of the story as it advanced, and that they
missed it because of a curious American trait: looking mainly for how
the story affects Americans. V. K. Narayawan, editor-in-chief of India's
Tribune, puts it this way:

The Americans were so concerned, because the loss of a human being is more
greatly valued in America than in the Third World, and they wanted to know
if Bhopal could happen there. We have such a profusion of people. U.S. journalists were never fair about it. The American idea is that a loss in the Third
World doesn't affect them. That feeling I could see come through in their reports.
They were only worried about whether it could happen in America. I think an
American life is worth more to them.[37]

But Victoria Graham, former New Delhi AP bureau chief, disagrees.
"That's wrong to say we don't care about the loss of Indian lives. But

... say there is a train crash and two people are killed. Pass it. And we do pass it. We pass it all the time. Indian railroads aren't that good, and they're always running away. It's not because it's Indians that we pass; it's because it happens over here all the time."[38]

That may be but, even so, it still provides witness to one reason that the atrocity stories of the Hitler reign of terror went largely unreported in America: There were just too many of them, and they ceased to become news, according to traditional U.S. news criteria.

That's all one aspect of American ethnocentrism. But there is at least one other affecting American reporting of foreign countries. We seem to feel that all movements toward freedom—or at least away from Communism—resemble America's democratic birth. Indeed we seem to feel that they are modeled on our own brand of democracy. So we see events—*tips of icebergs*—in Tiananmen Square occurring and we rush to the judgment that China is at once throwing off decades of a repressive government and will be building a permanent statue of liberty, that will probably look like ours, very soon. Shortly afterwards, they will probably be setting up a bicameral legislative body and installing a democratically elected president. Naivté personified, and the U.S. news media should be pointing out the improbability of it rather than reinforcing a distorted sense of reality. Yet because of an abbreviated sense of history, coupled with a limited world view, many reporters just don't get it.

An ABC "Nightline" program in November 1989 brought home this whole aspect of ethnocentrism in clear terms.[39] A couple of weeks after the East German government decided to nullify the effect of the Berlin Wall and allow their countrymen free passage to the West, "Nightline" producers decided to get East Germans' interpretation of U.S. coverage of the event. Several of the East Germans interviewed said the U.S. media, although doing a fairly good job in presenting the facts, nevertheless overemphasized and overstated the desire of many East Germans to flee their homeland. After all, they said, this is their home. Most didn't want the Wall removed so they could all run away from their homes, families, friends, and careers. Several of those interviewed said, in fact, the issue had nothing at all to do with the doctrine of Communism or its abandonment by East Germans. Even the Communists wanted the freedom to travel to the West. Most, however, planned to return after the visits.

But U.S. journalists have to be able to spend time in a country to understand its people and to realize that what these East Germans were saying was true. It took a Canadian, ABC's Peter Jennings, to admonish a field of top broadcast journalists at a DuPont-Columbia Awards Program to "spend more time in country" in order to understand what is really going on.[40]

Too often the on-camera reporter is flown into a city or country just to do the stand-up, then whisked away to another venue. And, too often, reporters are sent into countries they really don't understand and haven't had the time to background themselves on the people, culture, or language. Absent that kind of background, reporters are often prone to reporting from an ethnocentric base, defining the colors of their new culture through a strictly American prism. As Herbert Gans would remind us, if you want to see what ethnocentrism is really like, look at how foreign news is reported by U.S. journalists.

Still another exhibit of ethnocentrism is discussed in Chapter 9 with the handling by U.S. publications such as *Time* of the 1983 Soviet shootdown of Korean Air Lines Flight 007. Even a casual glance at the coverage this incident received by much of the American media will show how quick U.S. editors are to assume the Soviets are so capable of murder and how purely innocent the U.S. government is of contributing to tragedies such as this.

Turning to the realm of fiction for a moment to illustrate reality, can one ever forget the bewilderment and unpreparedness of Mel Gibson's Guy Hamilton in the critically acclaimed film *The Year of Living Dangerously*? Here this Australian journalist was, far from home for possibly the first time, dropped into the mass confusion of Jakarta. His only orientation to this culture—to reality—was his predecessor in the job, who had already fled the country and left behind only a note saying in effect, "Good luck." Had it not been for the enigmatic Billy Kwan, the diminutive photojournalist who had a keen understanding of the country and yet who was so inappropriately underrated by his journalistic peers, Hamilton would have spent months wallowing in the mystery of Indonesia. He would have spent his time either sending back off-base accounts or looking over the shoulders of the wire service reporters for ideas and leads. Not that their accounts would have been any more reflective of life in this hellhole, because they themselves had fallen into the trap of focusing almost totally on Sukarno and his cronies for their news of the day. The official source syndrome at its best: focusing on the top of the hierarchy instead of those who have to live with the policies sent down from above. Hamilton's salvation came as he realized, through Billy, that he must change this traditional focus and factor in the people as well, trying to understand their problems and their intended solutions.

CENSORSHIP, VIOLENCE PLAY A ROLE

To be fair, distorted accounts of life abroad are not always the fault of the journalists themselves. Often they are the result of the oppressive conditions correspondents are asked to report under. Some earlier discussion focused on the role Soviet suppression of news plays in getting out an accurate account of life in Russia. In other countries, as well, reporters are operating under the watchful eye of government authorities, and sometimes stories must pass through some official government censor before being transmitted back to the states. Certainly this was the case with much of the reporting done in Hitler's Germany. Berlin correspondents were subject to automatic censorship, and all government media were state-owned. So U.S. correspondents either had to find ways to spirit their stories home past the censors or else soften their material to accommodate the state's official censors.

In recent history U.S. correspondents found how restrictive such censorship can be when, following the tragedy of Tiananmen Square in Beijing, the Chinese government blacked out all television transmission, both domestic and international. U.S. journalists were detained if they were found reporting or shooting pictures in unauthorized areas. The same has held true in recent years for such non-Communist countries as India and South Africa. Justifying such censorship as preventing more upheaval in a time of state-declared emergency, the Indian and South African governments have resorted to strict suppression of news via shutting down newspapers and/or jailing reporters and editors for indefinite periods of time. Never mind that the emergencies were brought about by the governments themselves. Conditions were now volatile, and many governments feel the first thing to do is silence the media or bring it in line with official government thinking.

During the summer of 1989, when student demonstrations in Beijing erupted into mass bloodshed when Chinese troops moved in to crush the dissidents, life was very dangerous for any journalist covering the action. In addition to blacking out reports of the violence in the streets, the Chinese government had ordered a news blackout on all events surrounding the demonstration. In fact, they cut lines that were feeding live coverage back to the states and left news reports in mid-sentence. Several reporters were arrested and detained before being let go; their cameras and notes confiscated.

Kyle Gibson, producer for "ABC News," noted the bullets were so close to his perch in Tiananmen Square that his two-way radio could pick up the sound. As he began to describe to anchorman Peter Jennings in New York what was happening, machine guns opened up on him. "I stopped broadcasting and tried to race for cover, but there was no place to run except straight down the boulevard," Gibson said. "The sound of approaching tanks was terrifying. Within minutes, I crouched in a ditch in time to watch the first tank from the east bear down and crush the tractor on which I had just been perched. Someone told me my radio would be confiscated in the hotel, so I tossed it in the bushes near the door before escaping inside."[41]

Mike Chinoy, CNN correspondent, said he and his colleague, Tom

Mintier, lived a night of horror that Friday evening. "Throughout the night, [we] struggled to control our horror as we telephoned live reports to CNN, using a hotel room we had dubbed 'Tokyo Base' in order to avoid revealing the exact location over obviously tapped phone lines. Now there were rumors that soldiers would soon sweep through the hotel looking for reporters and TV equipment. Already, plainclothes police officers had begun searching some of those entering or leaving the lobby."[42]

In Poland, when rulers imposed martial law on December 13, 1981, a brief respite of press freedom came to a halt as hundreds of newspapers were shut down, and some 2,100 Polish journalists were either dismissed or told they must resign.[43]

In Northern Ireland, police often issue a "tissue of lies" about incidents in which members of the Irish Republican Army are shot by undercover officers.[44] In covering one such 1984 shooting, involving the deaths of three IRA members, *New York Times* correspondent Jo Thomas says she was warned off the story by British officials and then was refused all official records, including transcripts of inquests and trials that had previously been open to the public.[45]

In some cases, this attempt to bring journalism in line with official government policy reaches the ridiculous level. Writer Barbara Mary Johnson describes how a young Chinese reporter for Xinhua News Agency was covering an innovative television series dealing with teenagers discussing their everyday problems in China. In one segment, the teens began talking about dating and teenage crushes. The problem is that, in China, this type of teenage boy-girl relationship is frowned upon as being counterproductive and taking students away from their studies. The story the reporter did also focused on other aspects of the program, including traffic problems, the difficulty of college entrance exams, and so on. As Johnson states, the entire story was nearly killed by government censors and squeaked by only when all references to the dating discussion had been deleted. "In wielding their blue pencils, Xinhua editors had demonstrated a keen sense of what was *not* news in China. As it turned out, the producers of the TV forum were of like mind. The program on dating was never aired," Johnson says.[46]

If China is that paranoid about such seemingly innocuous subjects winding up in the news, how does it deal with more weighty matters? What about any attempts at investigative reporting, for instance? Such reporting does in fact exist, but the results of it are seldom—if ever—published. A young Chinese journalist notes, "We just send the article direct to the council [the news censors], and the council corrects the problem that the reporter was writing about."[47] If any word gets out at all about the problem to the readers, it may be published in a later roundup article, according to Johnson.

My wife and I were in India a few years ago, doing an article on how Indian journalists perceive Western reporting of their country. I recall on several occasions feeling that various Indian editors in New Delhi and other cities were choosing their words very carefully and, in some cases, censoring themselves as they spoke. But one particular occasion serves to show how paranoid some journalists in that proclaimed democracy are of their own government and of foreign journalists. My wife and I were invited to speak to a gathering of journalists who comprised an area press council for the city of Chandigarh in the Punjab region of northern India. There were about 50 of us sitting in a living room, and I was discussing some views U.S. journalists hold about their craft. Then I turned the tables and began asking questions of them such as, "What degree of freedom do you feel you have to report news in India?" and "Have you ever felt coerced by your government to present a particular point of view?" Utter silence engulfed the room, as the journalists sat and stared expressionless at us. I tried to restart the questioning, but as I did, a man came up to my wife and asked if he could see the notes she had been scribbling in her notepad. Before she could answer him, he reached down and grabbed the pad off her lap, then turned and ran upstairs with it. We were dumbfounded and, being a guest at this event, I didn't know what to do or how to react. It seemed I should chase after him, because that notepad had the results of several days' worth of interviews of journalists both in Chandigarh and elsewhere. Yet I was unsure of how the other journalists in the room would view that behavior. I didn't want them to think we were trying to hide anything from them. In any event, the moment passed in stunned silence for us. The audience was as unruffled and quiet as they had been seconds before the incident, so I resumed my questioning, relying on the ability of our host to retrieve the notepad. As it turned out, it was the right decision. We got the notepad back about 20 minutes later, but I never got any answers to my questions about government control of the press. Instead, our host explained later that our audience thought it a strong possibility that Diane and I were CIA agents, either working for the Indian government to find out who its allies and enemies were in the press or on some equally troublesome mission. As for the man who took the notepad, it was questionable as to whether he himself was a government agent or, like the others, just overly suspicious of us. Later in our trip we found the government's immigration bureau had been following our travels by calling people with whom we had visited. Giving them the benefit of the doubt, they may have only been concerned for our safety. But, by then, we were becoming paranoid ourselves and were thinking we were the objects of the government's scrutiny for other reasons.

Part of the difficulty journalists have in reporting in Third World countries is that their censorship may actually be more stringent than in Communist countries. Most of the world's 100-plus Third World nations were listed in a 1980 report from Freedom House (which monitors political rights and civil liberties worldwide) of countries having a significant or dominant voice in determining what does or does not appear in the media.[48] So even though the print media are free in many Third World countries, like India for instance, their content is watched carefully by the government in power. There are direct and indirect controls that can be exerted if a newspaper gets off-track, and these controls range from withholding newsprint (and in India, the all-important government advertising) to jailing the offending editor.

Most Third World countries practice a form of journalism known as "development journalism," a practice encouraged by UNESCO. That agency has called for the establishment of national communication policies in all Third World countries and has encouraged these countries to use their media in the economic and social development strategies. As defined by Sussman, development journalism is a "concentration by objective journalists on the news, the newness, of developments in education, agriculture, industry, communications, and applied science; developments that leaders hope will eventually produce economic success and a secure sense of national unity."[49]

The problem is that UNESCO's "new world information order" was never defined. As Robert L. Stevenson, author of *Communication, Development, and the Third World*, states, it became an omnibus slogan for a developing-world wish list of desires ranging from vaguely expressed "self-sufficiency" or "independence" to "just the good news, please" to harsher things, depending on who was speaking.[50] Commenting on Stevenson's point, former *Washington Star* foreign editor Dana R. Bullen says:

The more radical ideas—licensing of journalists, an international code of conduct, prescribed news agenda, etc.—threatened press freedom, everybody's freedom, and especially the right to know of people living in developing countries. Independent news media and countries believing in uncontrolled news— a "free flow of information"—now themselves mobilized and fought to preserve these freedoms. The resulting war has raged for more than a decade.[51]

Although UNESCO came out with an encouragement in the fall of 1989 for all Third World countries to allow the free flow of information, it remains to be seen what effect, if any, that will have.

Many Third World governments go beyond even questionable manipulation tactics to use the media as instruments of political power. In so doing, they conscript journalists to help stabilize existing governments, whether those governments should remain in power or not.

Foreign journalists reporting from such Third World sites encounter a range of similar restrictions, and some countries like Costa Rica require journalists to be licensed by the government before doing any reporting at all. In 1980, for instance, U.S. journalist Stephen B. Schmidt was charged in Costa Rica with the "illegal practice of the profession of journalism." His case before the Inter-American Court of Human Rights, now a decade old, has turned into a major test of Third World licensing.[52] In his case, he was arrested for not belonging to the country's Colegio de Periodistas, or journalists' association. To join the Colegio, a journalist must have graduated in journalism from Costa Rica's state university. Schmidt graduated from another university.

In a way, Schmidt is one of the lucky journalists running afoul of Third World governments. A 1988 Freedom House study of 159 countries found 26 journalists were killed while working in 11 countries that year. Some 238 journalists were arrested or detained, 50 more than in 1987. Another 14 were abducted, 53 were assaulted, and 43 were threatened with death.[53]

In one such country, Kenya, four foreign correspondents covering student protests at the University of Nairobi were beaten and arrested. Patrick Moser of UPI, Didrikke Schanche of AP, Lindsey Hilsum, who freelances for *The Guardian* and the BBC, and Peer Menert of Deutsche Press-Agentur were questioned by police, detained for three hours, and then freed after authorities confiscated their notes. Hilsum suffered severe bruises and a fractured bone in her neck, and Moser had a concussion and a perforated eardrum.[54]

Other evidence of intimidation comes from the Middle East and includes:[55]

- Several killings of correspondents in Syria after writing stories that government officials didn't like. Others have exited the country, often after death threats.
- Continuous threats against correspondents in Arab countries and Iran to keep them in line. In addition, these countries practice strict censorship that makes it virtually impossible for the media to cover some important events. For example, when the Syrian city of Hama was virtually destroyed in 1982 and upwards to 30,000 residents were killed, the story went unreported for months and then received only scant coverage.
- PLO killings of correspondents and threats against others who step outside the political boundaries of the PLO.
- The detention in Lebanon of U.S. correspondent Terry Anderson, who has been a prisoner there for years.

To be sure, this kind of intimidation, coupled with outright government censorship, does not help the correspondent intent on portraying a truthful account of reality in these countries.

SUMMARY

Truth is an elusive enough commodity even in a country that a reporter understands well. But in a foreign land, truth becomes even more shadowy; at times invisible. Because of an abundance of reasons, some for which U.S. correspondents have been responsible and others not, the U.S. news consumer has not always had the most truthful of portrayals from other countries. There is, however, one thing the U.S. journalistic community can do something about. That is to increase its interest in things foreign and to hire more reporters who understand both the culture and language of the countries that need coverage. It is no secret that most foreigners, when they come to the United States, find the paucity of foreign news here alarming. Editors' interest—as well as the public's—in foreign news has been characterized by Paul M. Davis, former national president of the Society of Professional Journalists, as only a "casual disinterest." He notes:

It is a bit embarrassing to face the fact that, for an educated nation, we aren't very sharp on foreign affairs . . . and don't seem to care, either. We have not been good at anticipating change in the world, and we have been remarkably quiet in reporting that we may have won the Cold War. . . . We are rarely aware of the ties of our local communities to other parts of the world. *The New York Times*, pre-eminent in coverage of international news is said to have international copy in only 14 percent of its news hole. Networks have cut back on foreign bureaus, wire services have reduced foreign staffing, many world-class newspapers have shrunk their distant staffs, and there is little complaint from the viewers and readers.[56]

This last observation is true, one might add, until another Adolf Hitler is threatening war against the United States, or the price of gasoline at the American pump seems—overnight and without warning—to have jumped 100 percent, or the East German government suddenly opens its borders for its own citizens to travel freely to the West. Then, absent coverage leading up to these events, we are left scratching our heads and asking "Now how did that happen?" And finally, "Where were the news media?"

NOTES

1. M. R. Montgomery, "Reporting on the Third Reich," *Boston Globe, Magazine*, January 30, 1983, pp. 11–13.

2. Ibid.

3. Ibid.

4. Deborah E. Lipstadt, *Beyond Belief: The American Press and the Coming of the Holocaust* (New York: Free Press, 1986).

5. Ibid.

6. Montgomery, pp. 11–13.

7. Ibid.

8. Ibid.

9. Ibid.

10. Jim Willis, "The American Press and Adolph Hitler: A Comparative Study of the *New York Times, Boston Globe,* and *Christian Science Monitor,*" unpublished paper, 1985, p. 7.

11. Montgomery, p. 13.

12. Ibid., p. 13.

13. Ibid., p. 13.

14. Curt Riess, *Joseph Goebbels* (New York: Ballantine, 1960), p. v.

15. Arnaud de Borchgrave, speaking at a Conservative Political Action Committee seminar "The Press and East-West Relations," Washington, D.C., 1987.

16. L. John Martin and Anju Grover Chaudhary, *Comparative Mass Media Systems* (New York: Longman, 1983), p. 124.

17. Martin, pp. 124–125.

18. Ibid.

19. Ibid.

20. Martin, p. 71.

21. Ibid.

22. Rick Ackermann, quoting Hedrick Smith, in "The Problem With Pravda," *Washington Journalism Review,* July 1986, p. 45.

23. Whitman Bassow, *The Moscow Correspondents: Reporting on Russia from the Revolution to Glasnost* (New York: William Morrow, 1988).

24. Ackermann, p. 45.

25. Paul McMasters, "Soviet Journalists Soar on Glasnost Wings," *Quill,* July/ August 1989, p. 7.

26. Reese Cleghorn, "Look Who Wants to be a Journalist," *Washington Journalism Review,* July/August 1989, p. 2.

27. Richard O'Mara, "Life Without the Red Menace," *Quill,* January 1989, p. 17.

28. O'Mara, quoting Cohen, p. 17.

29. O'Mara, p. 18.

30. O'Mara, p. 19.

31. Ken Silverstein, "The Panama Story, or Here We Go Again," *Columbia Journalism Review,* March 1988, p. 20.

32. Ibid.

33. Ibid.

34. Tsan-Kuo Chang, Barry Pollick, and Jae-won Lee, "Constructing the World: Newspaper Editors and Their World View," paper presented to the 1989 annual convention of the Association for Education in Journalism and Mass Communication, Washington, D.C., August 10–13, 1989, p. 5.

35. Meg Greenfield, "Misled by the Facts," *Newsweek,* June 26, 1989, p. 76.

36. Ibid.

37. Jim Willis and Diane Willis, "India: A Case Study in International Reporting," *Nieman Reports* 42, no. 4, Winter 1988, p. 28.

38. Jim and Diane Willis, p. 29.

39. "Nightline," ABC, November 13, 1989.

40. Peter Jennings, speech at DuPont-Columbia Awards Presentation, New York City, April 17, 1986.

41. "In Beijing, a Month of Living Dangerously," *New York Times*, June 29, 1989, p. 29.

42. Ibid.

43. Jane Leftwich Curry, "Poland's Press—After the Crackdown," *Columbia Journalism Review*, September/October 1984, pp. 36, 38.

44. Jo Thomas, "Bloody Ireland," *Columbia Journalism Review*, May/June 1988, pp. 31–32.

45. Ibid.

46. Barbara Mary Johnson, "Polishing the News," *Quill*, December 1987, p. 25.

47. Johnson, p. 26.

48. Martin, p. 153.

49. Ibid.

50. Robert L. Stevenson, *Communication, Development, and the Third World: The Global Politics of Information* (New York: Longman, 1988).

51. Dana R. Bullen, "Third World Media—Watchdog not Lapdog Role," *Nieman Reports*, 42, no. 2, Summer 1988, p. 39.

52. Doyle McManus, "Reporting Without a License," *Washington Journalism Review*, December 1985, p. 10.

53. "Incidents Against Journalists Reported Higher in 1988," *Presstime*, February 1989, p. 41.

54. LeeAnn Stauffer, "Crackdown in Kenya," *Columbia Journalism Review*, November 1987, p. 12.

55. Ze'ev Chafets, *Double Vision: How the Press Distorts America's View of the Middle East* (New York: William Morrow, 1984).

56. Paul M. Davis, "Foreign News: A Casual Disinterest," *Quill*, April 1989, p. 43.

5

Asleep on NASA, HUD, and the EPA

Chapter 4 addressed the question of how alert the U.S. media have been on foreign developments. This chapter will look at how awake the same media have been in covering strictly American institutions and agencies. To begin the discussion, we will focus on recent events involving the National Aeronautic and Space Administration, Department of Housing and Urban Development, and Environmental Protection Agency. As before, the discussion will focus on common threads that seemed to influence the reporting on these agencies.

NASA COURTS THE PRESS

There is a scene late in the offbeat western, *The Man Who Shot Liberty Valence*, where Rance Stoddard, the local hero who has risen to the U.S. Senate largely on his legendary victory over the dreaded Valence, reveals to a reporter what *really* happened. Stoddard didn't shoot the gunslinger at all. Instead, it was a friend who fired from the shadows at the last minute to save Stoddard's life. The reporter began scribbling notes furiously, whereupon his editor—an admirer of Senator Stoddard—grabbed the notebook from his reporter's hands, tore out the poison page, and ripped it up. "When the legend becomes fact," the editor philosophized, "print the legend."[1]

In Tom Wolfe's *The Right Stuff*, the media are seen as a group of doting admirers of NASA's boy-wonder astronauts who perform the same deed. Indeed, the press appears star-struck by the whole sweep of the spaceshot program. The 1960s offered a chance for all of us to fantasize about sitting atop a rocket and being shot into outer space. If we could beat the dreaded Russians in the process, how marvelous! Journalists were no exception to this thinking. In fact, they probably lived as vicariously through the pilots they covered as anyone else. Maybe even more. Here is the way Wolfe describes their actions when being introduced to the Mercury Seven team for the first time:

With that, applause erupted, applause of the most fervent sort, amazing applause. Reporters rose to their feet, applauding as if they had come for no other reason. Smiles of weepy and grateful sympathy washed across their faces. They gulped, they cheered, as if this were one of the most inspiring moments of their lives. Even some of the photographers straightened up from out of their beggar's crouches and let their cameras dangle from their straps, so that they could use their hands for clapping. But for what?[2]

Wolfe asks this because these seven men were unknowns to all present. Their previous achievements as flyers, some dubious indeed, were unknown. Their introduction by NASA officials had said nothing about their being chosen because of their piloting abilities. Only because they were "adaptable" to this new program. After all, the test pilots at Edwards Air Force Base—or anyone else who even tried to find out—knew these were not even the military's seven *best* pilots. Some had not flown test flights, some had not flown combat, one had relatively few hours in jets at all. Indeed, if any reporter had been enterprising enough to discover, these men were not even going to *fly* their space capsules at all. Before they would even get a chance at going up, the first shots would be manned by monkeys! And what happened when this fact was pointed out to the media as Chuck Yeager did in Phoenix prior to the initial launches?

The press, the eternal Victorian Gent, just couldn't deal with what he had said. The wire services wouldn't touch the remark. It ran in one of the local newspapers, and that was that.... Here was everybody talking as if the Mercury astronauts would be the first men to ride rockets. Yeager had done precisely that more than forty times. Fifteen other pilots had done it also, and they had reached speeds greater than three times the speed of sound . . . and that was just the beginning. *All of this should have been absolutely obvious to anyone, even people who knew nothing about flying*—and surely it would become clear that anybody in Project Mercury was more of a test subject than a pilot.[3]

But by now, even before the first suborbital flight was launched, the press had made the Mercury program a legend. And, as the editor said before, "When legend becomes fact, print the legend."

Okay, but that was all when the idea of space flying was new, when the whole idea of having a man in orbit was mind-boggling. Things are different now, right? The space program is three decades old, and reporters are wiser and more leery, right? If that is so, then how do you account for the distorted picture the media were painting of NASA's safety record right up to the most tragic disaster in the agency's history: the January 28, 1986, explosion of the space shuttle *Challenger*? Part of the answer lies in the effective way NASA managed and massaged its all-important media.

Lest anyone forget, the *Challenger* disaster claimed the lives of seven pilots and passengers including Christa McAuliffe, the New Hampshire high school teacher who was to become the first ordinary American to go into space. Were there hints of the tragedy to come prior to that January day? Or would we simply be using hindsight to criticize media that were doing the best they could in alerting the country to the dangers NASA was downplaying? Several observers feel there were many hints lying around for observant reporters to pick up. One such veteran reporter of numerous shuttle launches was William Broad of the *New York Times*. Broad told *Columbia Journalism Review* contributor William Boot, "Clearly, knowing what we know now, if [journalists had] really dug into it they might have been able to save seven lives. Standing back, it looks like the whole edifice [NASA] was rotten to the core."[4]

It that criticism sounds too severe, take a look at the facts. According to several reports, NASA had known for some time that the malfunctioning O-rings had some problems. The agency had also been advised by engineers of Morton Thiokol the night before the fatal launch that, due to the extremely cold weather in Cape Canaveral, the O-rings might malfunction and the launch should be cancelled. NASA also seems to have soft-pedaled the problem with the O-rings to secure a speedier launch date and remain on schedule. In these and other ways brought out in subsequently televised hearings, NASA appeared to have been mismanaging the launch program for years, while managing the media and its own image much more effectively.

Still, even if NASA officials and its relatively small corps of information officers were aware of problems, how could the media detect such problems without a leak in the agency? Obviously it was difficult, so NASA must share the blame at keeping the nation uninformed about the safety issue. Still, journalists don't get off scot-free. Another *New York Times* staffer, John Noble Wilford, says, "Everybody knew sooner or later there'd be an accident."[5] And Thomas O'Toole, NASA reporter for the *Washington Post*, said, "Something was amiss, but we couldn't put our finger on it."[6] So, lacking any whistleblowers and confronting the twin problems of a unified bureaucracy and a public eagerly awaiting the Christa McAuliffe chapter in space history, most of the media followed NASA's lead. Boot recalls ABC's Lynn Scherr telling him that her own editors failed to see how shuttle launches were any more dangerous than takeoffs of 747s. Even *Chicago Tribune* columnist Bob Greene wrote of Sally Ride's 1983 flight, "We feel we can talk casually about her because there's no doubt that she's coming back safely."[7]

Couple this attitude with NASA's experience in media management and toss in one other factor—the media's needling of the agency to keep on schedule—and you come up with the blueprint for tragedy.

But not all the media were looking the other way. In 1979 and 1980, two articles appeared in *Science* and the *Washington Monthly* challenging the safety record of NASA and asserting the agency was succumbing to budget pressures in cutting safety measures. In the *Science* article, R. Jeffrey Smith noted a decision by Rockwell International to save time and money by not testing engine parts separately. Smith noted this resulted in nearly a half-dozen engine fires during these tests. His conclusion: "a shuttle that many feel will be the most risky spacecraft ever launched."[8] In the *Washington Monthly*, writer Gregg Easterbrook noted there were no ejection seats for crew members, but there were plenty of used rocket parts—in some cases ones that had been used 100 times—despite space wear and tear.[9]

Despite these articles, there is no evidence they inspired any other pieces in other publications nor, notes Boot, were the articles even cited elsewhere.[10]

Several more red flags appeared from 1981 to 1985. Yet Boot's survey of six major publications including *Time*, *Newsweek*, the *Philadelphia Inquirer*, the *Christian Science Monitor*, the *New York Times*, and the *Washington Post*, shows these episodes were reported in only piecemeal fashion. As a result, we are left to wonder why reporters missed the boat. The following have surfaced as some possible reasons:

• Until the *Challenger* disaster, the media saw themselves more as popular science writers than investigative reporters.

• Space reporters, like police reporters often do with police departments, let themselves get too close to NASA and were blinded by the light of NASA's well-managed glow.

• A lot of editors and producers felt astronauts and fiery launches were infinitely more interesting than stories about questionable rocket parts.

• Several reporters, feeling that an accident *might* one day happen, got caught waiting for it to happen and then reacting to it instead of following up clues that an accident might be in the offing.

• The ranks of space reporters—like many other news beats—are filled with too many reporter generalists and not enough specialists. It might be more difficult to mislead a reporter who also happens to be an engineer by training.

• NASA has successfully managed to promote an impeccable image over the years. Even with its previous launchpad tragedy, this agency had maintained a spotless reputation among the press and the public. After all, these were the people who put Americans on the moon.

- Some reporters wanted to dig deeper into NASA's safety record, but editors and producers didn't want to commit the manpower or money necessary to do the job.
- As some reporters note, there were few—if any—whistleblowers inside NASA to help expose problems.

Whatever the reason, the reality of the shuttle's dubious safety measures went largely unreported in the years leading up to the *Challenger* disaster. Once again, most of the media presented shadows in place of substance. Reactive reporting was the order of the day, leaving us with a post-*Challenger* media that Boot describes this way:

The record of near-accidents and engine "glitches" and soaring costs suddenly seemed more sinister—a jolt in perception that brings to mind M. C. Escher's famous print of angels and devils. If the viewer concentrates on the white areas, he sees a pattern of angels. If he focuses on the black shapes, he sees a pattern of devils. News organizations, transfixed by NASA's angels before the Challenger explosion, are now seeing devils.[11]

One year later, AP aerospace writer Howard Benedict looked back on what the media have learned from the *Challenger* disaster, and he gave journalists mixed marks. In short, he noted that reporters were covering the space program with new aggressiveness and skepticism, but he wondered how long it would last.[12] He added that NASA was doing a better job a year later in keeping reporters abreast of the shuttle redesign effort. However, he noted that two of the media's best group of sources within NASA—middle managers and contractor managers—were afraid that they would lose their jobs if they spoke openly to the press. And in asking the same question that Boot did—namely whether better reporting could have deterred NASA from launching the *Challenger*—he was unsure. "As the commission learned, the engineers who knew about the booster rocket and cold weather problems didn't tell the astronauts or key agency decision-makers who could have stopped the *Challenger* launch if they had known," wrote Benedict.[13]

And, as to whether reporters would do a better job in future reporting on NASA, he was also unsure.

Will reporters and the Congress continue to keep a watchful eye on NASA, or will the old complacency again set in, after say, another string of 24 straight shuttle flights? It's difficult to say, but there is an historical precedent. After the Apollo 1 launch pad fire killed three astronauts in 1967, reporters and congressmen dissected the agency. Then along came a streak of brilliant Apollo flights, culminating with moon landings, and the vigilance vanished. NASA again could do no wrong—until that cold January day a year ago when the Challenger exploded.[14]

Chapter 8 will look at the role that official lies and secrecy played in this disaster. That secrecy came to an end when NASA lost its effort to control the investigation of the *Challenger* disaster, and the 120-day inquiry into the destruction of the tragedy was played out in public, much of it on television.

HUD SLIPS ONE BY

In a similar reactive vein, much of the nation's media managed to miss a series of red-flag warnings that corruption was running rampant in the Department of Housing and Urban Administration during the mid- to late 1980s. Despite the presence of thousands of reporters in the nation's capital, this gigantic agency succumbed untouched to influence peddling, payoffs, and backscratching for years until the media decided the agency was worth covering in a deeper way. Ironically, it now seems that many Washington insiders knew it all along, and the media, with their legion of leaks, was so late in catching on. *Time* magazine's answer? The press was sleeping.[15]

"Everybody who talked about HUD knew there was money to be made," says Republican political consultant David Keene.[16] Everybody but Washington journalists, it seems. In fact, it took an internal investigation of HUD to find what enterprising journalists could have found earlier. The *Washington Post*'s Bob Woodward said, "Somebody, an editor or a reporter, should have said, 'Where is the money going?' "[17]

It wasn't as though there were no stories sending up red flags. There were, but they, like the NASA safety stories, appeared in specialized publications that apparently got past the beat reporters in Washington. For instance, a July 1988 edition of *Multi-Housing News* published an article on influence peddling in HUD's Moderate Rehabilitation program, detailing the $2 billion scandal that eventually emerged by way of the internal probe. Part of the reason this and other stories were missed by Washington-based reporters is that they apparently grew tired of covering HUD after the Reagan cutbacks early in the decade. It was perceived now as a relatively low-budget agency with no earthshaking stories.

The reporters' cause was not helped by the fact that Congress was looking elsewhere as well. Those who weren't didn't see much new in the influence peddling at HUD since such practice seems common, to some degree anyway, at most governmental agencies. In other words, they weren't sure there were any actual laws being broken at HUD, so why stir up trouble with the administration?

At its best, covering Washington is a difficult task. At its worst, it is impossible. Despite the presence of a couple thousand reporters, there are hundreds of thousands of government and agency officials who are dealing with millions of constituents and lobbyists each day. The preponderance of possible influence peddling cases can reach astronomical proportions in any given week. However, one would think that some enterprising journalists would be able to detect a pattern from such an agency as HUD over a period of several years. Unless, that is, most of these reporters are following the government's lead, waiting for *it* to set the agenda, for *it* to start its own investigations, for *it* to provide the events for the press to react to. In the case of the HUD story of the 1980s, that is what happened.

A FAMILIAR STORY AT THE EPA

During the first two years of the Reagan administration, the Environmental Protection Agency was a strong candidate for media scrutiny that failed to come until Congress decided it was time to act. As later congressional probes would show, the agency was riddled with incestuous ties between top EPA officials and the officers at the industries the EPA is mandated to regulate. Then, as with similar cases, the reporting corps jumped in with both feet, as if to compensate for those tracks it failed to make while the corruption was at its height. One reason for the paucity of coverage given to agencies like the EPA is the pecking order that exists in Washington journalism and of how some beats— like the environmental beats—are seen as career stoppers. Even Sam Donaldson, upon leaving the White House beat to co-anchor ABC's "PrimeTime Live" program, is said to have quipped to fellow journalists, "It's not like I'm being fired or sent to cover the ecology beat." And ABC news president Roone Arledge said getting reporters to cover certain beats is difficult, because reporters perceive them as some sort of punishment. He noted that ABC wanted to set up a new beat involving Treasury and the OMB but explained, "We had a heck of a time with a reporter who felt like he was being sent to Siberia because he had no home base to go to each day."

This avoidance of beats like ecology is seen in an analysis of television reports. A study of network newscasts for 1981, for instance, showed a mere 16 stories done by the networks on the EPA. In 1982 that total was up to only 28 until December of that year, when things started breaking in the congressional inquiries of the EPA and its director Anne Burford. It was in that month she was cited for contempt of Congress, and the networks outdid their total number of stories for 1981, airing 18 stories on the EPA (including 10 on Burford herself) during that month. But that number was dwarfed by 116 stories the three networks did during the first three months alone of 1983. Six months later, the networks were back to their nominal treatment of the agency as if nothing had happened.

So in 1983, media overkill of the EPA became the standard, whereas during the two previous years, the agency was seen by the media as being as dull as HUD. Part of the problem for the scant attention the EPA received, however, arises from the fact few journalists can decipher complex and confusing chemical information regarding toxic wastes, pesticides, and air and water pollution. Once again, as in other cited cases, reporter generalists are sent to do the work of a specialist reporter. Simply calling a reporter an environmental reporter does not make him or her knowledgeable enough to go head to head with chemists at the EPA. That may take a major, or at least a minor, in chemistry.

Like the case with HUD, NASA, and a hundred other federal agencies, there are not enough journalists to produce daily stories and yet still do the deeper, enterprise pieces that can result in proactive journalism. As a result, the 20 or so regular reporters covering the EPA focused instead on the more obvious stories, like the budget wrangling with the Reagan White House. However, the press often seemed to focus on the *size* of the EPA's budget cuts rather than the *nature* and *impact* of those cuts. Because those questions went largely unprobed, reporters were easier prey for White House officials who insisted the cuts would have no negative impact on environmental standards. Or, if the media did try to check out these angles, their inquiries took them only as far as official press conferences conducted by environmental organizations or the EPA itself rather than to their own enterprise reporting.

An analysis by R. Jeffrey Smith, for instance, found the following typical broadcast and print stories in 1982:[18]

- A "CBS Evening News" story that went, "A coalition of environmental groups claiming more than one million members today accused President Reagan of 'giving away our natural heritage.' "
- A *San Francisco Chronicle* story headlined "10 Environment Groups Attack Reagan, Aides."

The point is that these stories focused on the give-and-take of accusations from official advocates representing each side of the issue. In terms of fairness, the media didn't do a bad job. But in terms of trying to verify which side was more accurate, they did a terrible job. Reporters once again adopted the classic technique of reactive reporting, of waiting for press conferences or formal statements and then reporting their contents without investigating the charges themselves. In this sense, journalism has not learned a great deal from the straitjacket journalism days of Sen. Joseph McCarthy.

Most of the media failed to get beyond a primary focus on Burford, to others in the EPA who were involved in equally curious dealings. One such subordinate was James Sanderson, an attorney for companies interested in water development and toxic waste disposal. Sanderson was third in line at the EPA and helped hire Rita Lavelle, who helped regulate the solid waste industry. He was also in on talks dealing with solid waste and their relationship to the Clean Water Act. Despite his heavy involvement in these official proceedings, he continued to represent waste and water clients outside the agency. Burford apparently saw this as no reason to fire Sanderson, and he left the agency voluntarily in 1982 to represent his clients on a more full-time basis.

According to Smith, the media could have easily uncovered Sanderson's activities by reading a seven-volume inspector general's report which was readily available months before Sanderson took his leave. In addition, Smith found:

From June [1982] onward, Representative Patricia Schroeder of Colorado, who chairs the House subcommittee on civil service, tried repeatedly to interest the media in the story. At one point, a number of congressional aides passed around copies of a letter to the U.S. attorney general from five subcommittee chairmen, detailing discrepancies between the inspector general's report and the cover letter, as well as listing some promising ideas for additional investigation. But Sanderson's behavior failed to attract any significant attention.[19]

Similar stories should have been followed up on Lavelle, who once said of the dioxin-contaminated Times Beach, Missouri, story, "I'm confident there is no emergency situation down there. If there was an emergency situation we would have moved in immediately."[20] Lavelle was finally fired in February 1983 after almost two years of questionable activity. In the end, of course, all of these EPA officials, including Burford herself, fell from grace. By this time, the media were all over the story, chasing everything that even looked like a lead. One might say they were in on the kill but were looking elsewhere when the entirety of the offenses was being committed.

COMMON THREADS OF DISTORTION

What are some of the common threads in these stories that resulted in such incomplete portrayals of reality? The following come to mind not only for these stories but for other similar ones as well.

1. *Media Manipulation.* For openers, a significant unifying factor among these and other stories is the effective way the U.S. government manages to manipulate the media. Speaking of this manipulation by government policymakers, Martin Linsky noted, "They understand that what the press covers and how it covers the news can affect their . . . careers. As a consequence, for many policymakers, managing the press has become an integral part of their professional routine."[21] These stories provide evidence in support of this thesis.

So the press once again follows the lead of the government in setting a news agenda and in decoding events it is covering. Since the possibilities of stories are endless in Washington and reporters are always looking for easy ways to get a handle on stories, press releases are a treasure. For many Washington reporters, in fact, that's all there is time for: to chase down leads generated by press releases from various governmental branches. A former EPA press officer noted recently that most Washington reporters assigned to the EPA, for instance, have always largely depended on the agency's press releases. "A host of reporters produced a lot of EPA stories in those days," says Jim Sibbison of when he was with the EPA. "But all they had to do was rewrite our material and possibly call an environmental group for comment. It was a textbook case of spoonfeeding. The difference between then and now is that our press releases were more candid and newsworthy."[22]

Sibbison says that, under the Reagan administration, the EPA press officers were "encouraged to help the public forget about pollution." So, he says, they shut off the flow of significant news and handed out overly optimistic releases instead. And the result? "It is now clear that the tactic worked," Sibbison says. "Lacking press releases that rang the alarm, the Washington bureau chiefs downgraded the beat."[23]

The ex-EPA official concluded that enterprise stories are few and far between, even today, on the Washington environmental beat. Possibly some network reporting examples would help to underline Sibbison's point. In 1981, of the 16 network TV stories done on the EPA, 14 were stories on Reagan announcements concerning the Clear Air Act or reports generated by the EPA itself.

The possibilities for distortion go far beyond government press releases, reports, and official announcements, however. William Rivers, former Washington correspondent and Stanford media professor, cites at least six things that occur between a Washington news event and the news report.[24]

1. Something happens in government.

2. Government officials decide how to announce this occurrence. This may differ from (1).

3. Through a press secretary, the news reporters are presented with the government's announcement of the occurrence. This may differ from (1) and (2).

4. A reporter produces a story about the occurrence. This may differ from (1), (2), and (3).

5. A media organization processes the reporter's story for presentation to the public. This may differ from (1), (2), (3), and (4).

6. The public receives a report of the occurrence. This may differ from (1), (2), (3), (4), and (5).

So even when you get past the government's version of the story, you still have the reporter, his or her editor, and the requirements of the news organization. So all of the possible distorting factors listed in Chapter 2 come into play here including the reporter's orientations, values, and deadlines, editor's news values, and marketing require- ments of the news organization. One of these requirements for both reporter and organization is usually that this story be based on an *official source*, whether identified by name or not, and that need can grease the wheels for media manipulation. Rivers describes such reporting this way:

Learning about the national government from the news media is like watching a tightly directed play. The director features the president at some length, the leading congressmen as secondary players, and the cabinet and justices of the Supreme Court as cameos and walk-ons. There are seldom any other entries in the dramatis personae, although there are three million employees of the national government. Any effort to move beyond the stage to see the undirected reality is useless. We must understand this: that the *image* of government appears to us primarily through the news media, and that the *reality* of government is often quite different from that reported by the two thousand news correspondents who help to create that image.[25]

It's important to note that, although these governmental stage-man- aged stories abound in Washington reporting, they also exist at lower levels of government as well. In fact, they exist as much in the lower levels as in the higher levels of government. Two attempts at manipu- lation come to mind in my own reporting.

Several years ago we were doing an enterprise series on the quality of life in a Texas city. Included in this series were pieces examining voting district lines, police protection, economic potential, busing pro- cedures, and school financing. Obvious problems began surfacing in several of these areas, especially in the areas of voting lines and pos- sibilities for attending the city's better schools. In our reporting, we tried to move from the indicators themselves to the "unofficial sources" (those affected by the problems), to the official sources (the mayor, council members, and school administrators). Often, even before we got to the official sources, we would receive phone calls or newsroom visits from persons at city hall or the school district office. These would be congenial visits, but there would always be a request that, in the interest of peace and harmony, we back off our series or hold it until a later date.

I had a good friend working for the school district at the time. One afternoon I received a call from the school superintendent who was distraught over our focus on alleged educational inequities among blacks and whites in his district. He pleaded with me, as editor, to drop the series. When I told him I couldn't, he commented on my friend and said, "By the way, your friend is doing a really good job here." I thought it odd at the time that he would bring her into the conversation at all, since she had nothing to do with the series. I interpreted this as an implied threat that, if we did not back off the series, her future with the district might be in doubt. I still don't know for certain if that was his meaning, but I resented him bringing her into the issue at all. The series, by the way, went off as planned. She was not fired.

Another instance involving racial trouble surfaced in the same district a year later. It concerned a fight during a basketball game between two high school teams, one from a predominantly black high school and the other from a predominantly white high school. The next morning I received a call from an assistant superintendent who asked me to drop over for a visit. I'd heard about the incident from our sports editor, so I went. When I arrived, the school official was all smiles. Once he got beyond the pleasantries, he brought up the disturbance and tried to make light of it. Something on the order of "Boys will be boys." The problem was that, as I had heard it, most of the trouble was caused by parents in the crowd. Nevertheless, the administrator assured me that in order to achieve peace and harmony in the district, it would be wise if I could wait on the story until his office had a chance to investigate it. I would be the first one to get a copy of that report once it was completed, probably in a week or so. This was the last time I ever honored such a request. A week passed, two weeks, three weeks, and still no report. The incident, which could have been a signal of underlying racial trouble in the district, went unreported. Thus, to the public, it never happened.

From the most innocuous interview to the most elaborate plot to manipulate the media, people are likely to say and do those things which make themselves look good even though that portrait may be distorted from reality.

2. *The Official Source Syndrome.* This was alluded to earlier, and it can cause a host of problems for the reporter. This syndrome is at the base of a lot of problems in Washington journalism, as well as reporting done from other quarters. It can—and does—lead to reporters being fed one-sided accounts by way of stage-managed leaks who are considered "official sources" by editors and producers back in the newsroom. Often the editor or reporter is so in awe of the source or what he or she has to say, that the information—which may have been fed just before the deadline—is published or aired with little or not attempt at verification. It's as if the title of the person divulging the information is verification enough. Take the series on Texas blacks discussed earlier. If this series

had been based on what the mayor and the school superintendent had to say about conditions of the blacks in the city, the resulting picture would have been vastly different from what various social indicators (busing boundaries, voting district lines, racial patterns in residential areas, median family income, dollars spent per school, etc.) plus the stories of the blacks themselves reported.

A series done on the homeless by a New York television station is another example. In the series "Asylum in the Streets," reporter Gabe Pressman did his homework on various social indicators and interviewed many disadvantaged people affected by such things as an early-release policy by state mental hospitals. His results were shocking and showed New York needed to overhaul its mental health budget so that more money followed the patients into the streets. As it was, although the mental health budget was the largest of any state in the nation, most of it was going for jobs in the hospitals, despite the fact that there were fewer patients in those hospitals and more on the street than ever before. This was all documented with mental health department statistics. But Gov. Mario Cuomo, when interviewed, focused solely on the size of the mental health budget as evidence that New York was doing the best it could for the patients. He did not address the nature of the budget allocations and, had Pressman not done his homework on it earlier, the governor and his mental health program would have come across as looking a lot better—even though it shouldn't have—to the viewers. The same thing held true in an interview with Mayor Ed Koch who insisted very few homeless persons were uprooted by a city program to convert low-rent apartments into high-priced condominiums or co-ops. Yet the social indicators, such as the increase of persons needing shelter, seemed to indicate otherwise.

In the film *The Year of Living Dangerously*, Australian journalist Guy Hamilton's first impluse (which came from years of conformity to press traditions and pack journalism) upon arriving in Jakarta as a foreign correspondent was to try to secure interviews with top government officials. Yet he didn't realize until later that his best stories came from getting out with the people and discovering how deep and widespread Jakarta's poverty really was and how Sukarno's policies were doing little to relieve it.

Diane Willis, a Boston television reporter, accompanied Sen. Edward Kennedy and other reporters to Ethiopia during the height of the famine in December 1984. The footage they got was graphic, but reporting in the limelight of, and under the restrictions imposed by, a U.S. senator seemed to be distorting the picture somewhat. So while other reporters left after a week with the Kennedy entourage, Willis and her crew decided to remain on and do some grassroots reporting of their own. Eventually they worked their way into Sudan and up into the rebel-held territory of Eritrea where they became some of the first journalists to interview the Eritrean fighters and their families about how little foreign aid was getting through to them, due to their civil war with Eritrea. Indeed, the crew found that much of the aid to Ethiopians and Sudanese themselves was not getting through. But it was not until the television crew got away from the official sources (at least one of whom was interpreting the remarks of Ethiopian farmers to make his government look better) that they found out what was really going on. But it took getting out of the city, out of the Hilton, and into the desert camps of the refugees.

3. *Getting Too Close to the Source.* A study done in 1981 at the University of Missouri showed that two of the things reporters like most about their jobs is getting to meet newsmakers and being on the inside of things.[26] That attraction can be dangerous for reporters trying to paint a truthful picture of reality. The danger is they will be so enamored, so in awe, of these high-powered sources that their reporting will tend to treat those remarks as being valid because, after all, look who they came from! At other times, reporters find themselves becoming closely allied with the causes their sources are promoting and, therefore, their objectivity is compromised. It happens a lot in reporting, although the best reporters are those tough enough to resist the temptation and remember they are the public's eyes and ears and not the sources'.

Several years ago, a reporter for the now-defunct *Oklahoma Journal* was assigned to the police beat in Oklahoma City. The reporter took the beat very seriously and viewed his relationship with the police themselves as of utmost importance. He became very close to the officers he was covering, and he came to believe strongly in their cause and their methods. The police liked him so much, they made him an honorary sergeant. He even helped with arrests, at times, patting down suspects to help out the officer he was riding with. As a result, the reporter was let in on a lot of stories before other journalists, and he scored a lot of scoops. The only problem was that he did almost no reporting on internal problems within the police department, and this department had its share of them. Opposition editors, surely with some envy, criticized the reporter for not being objective enough and not distancing himself enough so he could discern good police procedure from bad. They had a point.

I recall a police reporter in Dallas when I was an editor on the city desk. He fit the mold of the *Journal* reporter, although he had been on the beat for almost 20 years. He, too, got involved with police procedure and once helped put down a demonstration among inmates in the county jail. John would revel in his descriptions of how the police bravely chased down suspects (whom he insisted on calling "bandits") and, despite the paper's policy of not using a suspect's race unless it was significant to the crime, John would talk about "the suspect with a large Afro." Always the police came off looking like heroes, and one was left to wonder if they never did anything wrong. Later, stories began surfacing elsewhere about inappropriate police procedures involving female suspects arrested for soliciting. The paper had to assign another reporter to the beat just to handle all the internal problems that were there all the time; John had just been too tied to the police to recognize them.

Certainly the reporters assigned to NASA got too close to their story. As Wolfe and later critics described it, these reporters idolized the astronauts they were covering. Although the EPA and HUD reporters didn't go that far, they did take for fact a lot of lies that were fed them by official sources in high places that they just got too close to. One of the reasons a beat reporter's job is so hard is he or she must somehow find a way to establish a good relationship with sources that the reporter may have to burn occasionally. Nevertheless, as many reporters insist, if the reporter does an accurate job with a story and is fair to those involved, the sources will ultimately understand and continue talking to the reporter. It takes an independent-minded journalist to pull this all off, however.

4. *Pack Reporting*. Journalists on these highlighted stories also found themselves in the same trap that many beat reporters do. That is looking for standards in a very ambiguous craft. Once again the image of Megan Carter comes to mind in the film *Absence of Malice* as she realized finally, "There are no rules; there's just me." Although beat reporters quickly realize it's not just them individually; there are a whole lot of other reporters covering the same event, issue, or person. So, in looking for a kind of standard as to what the news of the day is or how it should be reported, beat reporters spend a lot of time talking with their peers on the same beat, comparing ideas for stories and philosophizing on what is and isn't news for the day. When you combine this "group sense" of newsworthiness with the skillful presentation of "pseudo-events" (more later) by highly paid media manipulators, you come away with the three network newscasts leading with basically the same story and same angle night after night. And, for national news, you find the same situation existing on the front pages of the major daily newspapers in the United States. Probably the one thread that ties this uniformity together more than anything else are the A.M. and P.M. budgets of the Associated Press discussed in Chapter 2.

Pack reporting may be most common in Washington where there are a limited number of "official sources" for a couple thousand reporters. So what happens is a kind of group consensus somehow emerges from the pack as to what is news and what isn't news on any given day, in any given governmental agency. As detrimental to editorial plurality as that may sound, it does have its good points. William Rivers, for instance, notes:

It is impossible for any news organization, no matter how large, to cover fully the entire federal government every day. . . . So the real question is not whether the media are at fault for not covering the entire government all the time, or for printing only a small portion of what is knowable about the government. The more appropriate questions are: How good is the judgment of the Washington press corps as to what parts of the government to watch and which of its actions to record or to investigate? And how good is the judgment of the Washington news bureaus and their outlets in deciding what information to print and to broadcast every day?[27]

So if these are the important questions, isn't it better to have reporters address them often as a group rather than individually? Other things being equal, it seems it would be harder to manipulate several beat reporters into covering a story than just one or two reporters. This is only true, however, if the group is making its collective decision on the merits, the historical context, and the impact of the story, and not on some organizational requirements such as whether the piece is visual or dramatic enough. Even then reporters must be alert to the possibility of going out on a limb alone to cover what seems to be a unique angle to a story. After all, at one time that was what reporting was all about.

5. *Covering the Pseudo-Event.* Like reporters rushing to cover the press conference on a new wonder drug for infertility, discussed in Chapter 2, Washington reporters seem mesmerized by governmental press conferences. Who would not show up and do a story dealing with a press conference called by an Anne Burford or one of her top assistants in the EPA during the early Reagan years? Who would not cover a NASA press conference as dutifully as the press has done all these years? What political reporter would not cover a press conference called by the head of a Senate or House committee? Of, if they have time, a press conference called by any U.S. senator? And what better way for politicians to manipulate the media than by having their aides plan, engineer, and coach their bosses through press conferences? Reporters have only so much time in a day and their editors/producers have only so much room for Washington news. So if they're going to file a story on a press conference, they probably will not file anything else from their beat that day. If so, chances are it won't be used. And who wouldn't file a story on a press conference called by an agency head or top U.S. senator or congressman? Especially if there were even a hint of news in it? Who wants to look like they're the only reporter in town who didn't show up?

Take the best show in town—the presidential press conference, for instance. Is even this event worth the coverage it gets? According to Martin F. Nolan, editorial page editor of the *Boston Globe*, only if you enjoy presidential filibustering. Ronald Reagan, like many presidents before him, seemed to specialize in taking up valuable time in either overexplaining simple answers, using elongated anecdotes that sometimes went nowhere, or dodging the question altogether. Since the average presidential press conference runs only a half-hour and since there are so many earnest souls pleading to be recognized for their questions, such filibustering seems to defeat the purpose of the press conference in the first place. Unless you are the president himself, that is. Describing the general pattern that seems to emerge from first-term presidents especially, Nolan says:

First, they put on a bravura opening-night performance with crisp, snappy and numerous answers accompanied by a promise to hold regularly scheduled press conferences in the future. Then post-honeymoon reality intrudes. Press and president complain about each other. New questioning formats are tried. As the press conference ritual deteriorates, the president begins to call on "softball" questioners—actual "planting" of questions is considered too risky and corny. The president may deliberately choose a bizarre query as an opportunity for a lengthy reply—and fewer questions.[28]

Even a commission at Harvard University's John F. Kennedy School of Government recently found the presidential press conference to be "in a serious state of repair."[29] The report, released just prior to the 1988 presidential election, encouraged the next president to restore the habit of "frequent, routine and undramatic" news conferences. The report noted that this type of press conference has not really been around since the days of Dwight D. Eisenhower. As yet, President Bush has not endorsed the commission's report. Although laying much of the blame for the sad state of presidential press conferences at the feet of the last three or four presidents, the report is also critical of broadcast journalists covering the event. It points out that television reporters don't really expect for the president to reveal anything new at these conferences; they just want him to confirm earlier statements or get him to say something that can later be verified or debunked. "The print media," the report says, "have slightly different interests. Obviously, they are less concerned about visual images, and more concerned about the substance of what is said."[30] Since presidential press conferences are played almost totally for television, the modern-day version of it now features a great deal of theatrics and very little content, the report concludes. And, in that, you have what Daniel J. Boorstin terms the classic "pseudo-event."[31] That is, you have an event designed to be dramatic, to attract the media, to deliver the illusion of substance, but very little significant content.

In the hands of other governmental agencies, the press conference fulfills the same purpose. That was a contributing reason that reporters spent so much time following the lead of NASA, the EPA, and HUD, when they should have spent more time looking for the real stories in these agencies: the stories that eventually surfaced through either trag-edy, congressional inquiries, or both.

Aside from the presidential press conference itself, who actually gets to have a one-on-one or group interview with the president? According to Larry Speakes himself, the Reagan White House used two criteria for deciding what reporters even get a chance to query the president in a press conference:

1. "What suits us."
2. "Kind of when your turn comes up and so forth . . . "[32]

What does that mean? It means, Speakes continues, that his staff or other top aides in the White House will have the president call on whomever they want and base the selection on the impact on "the constituencies we may be trying to reach at a given time."[33] Thus, even the interviews themselves are staged and pitched to the most favorable media the administration can imagine. And the real ad-hoc interviews—short as they may be—come from the Sam Donaldsons of Washington who are kept 20 yards away from the president and who must shout their questions across the White House lawn. Thus, to the American public, the Donaldsons look foolish and boorish, while the poor presi-dent—seemingly straining to hear—is to be pitied for having to deal with these boors. How ironic, and how well stage-managed by the White House.

NOTES

1. *The Man Who Shot Liberty Valence*, Warner Brothers Films, 1965.
2. Tom Wolfe, *The Right Stuff* (New York: Bantam Books, 1984), pp. 184–86.
3. Wolfe, p. 128.
4. William Boot, "NASA and the Spellbound Press," *Columbia Journalism Review*, July/August 1986, p. 24.
5. Ibid.
6. Boot, p. 25.
7. Ibid.
8. Boot, p. 26.
9. Ibid.
10. Boot, pp. 26, 27.
11. Ibid.
12. Howard Benedict, "One Year Later," *ASNE Bulletin*, January 1987, p. 4.
13. Ibid.
14. Benedict, p. 6.
15. Michael Riley, "Where Were the Media on HUD?," *Time*, July 24, 1989, p. 48.
16. Ibid.

17. Ibid.

18. R. Jeffrey Smith, "Covering the EPA, or, Wake Me Up if Anything Happens," *Columbia Journalism Review*, September/October 1983, pp. 29–34.

19. Smith, p. 31.

20. Ibid.

21. Martin Linsky, *Impact: How the Press Affects Federal Policymaking* (New York: W. W. Norton, 1986).

22. Jim Sibbison, "Dead Fish and Red Herrings: How the EPA Pollutes the News," *Columbia Journalism Review*, November/December 1988, p. 26.

23. Ibid.

24. William Rivers, *The Other Government: Power and the Washington Media* (New York: Universe Books, 1982), p. 212.

25. Rivers, p. 16.

26. Jim Willis, "The Editor as a People Manager," unpublished doctoral dissertation, the University of Missouri, June 1982.

27. Rivers, p. 18.

28. Martin F. Nolan, "Filibustering the Fourth Estate," *Washington Journalism Review*, February 1984, p. 60.

29. Tony Mauro, "Harvard's Memo to Bush: It's Not Too Late to Save the Presidential Press Conference," *Washington Journalism Review*, January/February 1989, p. 36.

30. Ibid.

31. Daniel J. Boorstin, *The Image: A Guide to Pseudo-Events in America* (New York: Atheneum, 1985), p. 39.

32. "Many Call, Few Chosen," *Washington Journalism Review*, July 1986, p. 21.

33. Ibid.

6

Competition's Legacy: Billygate and a Reagan-Ford Ticket

A major concern among many journalists today is the shrinking competition among big-city dailies. Only a handful of cities remain with competing daily newspapers owned by separate companies. The newspaper wars of years past live now in only a few cities like New York, Chicago, San Francisco, and Dallas, while newspapers in other cities like Oklahoma City, Buffalo, Minneapolis, and Memphis have died, or have been merged into their sister papers, or have been united in Joint Operating Agreements like Detroit and Seattle. In some cases, papers have been joined in operation but one has still died. In St. Louis, for instance, the *Globe-Democrat* first was joined with the *Post-Dispatch* in a JOA, then died several years later.

The problem, say many media observers like the University of California's Ben Bagdikian, is that the number of editorial voices is shrinking. Thus the fire that is lit by competition is dying out in most of this country's cities. Therefore news coverage suffers, and a diversity of editorial viewpoints becomes a thing of the past. Bagdikian also feels there are only 50 men and women today who control most of the output of daily newspapers and most of the sales and audiences in magazines, broadcasting, books, and movies. He says they would all fit into a large room and, in effect, constitute a "private ministry of information and culture for the United States."[1] Although they may not be able to tell the reading and viewing public what to think, they can and do tell them what to think *about*.

Many observers, like Bagdikian, are worried because the gigantic size of the major media companies also makes them participants in the arena of international finance. Most are traded publicly on the New York or American Stock Exchange, and all are under stiff pressure to compete with other speculative industries in the world. That makes the bottom line extremely important and infuses executives in every department of the newspapers with that realization. Thus, some feel, news media are edited as much with an eye toward how the product will affect the bottom line as anything else. Allen Neuharth, former head of the Gannett Co., has been quoted as saying, "Wall Street doesn't give a damn if we put out a good paper in Niagara Falls. They just want to know if your profits will be in the 15–20 percent range."[2] Others, however, point out that it helps to put out a good newspaper in order to achieve that kind of profit.

While it is worth attending to the critics' warnings, there are countervailing arguments to the idea that less newspaper competition impedes the quality and diversity of news coverage. First there is the argument that the surviving newspapers are better and are being managed by the media groups better than ever before. Second there is the argument that newspapers actually have more competition than ever before in their race for news. That competition is just present in different forms than before.

Taking the initial argument first, let's look at a 1988 report by the American Society of Newspaper Editors on the future of newspapers.[3] That report acknowledges that there are some negative influences of newspaper concentration into media groups. Among these are:

1. Smaller newsholes as groups seek to cut production costs.
2. Sameness as some groups may strive for a uniform look or editorial philosophy.
3. Less local news by some cost-conscious groups because it costs more to produce than wire news.
4. More filler used by some groups for the same reason.
5. Blander content.
6. Declining circulation (which, by the way, is a problem affecting *all* newspapers).
7. Rotation of editors to other group-owned papers.
8. Editorial cost-cutting resulting from high purchase prices.
9. More attention paid to the bottom line for the same reason.

Having listed these negatives, however, the ASNE report points out that there are several positives associated with the groups. Among these are:

1. Better and more comprehensive training of the news staff.
2. Greater financial support from companies with deeper pockets than individual owners.

3. Quality improvement which occurs on many papers bought by groups from independents. One shining example is the *Dallas Times Herald* which underwent a metamorphosis and grew into a solid, Pulitzer Prize–winning paper under the Times-Mirror Corp. in the 1970s and 1980s before it was sold toward the end of the decade.

4. Better management with more modern management experience.

5. Higher profits which can lead to more editorial independence as the newspaper becomes less dependent on a narrower base of advertisers in the market.

6. Group discount rates on syndicated material that allows the reader to have a greater array of this material in the paper.

7. Group benefits to employees that include better savings and pension plans than most independents offer.

8. More chances for editorial promotion due to the fact that the group owns several newspapers.

9. Supplemental news services made available through the pooling of resources of the group's papers. This allows more voices from news services like the *Washington Post, Chicago Tribune, New York Times*, and other services to be seen in a single paper.

10. Internal group news services made possible by the pooling of reports from reporters and columnists within the group itself.

So the debate concerning group ownership and shrinking newspaper competition continues, academic as it may be, because it doesn't look like Congress is going to become involved in setting an upper size limit for newspaper groups.

The second argument against shrinking competition causing worse editorial content is that newspapers have more competition now than ever before. That competition simply comes from other areas such as:

1. Suburban newspapers.

2. Network and local television and radio news.

3. News, sports, weather, and entertainment cable channels.

4. Thousands of news, special-interest, and city magazines.

5. A growing list of alternative local newspapers.

6. A growing nonfiction book industry.

When we consider these competitors, we might indeed wonder what critics mean when they talk of shrinking editorial voices in a community. When has a community had *more* opportunity to indulge itself in news of the day than it does today? It is almost as if critics are saying the only worthwhile news and opinion comes from the metro daily newspaper. While we may get a more complete array and detailed analysis of it from this source, there are plenty of other sources for news and commentary in any city. Some of it is as detailed and as good as the local daily produces. And all of these competitive sources should serve to keep reporters and editors of the local daily on alert and striving for the same exclusives they did when they were under pressure from an opposition metro daily.

There is another thing to consider when pondering journalistic competition. Are we to assume that the mere existence of competition is always a healthy thing for truthful journalism? In many cases, it is not. In too many cases, competition leads to high-speed journalism, and that translates into a number of inaccuracies going forth to the public. In Chapter 9 we'll look at the distorted media frenzy surrounding the 1989 Charles Stuart murder case in Boston. In large measure, that frenzy was fed by media competition and the fear of getting beaten on the story.

So one of the factors distorting reality for the news media is competition itself. Despite the fact that many observers feel the media are mired in too much pack reporting and conformity in the way they do stories, the fact remains that competitive blood runs in the veins of the best American journalists. On the plus side, competition keeps reporters and editors on their toes, always looking for the unique angle to a story or uncovering the story itself for the first time. On the minus side, competition causes too many statements to go unverified and too many stories to go "as is" for fear of being scooped by the opposition media. There is a truism in the news business that accuracy and speed mix about as well as oil and water. To a great extent, that seems true despite the fact that many reporters do their best writing on deadline. Like the football player taking to the field on game day, the adrenaline is pumping and stories emerge miraculously in the final 30 minutes before deadline. However, while they may be well written, the content may indeed suffer from such speed-writing.

Competition also has produced some amusing and intentional efforts at causing the opposition to come up with a faulty or incomplete story. I recall once, while working at the *Dallas Morning News*, such an incident occurred involving a suspected kidnapping of a young boy. The story broke in mid-afternoon. Later that evening, our police reporter had located the lad thought to have been abducted and found that the boy had just gotten angry at his parents and had hidden in his own home. By late evening the police and parents knew about it, and our reporter did everything he could to keep his opposite number away from police headquarters on that Saturday night, because we were going to run a front-page story on the incident the next morning. Up until this point, we had a scoop with the fact there was no kidnapping involved. Actually, the plan worked better than anticipated. Not only was our reporter successful in keeping the rival reporter away from police sources that night, but the competition's photographer had gone to the parents' home that afternoon and shot a picture of them in sorrow sitting on their bed. This photo was shown prior to the parents' discovering their son's mischievousness, but the competition was blissfully unaware of the new developments. To make matters even more embarrassing for the opposition, the boy was actually hiding under the bed on which his tearful parents were sitting. So, on Sunday morning, we had our front-page story of the son's mischief, and the competition had its off-base, front-page story and picture which, to its embarrassment, was later shown to be ironic indeed.

Competition also causes a distortion of news in some media because of the intense fear of getting beaten on a story, even if that story isn't worthy of the heavy attention the media give it.

BILLYGATE AS A NON-STORY

One such story was the ongoing saga of the late Billy Carter, the somewhat amusing and unpredictable brother to President Jimmy Carter. This particular story involved Billy Carter's ties to the Libyan government and his accepting payment from President Moammar Khaddafi to act as a U.S. agent. The story ran for much of the summer of 1980 and resulted in an hour-long presidential press conference and a Senate investigation that, ultimately, found no laws were broken by Carter. *Washington Post* columnist David Broder notes that, during the four-month time between Carter's registering as an agent with the Libyan government and the Senate report which surfaced in October, the *Post* published almost 120 stories on the subject. Nearly 50 of them ran on the front page. Even so, Broder recalls that the now-defunct *Washington Star* published an average of three stories a day on "Billygate," as it came to be called during the peak run of the incident during July and August. It was later revealed that the *Star*'s editor, Murray Gart, had pushed his reporters so hard on the story in the belief that it would do for the *Star* what Watergate had done for the *Post*.

Competitive pressure aside, some would ask why use this incident as an example of a "non-story" that arose from such pressure. What could be more interesting than a president's brother representing a self-sworn enemy of the United States?

The point is that, while Billy Carter's connection to the Libyan government was news in its best sense, the *Post*'s and *Star*'s drenching treatment of the story over the next four months seemed unjustified. What Billy Carter had actually been hired to do was act as a liaison to help increase the Libyan oil allotment of a *domestic* firm, Charter Oil Co. As U.S. law requires, he registered with the Justice Department as such

an agent, and then he accepted payment for his services. But the *Post*—
and certainly the *Star*—editors thought they smelled more. Was he really
being used to further Libyan interests at the expense of the United States?
Was he being used to influence his brother's thinking and policy toward
Libya? Certainly a possibility, although Billy's reputation as being a bit
unstable and his strained relationship with President Carter seemed to
make that notion a hard one to believe. And where was the proof?
Finally, lacking the proof, where was the proper proportion to the stories
that emerged and flooded the country in the summer of 1980?

This was a continuing series that kept coming despite editorial comments from both papers in late July that the story was being overworked.
For instance, on July 31, foreign affairs columnist Philip Geyelin said,
"Billygate . . . may turn out to be something of a bust, . . . the uproar over
the Libyan connection looks all out of proportion to the available evidence." The next day, however, the *Post* carried no less than five stories
and the text of the State Department cables concerning Billy's excursions
to Libya. The heavy treatment continued despite what many observers
felt was a watering-down of the whole story by a very accessible Jimmy
Carter who, on August 4, met with reporters for an hour, answering
their questions and sending a lengthy report on the case to the Senate.

Commenting later on the Billygate story—or non-story—Broder himself says he feels editors at both papers failed in abandoning their basic
editing responsibility and turning it over to their readers.[4] For his part,
Star editor Gart said the frequency and intensity of the stories resulted
more from over-eager reporters, the pressure of *Post* competition, and
the heat of Carter's political campaign with Ronald Reagan. Howard Simons, acting editor of the *Post* in Ben Bradlee's absence, also attributed
the heat of the series to intense competition and the fear of getting beat.
"So," he said, "you err on the side of overcovering it." He added, "It's
hard when you've got three reporters working on a story to tell them that
what they've got today is one story, not three. I'd ask at a story conference if we couldn't fold it into one story, and I'd get my head handed to
me."[5] *Post* reporter George Lardner, Jr., echoed Simons's thought and
said, "There were certainly points where I would willingly have said,
'I've got no story today'. But we were apprehensive about what the *Star*
might have, so we played defensively and kept writing."[6]

Broder says the pressure encountered in doing the Billygate story was
similar to that encountered with the Watergate story. The difference, he
notes, is that reporting and verification standards were kept intact during
the Watergate series. Reporters Bob Woodward and Carl Bernstein knew
they might be scooped any day, but they still made valiant efforts at
"triangulating" the documentation for their stories (getting at least three
sources for each key point). In Billygate, he says, distortion and exag-

geration took over and helped destroy some of those standards the *Post* is famous for.

In conclusion, Broder notes:

> We were all too eager to have the big story pan out, and we brushed aside anything that did not move the story along to what we thought should be its conclusion. We were not content to report what we knew—and to emphasize what was not known or what had not yet happened. We anticipated events, rather than reporting them. And so we ended up creating a largely false picture in the minds of our readers and viewers.[7]

Parallels can be drawn from this story to the media's treatment of John Tower during his doomed confirmation hearings nine years later for Secretary of Defense. In both cases the stories seemed to run ahead of the evidence, while rumors and unsubstantiated reports seemed to play a large part in creating the illusion instead of delivering the reality of the situations.

REAGAN'S CHOICE: FORD?

Anticipating a story can be good in one respect, bad in another. If a journalist is engaging in social indicator reporting and, for instance, spots a clear rise in homebuilding costs in the community based on the average amount of homebuilding permits last year versus previous years for the same size home, then she or he can assume the cost of housing is escalating. That might lead the reporter to anticipate the cost of next year's housing will be even higher—other things being equal—and that is good anticipatory reporting. Bad anticipation results from stories like most of the Billygate stories in the summer of 1980 and, most strikingly, from the media's rush to judgment on who Ronald Reagan would select as his running mate in July of that same summer. The fact that CBS, ABC and NBC said the choice was former president Gerald Ford shows how far competition can push newspeople in errors of judgment and how highly prized speed is in television news, even if accuracy might suffer slightly. In this case, however, accuracy was trampled on. NBC's John Chancellor summed up the scene as "politics out of control in the electronic age."[8]

The story arose out of the Republican National Convention in Detroit. As has become the norm for these media events, this one was played primarily for the television cameras. Early on in the convention, Ford told CBS's Walter Cronkite he might consider saying yes to a vice-presidential nomination. That was all that most of the reporters needed to run with the story and turn it into a number of stories based strictly on that remark and surrounding rumors. No pact had been reached between Ford and Reagan at the time of Ford's remark to Cronkite. Despite that, the story gathered momentum. Dan Rather reported a rumor that Reagan would come to the convention Wednesday night with Ford. He also quoted unnamed Reagan aides as saying Bush was out of the running. Finally, he said "the best source I have had all day long" confided in him that Reagan had conceded to most of Ford's demands for coming aboard, and that he wanted Ford's answer within 30 minutes.

Then, at 10:10 P.M. on Wednesday, Cronkite took the story to the limit, saying CBS had learned of a "definite plan" for Reagan and Ford to be running mates on the fall GOP presidential ticket. ABC was not far behind, airing stories that speculated such a deal was imminent, with reports from Reagan aides who alternately confirmed and denied the Ford selection.

Then came NBC with a report from Iowa Gov. Robert Ray confirming the deal. David Brinkley then reported that several good sources had said Reagan and Ford would be appearing on the rostrum later that evening.

Around 10:30 P.M., denials started coming from different quarters on the convention floor. Then the pollsters got into the story as Tully Plesser said, "There is no doubt that there will be a Reagan-Ford ticket."[9] Nevertheless, all three networks began backing off the story a half-hour later, and within another hour a Reagan aide yelled to GOP delegates that Bush had won the spot instead. Then, just as it had announced two hours earlier that Ford would be the running mate, CBS now was announcing it would be Bush. Viewers who had tired of the convention coverage by 10:30 or so went to bed thinking Ford would be the first former president to accept a new vice-presidential job. And early editions of newspapers like the Chicago Sun-Times would banner their Thursday morning front page with the news, "It's Reagan and Ford."

The ironic thing is that, according to Newsweek writers, most of the CBS crew "had no apologies for their performance" on Wednesday night.[10] "I was very proud of our coverage," said CBS's Bob Schieffer. "We were all over that goddamn story. We outhustled everybody."[11] Others, however, were not so sure and wondered if the network correspondents had run ahead of the story. Had the television demands for immediacy caused the networks to jump on a story it should have waited for? Had the force of competition done the same? Were the politicians using the media to test trial balloons or to escalate delegate pressure on Reagan to, in fact, choose Ford? Finally, did the story affect the outcome of the vice-presidential selection process? Jack Kemp told Newsweek, "Television literally affected Reagan's decision. I got the feeling Walter Cronkite was in the middle of history. And that's rather a special role for a network—to be such a force for change in the history of this nation."[12]

Those, like Kemp, who felt television affected Reagan's choice base their belief on the notion that, since the rumor was out, Reagan backed Ford into a corner for a quick answer, an answer Ford could not give without further consideration. When the deadline passed, the theory goes, so did Ford's chances. If that theory is true, then reporters both in television and print (AP and UPI were also running stories that Ford was the man) had something to be embarrassed about. As *Washington Post* veteran Haynes Johnson said, "There had been no story at all. We were stampeded. It had a life of its own. It's very hard to stop, because the perception becomes the reality."[13]

A RESEARCHER LOOKS AT COMPETITION

Media researcher George Sylvie of Kent State analyzed the influence of competition between the home-owned *Shreveport Journal* and the Gannett-owned *Times* (of Shreveport) in covering an explosion of racial tensions on September 20, 1988, in that city's Cedar Grove area. The racial trouble followed an incident where two white women allegedly tried to buy drugs in a grocery store parking lot. One of the women, 17-year-old Tamala Vergo, was reportedly robbed of her money and then opened fire into a crowd of bystanders. One of the bullets hit and killed David W. McKinney, 20, a black resident of the Cedar Grove area. The next day hundreds of residents burned two businesses, looted others, fired weapons, and threw rocks and bottles at police and firefighters. The study analyzed all sections of the final editions of each newspaper from September 21, 1988, to September 24, 1988.

Among the findings were the following:[14]

1. By a 2–1 ratio, both newspapers used more "unknown" sources than "known" sources.

2. The coverage of the larger-circulation *Times* had more source diversity than the *Journal*'s coverage. Also, the *Time*'s unknown source–to–known source ratio was larger than the ratio of the *Journal*.

3. Newspaper coverage of both papers emphasized manifestations of discontent and physical confrontation over the causes of the protest. Therefore, neither newspaper offered balanced treatment of all angles of the riot.

4. Both newspapers tended to have more of an order-authority orientation than an issue orientation. In other words, the papers emphasized things like physical confrontation and results of it, rather than stories dealing with causes or corrective actions.

5. The *Times* was found to devote more coverage to order issues than the *Journal*. In other words, the larger newspaper carried more ink dealing with activities of the disorder, results of the disorder, and reaction to the disorder than did the smaller *Journal*.

6. The *Journal* devoted more coverage to background issues than the *Times*. In other words, the *Journal* carried more news about causes of the disorder and corrective action than did the *Times*.

7. No significant difference in intensity of coverage was found between the two newspapers, nor did the amount of coverage differ significantly. For instance, Sylvie reported that the *Times* had 1,050 "square inches" of coverage while the *Journal* had 1,084.

8. Nevertheless, the *Times* devoted a smaller percentage of its overall newshole (8.9 percent) to covering the disorder than did the smaller *Journal* (15.8 percent). Also, the *Times* devoted less of its front-page newshole (19 percent) to coverage of the disorder than did the *Journal* (26.9 percent).

Discussing his findings, Sylvie said the results seemed to confirm earlier suspicions about competitive newspapers with the exception of one important one: that newspapers will generally rely on safe, "known," routine channels of information. This study found the opposite: that both papers sought out unusual, "unknown" sources for their stories. That is music to the ears of an innovative editor. It gets the reporters away from stereotyping and means they are digging deeper into the actual story than simply going to the official sources that may or may not know what really happened. It could be that such disorders produce more of an abundance of unofficial sources than the standard news story, so they are easier to find.

Concerning the wider array and diversity of sources in the *Times*'s stories than the *Journal*'s, it seems natural that the larger paper, with its greater resources to commit to reporting, would field more reporters who would be searching for more sources than is possible with fewer reporters assigned to the story.

Concerning the finding that the *Times* devoted more coverage to the riot itself and the aftermath rather than causes of it, Sylvie notes that this paper considers itself the "paper of record" for Shreveport and feels it must appeal to a larger and more conservative audience's desire for the status quo in the are of law and order. In contrast, the *Journal* sees itself as the alternative paper in the Shreveport market, promoting a more liberal orientation and championing minority causes. Therefore, its stronger issue orientation might have been expected. Concerning the fact that the *Times* devoted less overall and front-page space to the story than did the *Journal*, it seems consistent with earlier studies suggesting that the larger paper will perceive less of a need to attract new readers and can therefore afford to go with less coverage overall and to balance its front-page array of news with quieter stories.

In conclusion, Sylvie notes that

news values of conflict and order, as well as competitive and market factors, exert some influence on newspaper content. The results also tend to suggest that such influences win out regardless of the predominant usage of one type of source. Although there appears to be a degree of similarity among the two competing newspapers' total coverage, differences occur when the various aspects of coverage are examined. To wit, each newspaper tends to stress one area more than another.[15]

So on the basis of this study, it seems competitive newspaper environments do evoke some differences in content emphases, although the overall intensity, direction, and amount of the coverage remain about equal between the two competing papers. It should be noted, however, that *other* competitors, such as television and radio, were not covered in this Shreveport study. If they had, it seems possible that—in sum—all of the competitors would have provided a more well-rounded series of stories on the disturbance than any one or two media sources.

DALLAS: TWO SLEEPY PAPERS WAKE UP

Earlier we used the example of the *Dallas Times Herald* as a newspaper which was improved editorially when a large media group—the Times-Mirror Co.—bought it in 1970. But the purchase and overhaul benefitted not only the *Times Herald* but also its cross-town rival, the *Dallas Morning News*. This is another reason to avoid wholesale criticism of the phenomenon of media groups. Sometimes, when a group media group takes over a newspaper in a two-newspaper town and improves that paper, it will have a direct positive influence on the competitor paper. As a staff member of the *Morning News* during the 1970s, I recall vividly the jolt that shot through our newsroom when we realized we had a *real* competitor on our hands and we had to step up our own lax coverage of the city. *Time* magazine described the competitive battle as "a Texas-style shootout."[16] As a result of the fight, both papers wound up on top–25 newspaper lists, although the *Times Herald* faded from that elite list when Times-Mirror sold it after several years of carrying the fight to the *Morning News*.

Spearheading the changes at the *Times Herald* was editor Kenneth Johnson, who was hired away from his job at the *Washington Post* to breathe life into this paper which found itself in a distant second place to the *Morning News*. Within three years, Johnson hired 100 new staff members and moved out dozens of complacent veterans. He also began a new morning edition to compete better with the *Morning News*. In addition, he overhauled the design of the paper and gave it a cleaner look, adding new sections on sports, fashion, and travel. Following the philosophy of such media analysts as John Morton, Johnson realized he would have to commit revenues to the newsroom to improve the quality of the editorial product. This is heresy to many publishers who see the newsroom as a "non–revenue producing center" and wonder why you would want to pump more money into it. But Johnson realized that, if the editorial quality didn't improve, neither would the bottom line. So the editorial budget rose 157 percent in five years.[17] The result: Circulation rose 80,000 in two years, climbing to 280,000.

Then the *Morning News* began to catch fire with the appointment of Robert Decherd as executive vice-president. Decherd hired Burl Osborne as executive editor and increased the editorial budget by 25 percent. Like Johnson at the *Times Herald*, Osborne streamlined the look of the *Morning News*, made it more reader-friendly, started packaging national and international news together, and built a fine business section to serve the growing business boom in the Dallas area. More in-depth coverage and analyses were added, and reporters began specializing in areas like energy, electronics, entrepreneurship, and architecture. All these were subjects of strong interest to Dallas residents.

Both papers continued the fight in establishing more bureaus, both domestically and on foreign soil, and in beefing up existing bureaus.

Had not the *Times Herald* become a better product, the impetus for that improvement by the *Morning News* might never have come. In this case, competition proved valuable for not just the two newspapers, but also the readers in Dallas.

UNIFYING FACTORS AMID COMPETITION

In considering news media competition we must realize there are a number of unifying factors that create a certain sameness in coverage even among competing media. These unifying influences result from:

1. The Associated Press and United Press International.
2. The fact that many television stories, especially at the network level, originate from stories in the daily newspapers or a national newspaper like *USA Today*.
3. A similarity in thinking among editors and producers concerning what is important news and what is not and a strong desire to have everything the competition is going to have in its next day's newspaper.

Taking the first of these influences, AP and UPI, it is easy to see how they influence uniformity in the daily print and broadcast media. In a business where editors and producers are looking for standards as to what is newsworthy and what is not, AP and UPI often are chosen as that standard. Having a story appear on these wire service budgets is sort of like giving the story a Good Housekeeping Seal of Approval. If it's on the budget, it will probably wind up in the newspaper. If it is not there, and it is a national or international story, it likely will not appear in the paper or, if it does, few editors will go out on a limb to give it much play. The exception is, of course, when the editor knows it is his or her own bureau people who originated the story and those reporters have earned the editor's respect and trust. Even in this case, however, many reporters have a hard time convincing their editors the story is on the level and should be given good play.

So, with many newspapers and the networks, the national and international story agendas are set by AP and/or UPI. Not only are the agendas set, but the actual wire service stories that appear in hundreds of dailies across the country will be word-for-word the same story. Some papers will rewrite wire copy or combine it with local observations, but many will run it verbatim. So, even if we find a city with competing dailies, chances are the wire service stories on the front page of those papers will read the same. In this, there is much uniformity among competitors.

The second of these unifying factors is the degree to which television news springs from stories appearing in that day's morning newspaper. It is no coincidence that one finds so many open and rummaged newspapers lying about a television newsroom. Just as many newspapers seem to be looking at the wire services to set their agenda, so many television stations—and the networks themselves—take their lead from stories appearing in that morning's *USA Today*, *New York Times*, or *Washington Post*. Michael Massing commented recently that:

A great many of the stories you see on TV news programs have their genesis in our leading newspapers. Sometimes the borrowing is explicit, as when an anchorman begins a story, "The Daily Bugle reported today that . . ." At other times it is less direct, as when papers catapult a rather humdrum story onto the evening news by giving it front-page treatment. Two papers stand out for their influence: *The New York Times* and *The Washington Post*. Their power is so great that the mere likelihood of a story appearing on their front pages the next day often compels TV producers to pay attention to it.[18]

The third unifying influence—a similarity in news judgment among the nation's editors and producers and a fear of getting scooped—may be the strongest unifier of all. For although no two newspeople are likely to define "news" in quite the same words, nearly all journalists have similar ideas as to what news is and what it isn't. More than 80 percent of all newspeople now have journalism degrees, and there is surprising similarity concerning how these schools teach newswriting and reporting. Lest anyone should doubt this, just look at the similarity in teachings among the three or four most widely used reporting textbooks at the college level. They all list the same criteria of news (timeliness, proximity, impact, uniqueness, conflict, prominence, and human interest), and they all instruct students to write their news stories in the inverted pyramid, a format that breeds conformity in many ways as noted elsewhere in this text. Interviewing techniques are similar in these texts, and they all seem to paint a rather uniform portrait of the typical journalist's values and orientation to the craft. On this basis alone, it is no wonder that journalists develop similar ideas of news.

When reporters get out into the field they may start taking on different orientations and perspective to their craft, but to a great extent they and their editors retain and pass around to peers their uniform idea of what constitutes news.

COMPETITION CAN CHANGE A PAPER'S FOCUS

In order to survive economically, a newspaper must cover its own community. Most newspapers have always realized this, but the degree to which they cover the local news vis-à-vis national and international news has always varied. Some newspapers, like the *New York Times*, *Boston Globe*, *Baltimore Sun*, and *Los Angeles Times*, have always covered national and international news heavily, and that coverage has caused less space to be devoted to local news than if out-of-state news had been downplayed. Often, newspapers like these have had to pay the price in terms of readers lost to the competition. This loss has then caused some of these papers to reassess their emphasis in news coverage. A case in point is the *Los Angeles Times*.

Although the *Times* is now regarded as one of the best newspapers in the United States, that status has failed to impress many newspaper subscribers in its own backyard and neighboring yards. Although it has global journalistic goals, it is having a hard time fighting its smaller area newspaper competitors for readers in Santa Ana, the San Fernando Valley, and San Diego. The *Times* is now undergoing extensive self-analysis and, says publisher Tom Johnson, "is clearly in a period of great transition."[19]

We're talking about a newspaper that many would say has a lock on the Los Angeles newspaper advertising market, bringing in revenues of $1 billion a year, built on a circulation of 1.1 million Southern California homes. However, although the Los Angeles population has grown 25 percent over the past decade, the *Times* circulation has grown only 12 percent. Only a fourth of L.A. homes subscribe now.[20]

Part of the reason is that the *Times* has been losing out to local competitors which don't have near the journalistic stature of the *Times*. And the *Times* is losing out partly because it has relegated area news to secondary—and often tertiary—importance. The *Wall Street Journal* noted recently that "the *Times* has treated the regional sections as farm teams, whose reporters are occasionally able to move to the big leagues at Times Mirror Square, downtown."[21] But former *Times* editor Bill Thomas said recently, "I look on the zone editions as a picket fence to keep the competition out before the onslaught comes."[22]

Still, the *Times* has been slow in responding to such challenges as that posed by the *Orange County Register* and is paying the price in many area communities. Now, however, it is stepping up its battle there by expanding into markets like San Diego and elevating local and regional news in importance. That leaves the *Times* with a problem on its hands: Will it continue to try and "posture to be the *New York Times*," as a local television writer said, or will it try to become more of a hometown newspaper? Or has it been beaten on both counts? If the city's *Daily News* is providing a solid alternative local and regional paper—and succeeding with the formula—and if Los Angeles readers find in the *New York Times* the heavy diet of national and international news they want, does that leave much growth room for the *Los Angeles Times*? Possibly, but if so, papers like the *Times* will have to confront readers like those in the Santa Clarita Valley who, the *Wall Street Journal* notes, "saw a *Daily News* front page recently that covered not only President Reagan's farewell address and some U.S. immigration-quota changes but also a town council's potential opposition to new residential development. Conversely, of the ten stories on the *Times*'s front page that day, six came from Washington and one from Havana"[23] and none concerned Los Angeles, let alone the Santa Clarita Valley.

So it may well be that forces other than a consideration of what is really important in the world will force newspapers like the *Los Angeles Times* into changing its definition of news somewhat or at least changing the emphasis of the front-page newshole. That constitutes an influence that may mean passing off celebrations in the Santa Clarita Valley as more important than Third World peace negotiations. And that could translate into the elevation of shadows over substance.

Then there are newspapers that feel they must be different from their competitors to interest another segment of the readership that is dissatisfied with the competition. This situation obviously arises in two-newspaper cities, and New York (the only city with four metro dailies), Chicago, and Boston are prime examples of how it is played out. In each of these cities, there is a traditional broadsheet daily and an alternative tabloid daily under separate ownership (in New York there are three major tabs). The "alternative" description applies not only to the fact that a second paper is available, but also applies to the alternative style of news and format the second paper offers readers. Australian-American entrepreneur Rupert Murdoch has figured strongly in all three of these markets, bringing each city a racy alternative to the more traditional paper. In Chicago, for instance, he purchased the *Sun-Times* and gave the city a kind of newspaper it had not had for many years. The paper resurrected memories of the heyday of Chicago journalism where slam-bang tabs with punchy and near-libelous black headlines beckoned pedestrians to drop a nickel into the street box for more sensationalism inside. Sports, crime, gossip, and graphic pictures were the big draws and still are with Murdoch-style alternative tabloids. Three Northwestern graduate students did a study that showed news space dealing with rape stories jumped almost 100 percent during the first 30 days of Murdoch's ownership of the *Sun-Times*.

So newspaper competition can influence changes in two ways: by making other editors and papers desirous of conforming or by making them want—and need—to be different. In neither case is the criterion for news value purely based on the merits of the story. Instead, that is supplanted by marketing criteria where the target audience gets to set the newspaper agenda either directly or indirectly. The same thing happens in television—especially local television—and on a more routine basis. While individual news stations hate to get scooped by a competitor on a story, they will not hesitate to give their newscasts a different look or overall content mix if they feel the alternative style will draw more readers. At a recent staff meeting of television news personnel in a large midwestern market, the news director pointed out to his charges that this station needed to be different. "We can't just be a clone of Channel 8," he said. "We have to look at our network's programming and see what it says about our audience. Research shows the network's programming is breeding an audience that doesn't really care much about hard news. Oh, there are some news junkies out there, and we should remember them in our newscasts. But what our viewers want is a sexier and more sensational newscast with items that make them say, 'Gee Whiz!' So we need more stories to make it appear as though we're everywhere on a given night, but these stories must be short and lively."

Television, in fact, has gone even further in clouding the distinction between shadow and substance with its docudramas and staging or recreating events for the evening network newscasts at times. Although most of the networks have announced they are out of the re-creation business, NBC found a unique way of combining news and a dramatic series on drug wars in January 1990 by tagging news anchor Tom Brokaw onto the end of each segment with from 5 to 15 minutes to discuss the drug problem and how it is really being fought.

INTRAMURAL COMPETITION IN THE NEWSROOM

All media competition is not confined to the inter-media arena. Much of it can be found in the same newsroom, and many editors and news directors try to inject competition into their newsrooms, believing that will keep reporters on their toes. Those who have read the book *All the President's Men* remember the effect that such competition had in bringing together the team of Woodward and Bernstein. Although the story was originally Woodward's, Bernstein could not tame his craving for it and finally convinced Woodward to take him on as a partner. In this case, competition caused a good team to be formed and resulted in stronger documentation for most of the stories that flowed from that team.

What about the cases, however, when intramural competition causes reporters to step over the line and file stories that lack such documentation or—worse yet—to actually create stories out of whole cloth? It is ironic that this latter phenomenon occurred in the same newsroom where competition had earlier worked toward a positive goal. In Chapter 9, the case of the *Washington Post's* Janet Cooke will be discussed. Here was a reporter who, despite working for one of the best newspapers in the country, felt driven to fabricate a story because of the intense competition that existed in the *Post* newsroom that threatened to short-circuit her own journalistic ambitions. It has happened in other newsrooms as well. Is this a reason to downplay newsroom competition? Probably not, but it is an example of what can happen if it is overplayed by editors eager to keep reporters on their toes and setting them against one another to reach their individual career goals.

NOTES

1. Ben H. Bagdikian, *The Media Monopoly* (Boston: Beacon Press, 1983), p. xvi.
2. Bagdikian, p. xvii.
3. James H. Ottaway, Jr., "Trends in Newspaper Ownership and Economics," *The Next Newspapers* (Washington: ASNE Foundation, 1988), pp. 43–47.
4. Davis S. Broder, "Billygate: Anatomy of a Non-Story," *Washington Journalism Review*, May 1987, p. 46.
5. Ibid.
6. Ibid.
7. Ibid.
8. "TV's Rush to Judgment," *Newsweek*, July 28, 1980, p. 72.
9. "TV's Rush to Judgment," p. 75.
10. Ibid.
11. Ibid.
12. Ibid.
13. Ibid.
14. George Sylvie, "Study of a Riot: The Effect of News Value and Competition on Coverage by Two Competing Daily Newspapers," paper presented to 1989 Association for Education in Journalism and Mass Communication Convention Newspaper Division panel, Washington, D.C., August 13, 1989, pp. 8–11.
15. Sylvie, p. 14.
16. Janice Castro and Anne Constable, "Shootout in the Big D," *Time*, September 7, 1981, p. 58.
17. Ibid.

18. Michael Massing, "The Network Newscasts: Still Hot Off the Presses," *Channels*, January/February 1984, p. 47.

19. Frederick Rose, "Illusory Monopoly: Los Angeles Times, A Publishing Power, Is Beset by Small Rivals," *Wall Street Journal*, February 7, 1989, p. 1.

20. Ibid.

21. Ibid.

22. Ibid.

23. Ibid.

7

Is There a Specialist in the House?

One piece of advice that is often ignored by college journalism students is that they complete a second major along with their degree in journalism. The idea, I've counseled over and over, is that they get a specialty to write *about*. We can train students in journalism school to write, and their liberal arts education will give them a broad overview of the things to write about. But a couple of courses in earth sciences are not going to make a journalism graduate able to delve very deeply into the subject of ecology. Fairly soon that graduate will run up against information so technical that he or she will either guess in deciphering it or ignore it altogether. And that's just in ecological stories. In stories dealing with medical research, the journalist may announce prematurely the cure for some dreaded disease because the subtle qualifications of the scientific method have been lost on the writer who never really understood the method in the first place. And in business and economic reporting, the graduate may wind up focusing on the wrong thing altogether and leave his or her readers unprepared for the next recession.

THE STATUS OF BUSINESS REPORTING

For much of the nation's media, business reporting goes in one of these directions:

1. Toward a quick summary of the nation's leading economic indicators, followed—maybe—by an analysis of how those indicators might affect a certain industry.
2. Toward daily quotations of stock market reports.

3. Toward stories of new businesses, industries, or unique products businesses are marketing. In much of this reporting, the newspaper or television station becomes little more than a public relations agent for the business being featured.

4. Toward limited-view consumer action stories that spotlight such things as a particular tire dealer selling faulty tires to a customer.

5. Toward broader-based consumer stories that cover the Consumer Products Safety Commission reports on unsafe products and toys.

6. Toward stories of labor strikes and other union-management disputes.

7. Toward a focus on celebrity businesspeople such as a Lee Iacocca or Donald Trump.

There is a place for all of these stories in the news media, but the range of business reporting needs to be broadened greatly. For instance, although it is titillating to talk about how much Donald Trump has made or lost on his latest deal, it really affects few people other than Trump himself. Further, in reporting the daily trends of the stock market, many readers and viewers have no idea that such daily averages have little impact on society, that it is the longer-term trends that are more important. Third, concerning the trend of smaller newspapers in doing stories on new or unique businesses in town, many of those businesses should take out ads to spotlight their ribbon-cuttings. They also can run stories in special, year-end progress editions that many newspapers publish just for this purpose or run their stories on a special business page that is connected to the advertisers appearing on it. As for consumer news, while it is important, many consumer stories show the media's penchant for personifying the huge institution of business, of bringing it down to the level of how one dealer or product affects the public. Again, that is important, but it doesn't do much toward educating the public on the greater impact business is having on the country every day of the week.

In many cases, the media are trying to do more in-depth business stories. Some excellent magazines like *Business Week* and *Fortune* cover the major trends, while *Inc.* focuses on smaller businesses. In addition several major newspapers are doing more and more in-depth business stories with enlarged weekly business sections. And the *Wall Street Journal* and *Barron's* represent some of the best in business reporting. So what is all the commotion over poor business reporting? It centers on the fact that most newspapers and nearly all television stations do so little business news and that when it is done it falls into the category of banality or stereotyped superficiality.

Newspapers should bring more business news out of the neatly compartmentalized business sections and onto the front page. Television must do more with business news than show a graphic of today's stock market movement in the break between news show segments. If for no other reason, editors and producers should realize much business news is important because the tradition of responsible capitalism is one of the deepest enduring values most Americans have. Stories should be featured both on companies and individuals upholding this value as well as those who would violate it. And more of these stories would be believable if reporters and editors were slower to adopt stereotypes of the U.S. businessman and more careful to avoid oversimplification of corporate America. Instead, why not stick with the facts as they come to light? Also, the news media might catch more stories in the making if they were to provide greater play to business stories and were to follow the right indicators and decipher them correctly. Business is an institution and thus is a body of persons working through mechanisms they have designed and control to serve common interests which they have defined.[1] Therefore, institutions are created by people and make their own rules. They have a power and inertia of their own. Reporters should focus more of their investigative reporting on the institution of a given business or group as opposed to the individuals. It is these institutions that generally condone, fail to control, or even foster corruption. Any meaningful change in the system is most likely to come from these institutions, not from any one or two individuals.

For instance, in many business stories, the focus is on an individual who is either being applauded for a business's success or being tapped to single-handedly pull the business out of deep trouble. Many stories that have been done on Chrysler and on Southwest Airlines would fit that bill. In politics, the same holds true. In Watergate, the focus may have been too much on the key players in the drama and not on how such a thing could happen in the White House in the first place. Also, in the Pulitzer Prize–winning story on the U.S. Marine from Lufkin, Texas, who was wrongfully killed in basic training, the focus was again on the key players and not on how the Marine Corps could let that happen at all. Finally, when a television investigative series aired in St. Louis in 1982 about a couple of local tax collectors freeloading off the government and being paid for doing nothing, the focus should have been on how the patronage system in the city allowed for that to happen in the first place. Many of the stories aired weekly on the popular "60 Minutes" also focus on people guilty of corruption instead of the system that either condoned or fostered that corruption.

This is not to say that less reporting should be done on corrupt individuals. If nothing else, that individualized corruption often leads the reporter to find institutional corruption. If it does, and if it is reported on, then an institutional-wide cure may be put into place instead of just discharging individual executives. While that is probably needed, more sweeping changes usually are called for. One example of how the news media were late in arriving at a story on institutional corruption was found in the savings and loan crisis of the 1980s.

The S&L Crisis and the Media

The savings and loan industry fiasco of the 1980s was a story of many of the nation's S&Ls going under and of the nation's taxpayers having to bail the industry out of deep financial trouble. The crisis was a result of government deregulation which had spun out of control, of a savings industry making highly questionable investments with little or no fear of personal financial loss, of politicians with questionable ties to an industry they were supposed to legislate, and of an industry ultimately under the regulation of a man they chose themselves.

Conservatively speaking, it will wind up costing every person in the United States some $600 to amortize the savings and loan fiasco of the late 1980s.[2] However, if the news media had spurred Congress into halting the looting of the S&Ls in 1986, no one would have to pay anything to solve the problem. It simply would not have existed. But, to a large degree, the nation's press didn't notice what was happening, and Congress missed its chance to act early.

As Stanley Cohen, former Washington bureau chief for Crain Communications asserts, the S&L lobby exploited loopholes in federal laws, manipulated government officials, and did it all under the sleepy eyes of the U.S. news media.[3] Cohen notes that a few of the themes that should have been plumbed by the media were:

1. *Deregulation*. Did it make much sense for the Reagan administration to decrease the number of S&L auditors at the same time it was freeing the institutions to make a wider range of investments and riskier loans? So did deregulation set up an atmosphere in which looting from the S&Ls could take place?

2. *Ethics*. Was it ethical for then Speaker of the House Jim Wright to hold back on important legislation affecting S&Ls until such time as pesky auditors were removed from his home state of Texas?

3. *The Wall Street connection*. Highly regarded Wall Street investment firms backed shaky financial institutions, knowing insurance law loopholes allowed money brokers to deposit millions of dollars, risk free, and get high interest rates in return. In fact, the government actually helped out by ignoring these loopholes.

4. *Campaign contributions*. According to Rep. Jim Leach, R-Iowa, "3,000 S&L executives were able to buy Congress."[4] Was there a spurious connection between a system that permitted corrupt campaign contributions and the corruption of the S&L reform legislation?

5. *Cronyism.* The S&L lobby seemed to control the White House and Congress. And, at the height of the crisis, Reagan put the regulation of the S&L industry under the direction of a man chosen by the industry itself.

Part of the problem is not that S&L stories weren't done during the 1980s. It's that the lion's share of them wound up in the business section which has a limited audience on any newspaper. Few wound up on the front page until the crisis hit in 1988. Hobart Rowen, assistant editor and financial columnist of the *Washington Post*, noted, "The media more or less instinctively reach for stories of sex, politics, and intrigue ahead of the more pedestrian financial issues. That's the way it is."[5]

So Gary Hart's escapades became front-page news, while the ailing S&L industry went inside. Only when it became plain it would wind up costing Americans so much to bail it out did it become front-page news. In assessing the situation, Cohen comments:

Press historians and critics may puzzle over such attitudes. They may recall the journalists of yesterday, honored for exposing the Credit Mobilier railroad financing scheme, the Tweed Ring in New York, and the Teapot Dome oil scam. If yesterday's journalists could arouse semi-literate farmers, why should today's journalists, with all their training and technology, be ineffective with complex stories? Today's editors generally operate on the conviction that even relatively intelligent readers won't read long stories on serious topics.[6]

Still, is that a truism or an untested theory? If few newspapers are publishing the in-depth stories on serious subjects like the savings and loan debacle of the 1980s, and if newspaper circulation is decreasing, couldn't there be a connection? In any case, public attention is being turned toward sexier stories that—in many cases—have much less significance than issues which wind up costing us that $600 apiece. Once again, shadows triumph over substance. Part of the reason has to be that there are too few financial specialists in the ranks of reporting and those that are there are allowed to write solely for the business and financial section. Newspaper compartmentalization, deemed so vital in media marketing, may actually help keep many readers in the dark about the reality of the day because they just don't get into those special sections. To a great extent, however, that is the fault of the reader and not the newspaper, assuming the editor makes those sections reader-friendly and enticing.

Understanding Is the Key

For the media and business to avoid destroying each other through public criticism and ignorance, which leads to distortion and avoidance tactics, each must understand the other better. This understanding is important not just so the two institutions can get along with each other, but because the public needs to become better served by better economic reporting.

Journalists must know how business operates and what really motivates it. The business world is pragmatic and realistic; the theories of Adam Smith, Karl Marx, Emmanuel Kant, or Jean-Paul Sartre do not mean a great deal to business executives unless those theories can be translated into improving the bottom line. Journalists should be able to understand this by taking time to view the operation of their own newspaper or television station. If they take this time, they will come to the realization—sad though it may be—that their own cherished news medium is actually a *business*. As such, its operations are funded by income derived for services performed. The bottom line, profit margin, return on assets, cost-effectiveness of expenses, and so on are all of uppermost importance to the publisher or general manager. It's not that these executives don't respect the canons of good journalism and want to uphold them whenever possible, it is just that often these canons are balanced by the reality of profit and loss figures. And, if entertainment or soft news is found to bring in more readers or viewers than investigative reporting, the resources will often flow to entertainment reporting.

A vivid example of this comes to mind from my days at the *Dallas Morning News* in the 1970s. Promotion executives at the *News* decided to begin installing billboards around the city touting the paper. This was becoming increasingly important because of the stepped-up competition with the *Dallas Times Herald* (see Chapter 6). In looking around for aspects of the paper to promote, *Morning News* readership surveys apparently showed the newspaper derived much readership from the comics. This is true at many dailies, in fact. So several of these billboards went up around the LBJ Freeway and elsewhere asking passing motorists, "Why Should You Read *The Dallas Morning News*? Funky Winkerbean!" This was not uncommon—and still isn't in newspaperdom, as comics are a big predictor of readership, and promotion departments like to capitalize on them when they can. Obtaining exclusive rights to a popular syndicated comic in a competitive market is considered a mark of good success to any newspaper. All the *News* was doing was touting its success and the fact it had Funky Winkerbean. Nevertheless, it left a lot of reporters and editors who worked extremely hard everyday scratching their heads as to why the paper didn't promote their own work instead of some mythical cartoon figure. The answer was apparently that you promote what is selling well, and Funky Winkerbean was selling well. So the answer was influenced by business considerations. In fairness to the *News*, the company later began promoting individual *News* writers on billboards placed in similar places.

The point is that business is pragmatic, and theory benefits it only to the extent that it can act as a predictor of what causes people to read or tune in the product.

In an ITT-sponsored lecture at the University of Missouri, former *Business Week* editor Lewis H. Young described a familiar scenario facing reporters and gave his views on how to overcome it and obtain more accurate reporting.[7] In the real world, he said, interviewing a half-dozen corporate board members after a tumultuous meeting, a journalist will hear as many meetings described as there are board members. Each has viewed the meeting from his or her own perspective, and the journalist must wonder: Did all these people attend the same meeting? Which meeting should he write about? Using his judgment, experience, and intuitive sense of which director was closest to the truth, the journalist synthesizes his best interpretation of what really happened. It may be a unique view of that meeting, putting it into a perspective that nobody who was close to it could see. That is possible to do because the journalist should have no vested interest in what took place at the meeting. Or it can be dead inaccurate because the journalist was swayed too much by an articulate director with a sharp axe to grind. The same risks apply to every story, whether it be a business meeting or a meeting of the city council. What is important, according to Young, is that a good journalist does more than just record what many people tell him. A tape recorder can do that. The journalist .nust bring his own insight, interpretation, and meaning to every story he reports.

But to bring all these to a story, the reporter must have some technical knowledge and experience dealing with such stories and be willing to do *all* the reporting. He must be able to read a corporate operating statement and balance sheet instead of having them interpreted by a board member with a vested interest. The journalist must understand how marketing is carried out, how management operates in the real world, and know something of the technology and corporate culture involved. He cannot make judgments solely by the seat of his pants, the way one might evaluate a high school football game.

Another threat to a truthful portrayal of reality in business stories is the reporter who is simply biased against big business because of stereotypes from the entertainment world that he or she might have grown up with or from some other stimulus. In fairness to business reporters, however, a 1984 study found that many business and financial editors have even more favorable attitudes toward capitalism than the public.[8] The study was based on more than 450 responses from business and financial editors and more than 1,500 responses from the general public. More than two-thirds of the business editors said the media is unbiased toward business, and almost nine out of ten in this group claimed that their attitude has become more positive toward business in recent years. Conversely, only half of the public surveyed said their attitude toward business has grown more positive during the same time frame. They also felt that much of the bias perceived in certain business stories was actually probusiness. That could be account for by the large number of smaller newspapers that put a great deal of effort into publicizing ribbon-cuttings for new businesses in town, changes in management and employees, and chamber of commerce stories. That, in effect, is the definition of business reporting for many of the nation's news media.

Nevertheless, it is no secret to any journalist that there is a certain degree of antibusiness bias present in any newsroom. Young acknowledges this and says many reporters "do not like business because they think corporations are unresponsive ogres which are interested solely in profits."[9] Or, if not this, they consider business reporting to be dull and somewhat grubby in comparison with crime, politics, or foreign affairs.

If this is true among editors, it is also true among those training to become reporters or editors. I can count on one hand the number of college journalism majors over the past ten years who think enough of business reporting to take *elective* business or economic courses, let alone try a second major in business.

Young sees two other kinds of reporters who exacerbate the problems existing between business and the media:

One group is insensitive to money; their real target is power. They want to redistribute the power in the world so that they have a bigger voice in making decisions. To these people the business establishment is a threat because of its strength and power. A second group of journalists uses reporting as a form of psychotherapy, to relieve themselves of personal frustrations. They use the printed word or the television show to attack those bigger and more powerful than themselves.[10]

However, only some of the problems in business reporting are caused by errant or ill-informed journalists. Many are caused by business itself. Because the corporation is an autocracy, the chief executive officer will shape its approach to the news media. It makes little difference what the public relations department feels about media relations or how good they are. If the CEO does not want good relations with the press because he has his own set of stereotypes about reporters, relations on both sides will be bad. Sometimes a CEO will see absolutely no need for good media relations, because he or she doesn't understand the role the media play in society and in the business world.

Many CEOs may even expect the media to respond to them the same way subordinate officers do, and it is a hard pill to swallow when they don't. They may see the role of the press as one of a mouthpiece for their business, as an extension of their public relations effort. A frequent complaint heard from CEOs to editors about stories is "I told you what the story was. Why did you talk to anybody else?"

To their credit—but also at times showing their cynicism—many of the best journalists go far beyond the CEO and other corporate chieftains to get the story. In a 1984 Columbia University seminar on media and business "60 Minutes" reporter Morley Safer discounted immediately the value of researching a company's press releases on its own officials. Giving a hypothetical scenario in which PR executive Herbert Schmertz starts providing handouts just as the reporter is beginning to probe the background of a company official who has been nominated for secretary of defense, Safer quipped, "You start by *not* reading the Schmertz papers. . . . I know what's in the Schmertz papers. . . . I've probably met Schmertz before."[11]

But sometime before the story is put together, the Schmertz papers had better be read, and it would be nice if they could be read with some degree of objectivity and a sense that what's in them *could* just be accurate after all. It is this open-mindedness that should characterize all of journalistic reporting.

In that same Columbia University seminar, the frustration of business executives over what they perceived as loose-cannon reporters became evident. At one point, Mobil Oil president William P. Tavoulareas said dejectedly, "I can't control what the media does. I learned long ago I can't control the media."

Frustrated or not, the fact remains that it is not the job of business to control the media. I once had a meeting with an angry CEO of a local company to discuss his view that my newspaper was prejudiced in its coverage of the corporation. The executive quickly went through a series of stories we had run with such comments as "You certainly didn't help us with that story" or "That story didn't do us any good" or "We didn't look good in that story." I finally told the executive he had me mixed up with his vice-president of communications. My job was not to make him or his company look good.

Another problem journalists face in covering business is that, often, business executives see no reason why they should reveal facts about their company to the media or tell the truth if they do say something. Wouldn't it be better for business executives to say things that will, instead, have a positive effect on future earnings? Companies do use several techniques to de-emphasize bad corporate news. One is to put out disappointing earnings reports at 8 A.M. when the business news wires open, before most people are at work, hoping the item will be lost in the pileup of newsroom copy. Or the company releases the news at the end of the working day so a morning newspaper has not time to do any reporting and has to confine itself to the contents of the press release. Or the negative news will be released late Friday afternoon for Saturday newspapers whose readership is probably the lowest of the week. And some companies will stall on getting answers back to a reporter, hoping that the company will be ignored because there has been no response.

Journalists simply have to learn more about business and economics so they can understand what they are writing. Gardner Ackley, former chairman of the Council of Economic Advisors, once said he wished reporters who wrote about economic affairs would have two qualifications: first, they had taken a course in economics, and second, that they had passed the course.

But even more specialization in the reporting ranks won't do the trick alone. Whatever stereotypes or biases against big business that exist in the newsroom must go out the window. If for no other reason, anti-business editors and reporters become easy targets for special-interest groups opposed to business who might themselves lead the media down a wrong road. It's just as wrong for a reporter to be used by a populist group as it is for him or her to be used by a probusiness group.

When it comes to television and business reporting, TV must learn to handle business news that goes beyond consumer reporting or tagging the stock market quotations to the teaser between two news show segments. Also, the idea that the only way to enliven a dull subject is to make a fight out of it is thinking that leads to distortion and mis-emphasis in business stories. That kind of format makes it impossible to educate the public about a basic economic idea in which there is no dispute. In fact, the only way the government can make the tough decisions it must in the economic area is if people understand what is really at stake. For instance, how many average people really understand that if a government is not going to raise taxes it cannot pay off the soaring national debt without cutting expenditures to other programs the public deems essential? This is basic stuff, but the message doesn't always seem to get through over the television set or on the front pages of the newspaper.

Finally, corporate CEOs have a responsibility to see their operations are portrayed accurately. While business may not be a government agency, most big businesses are publicly held and nearly all have an impact on society, with that impact ranging from unemployment to acid rain. There have been several examples of companies, like Johnson and Johnson during the Tylenol scare, doing first-rate jobs in disseminating information to the public, even though their first inclination might have been to close ranks and let the public figure things out for themselves. More of this thinking from CEOs is needed if accurate stories are to get through to the public.

A Grocery List of Causes

Finding causes for the incomplete and often inaccurate picture of business is easy. Finding solutions takes a little longer. Look at some of the causes that two economics writers—MIT's Lester Thurow (who has written economics columns for *Newsweek*) and Alan Reynolds (a frequent contributor to the *Wall Street Journal* and *National Review*)—feel are at the base of the shadowy reporting. It is interesting to note that, while some of their ideas regarding media coverage merge, few of their economic ideas do, since Thurow is seen as a liberal economics thinker and Reynolds is perceived as a supply-side advocate.

Thurow sees a major mistake in economics reporting in making insignificant events into seemingly more important ones.[12] He uses the stock market as a prime example, noting how discussion of it dominates most business sections. Most days, in fact, it is the only business news on radio and TV. Yet daily stock averages are relatively insignificant to society or even individual investors on most days. Even the analysis of why the stock market rose or fell is generally useless, Thurow feels, because the truth is we don't usually know why the market went up or down. It is simple speculation, attributed to "analysts" who are, themselves, guessing.

Concerning other economic indicators, Thurow cautions against placing too much value on short-term indices because the economy is subject to random fluctuations. Instead of looking at daily or even weekly or monthly trends, the media should focus more on three-month and six-month averages that do better in capturing major trends. To multiply the shorter-run numbers, converting them into annual numbers, only compounds the problem. Conditions next month or two months from now may be slightly or vastly different than now, and this month's average may not be indicative of any year-long trend.

Third, Thurow feels too much business news overemphasizes what is happening in Washington to public policies and to the financial markets in New York, and underemphasizes occurrences in the industrial economy. For instance, the war between Japanese and U.S. businesses to corner the market for 256K RAM chips is more significant over the long run than any congressional committee meeting. Still, the latter event more generally receives the media spotlight. Possibly because it is a preplanned event that the media can more easily schedule into their upcoming daily budgets of news.

Fourth, economists like Thurow believe more media attention must be paid to global economics in order to understand the significance of U.S. economic news. Business, in case anyone hasn't noticed, has become internationalized. If that isn't clear by now, after the Japanese have taken hold of such vast capital and companies in the United States, it will become even more clear by 1992 when the United States of Europe becomes a reality. America is now a nation that depends heavily on international trade and exports. Yet foreign correspondents—when news media field them—are generally political reporters who know little of economics or business. And that situation spells trouble, because the events they have a chance to observe in international business are even more important than events American business reporters are witnessing in the United States.

Finally, Thurow believes the media must help the public better understand economics news by providing them more background of distinct news events. For instance, do readers and viewers really understand that in one 30-day period, only about 4 million out of the 10.5 million unemployed workers are receiving unemployment insurance? That means the other 6.5 million are receiving little if any subsistence payments at all. Yet a large portion of the public probably feels most unemployed workers are receiving unemployment insurance. A little background would help understand monthly unemployment statistics better.

Reynolds's list of reporting errors begins with the belief that journalism schools train students to treat information and nonsense with the same respect. His position is supported by such media scholars as William Rivers who points out that one key difference between the research method of journalists and social scientists in that journalists pursue every piece of information they can get their hands on, not knowing whether it is accurate or where it will lead. Reynolds says this philosophy leads to reporting more than explaining, often with confusing results. His list of errors runs as follows:[13]

1. *Reality by Consensus.* If there is a favorite expression that broadcast journalists use in trying to describe what is happening in economics, it is "most economists agree." Journalists, Reynolds says, treat truth as if it is the result of some sort of democratic process whereby reporters survey maybe five "experts" and go with the conclusion of three or four of them, whether they are, in fact, right or wrong. It is rare to find several economists agreeing about anything, and even if they did, there is no guarantee they would be right. If that were the case, then predicting the future and making a fortune on Wall Street would be easy. In like manner, many economics reporters will say something like "Wall Street believes," when they have spoken with only a handful of economists. Can a handful of economists really represent the beliefs of thousands of portfolio managers on Wall Street?

2. *Royal Expertise.* Who decides which economists or financiers are the "experts" anyway, and who decides which of them gets interviewed? As in most areas of reporting, the media decide all the way and often go with those "experts" they've used before or whom they feel are perceived as experts by the public because they have been featured in the news so many times. In other words, the media create experts on the basis of who has been featured enough in the news to become perceived as an expert by the public.

3. *Press Gullibility.* The media love studies and official reports coming from agencies like the Federal Reserve or the Congressional Budget Office as well as private think-tanks. Never mind the fact that a certain agency might have a point of view to push or a little propagandizing to do. What better way for an agency to enlist the support of the press in promulgating its philosophy than by putting it into an official-looking study or report? This, of course, happens in areas other than economics reporting. The president will make an issue of the sad state of public schools. He will appoint a "blue-ribbon panel" to investigate the condition of public schools. The panel will consider the matter and file a report. And what will the report say? That public education is in bad shape. In other words, if the president feels a matter is important enough to establish a panel to consider it, will they really return a report contrary to the chief executive's reason for establishing the panel in the first place?

4. *The Dangling Forecast.* While the media love economic forecasts, journalists are often at a loss to find solid underpinnings to those forecasts. Here, getting both sides to the story doesn't help much, because one economist might say deficits cause high interest rates, while another may say high interest rates cause higher deficits. Or an administration economist might say providing greater incentives to business will help the economy by creating more jobs, while another might say providing such incentives will put more of a burden on the individual taxpayer. As is the case with many other causes of distorted economic reporting, this is not the fault of the reporter. It is simply the state of disagreement and guesswork found among even the nation's best economists. But the public should know that and not have it interpreted as gospel.

5. *Fads and Fashions.* Often the media do react to this last concern by championing the anti-intellectual idea that economics is simply a matter of opinion. But then reporters will arbitrarily classify the camps offering these opinions into certain categories like "supply-siders" or "monetarists," much the same as political reporters classify politicians as liberal or conservative. The problem with the former labels, however, is that the public usually doesn't know what a supply-sider or a monetarist is. And the media doesn't have the airtime or space to explain it enough times so that enough people will understand the terms. What is worse is that many reporters don't understand the terms themselves.

6. *Errors of Omission and Commission.* Reynolds points out that reporters (often because they don't understand economic concepts themselves) misinterpret a lot of data coming from economic indicators. He points to a June 25, 1982, "Today" show when a reporter said "big deficits are inflationary." Still, wasn't the deficit big in 1932, Reynolds asks? Didn't nonfood producer prices *fall* that year? The point is that such sweeping statements regarding deficits or any other concept in economics are dangerous and are not always true.

In addition, Reynolds warns reporters against believing so strongly in the truth of some conclusions such as the policies of the Federal Reserve. It is not always flawless, he points out, and it should engender more suspicion from reporters than it does.

Finally, Reynolds feels there is much reliance on official sources and too much comfortable restating of the easy and obvious in economics reporting. Conversely, there is too little attention paid to truly innovative economic reporting. The best jobs, he says, are being done by the business magazines and some stellar newspaper business sections, and these have improved greatly over the past decade. But not enough of this solid reporting is around, and economic specialists in the media would help correct that.

When PR Is Good and Bad

We cannot discuss the causes behind shadowy business reporting without looking at the role institutionalized public relations plays in the process. Much of what the media know of the business world comes through press releases and regular contact with the large public relations or public affairs departments of business and industry. While these departments fill important functions in keeping the news media apprised of trends within the business and industrial environment, journalists must never lose sight of the fact that a key job of these PR practitioners is to portray their company in the best possible light. They are the image makers and, while the best of them will make that image conform as much as possible to reality, many do not or cannot because of edicts or media policies floating down from the CEO.

Several systematic studies were done during the 1980s regarding public relations practitioners and their orientations toward the profession. It is worth noting a few of those here as we look deeper into the influence of public relations on the creation and maintenance of the shadow world of business.

A study by Michael Ryan and David Martinson emerged in 1988 in which the researchers concluded, "[PR] practitioners acknowledge that journalists often view public relations negatively, and they accept some of the blame for those negative views." The researchers questioned 200 public relations people and found the following attitudes to be prevalent:

1. Practitioners say journalists' negative experiences with individual public relations people cause about 90 percent of the antagonism between the two camps.

2. Three out of four practitioners say journalists consider their work to be more important than the practitioners', and this also causes some antagonism.

3. More than half of the practitioners state the antagonism stems, in part, from journalists' inflated view of themselves, biases common to journalists, and journalists' fear of being used.

4. More than 65 percent of the practitioners believe the public relations industry is partly responsible for the negative attitudes that the media have toward PR.

5. Eight out of ten PR people surveyed feel public relations must police itself for unprofessional conduct.

6. About two-thirds say PR people are at fault because they do not care about journalists' need for clear, concise, and accurate information.

7. Practitioners, as a group, consider journalists' overall negative views of them to be unjustified.

8. Personality is important, practitioners say, in determining journalists' views of practitioners. Most say journalists think well of the PR people that they know, yet dislike the field in general.

9. In their order of importance, the factors influencing practitioners' professional attitudes are parents, early home life, educational background, public relations experience, religious upbringing, colleagues' behavior, and current family life.

Ryan and Martinson suggest that PR practitioners work harder to identify the causes of antagonism between the two camps, agree on a common definition and set of values for practitioners, and then conduct a PR campaign for public relations itself to educate journalists and diminish the antagonism.[14]

In another study, Ryan noted that the public relations practitioners can help corporate officers by acting as a kind of company conscience, standing up for strategy based on social needs as well as profits. Ryan's mid-decade survey of public relations people yielded the following conclusions:[15]

1. Ninety-seven percent agreed that being socially responsible is good business for the company.

2. A smaller number, but still almost 80 percent, agreed that pursuing social goals strengthens a business's ability to earn a profit.

3. Ninety-five percent agreed that a socially responsible corporation is a more credible corporation to the public.

4. According to 97 percent of the practitioners, social responsibility must stem from a firm, deep-seated conviction among the corporate officers that the company should act in the public interest.

5. Almost all of the respondents (98 percent) felt a management wanting to be socially responsible must act *consistently* in the public interest.

6. However, public relations practitioners may not be so committed to consistency and deep-seated convictions as one might think from the fifth conclusion. For instance, only 63 percent said management must act responsibly, no matter what the impact on profits. And 17 percent felt it is permissible for executives to have two ethical standards: one for personal use and one to be used professionally.

7. Seven out of ten practitioners believed they should act as their corporation's conscience.

8. Ninety-five percent said practitioners should share in defining the corporation's social role.

9. Eighty-five percent believed that practitioners should put personal conscience ahead of corporate obedience.

10. Nine out of ten respondents believed practitioners must work to ensure that the corporation does not use secrecy to hide company foul play.

11. Ninety-eight percent said a corporation should predict the social impact of its actions before approving them.

12. Only two-thirds said practitioners should present several sides to any issues about which they are disseminating information and give objective appraisal of conflicting opinions on that issue. This underscores the reality that the job of the public relations person is to put forth his or her own company's case—not the opposition's as well.

13. Indeed, just over half of the respondents felt that presenting all sides of an issue is the news media's job, not theirs.

14. No major differences were seen among PR practitioners with different titles or at different levels in their organizations.

15. The age of the responding practitioners did not appear to influence their philosophy of corporate responsibility to the public.

Assessing his findings, Ryan noted, "If public relations practitioners suddenly gained control of America's corporations, the public's negative views of corporate American soon would be reversed, and corporations would enjoy the kind of high credibility they have not seen for decades."[16] The researcher added quickly, however, that this would be true only if:

1. The corporation acts consistently in the public interest.
2. The public relations practitioners practice what they preach.

Many corporations, especially in times of crisis, try to manipulate the news media into portraying a favorable image of their operations. They do this in various ways. One such way is to turn a negative issue into a gray issue, causing much of the public to wonder if it presents much of a threat to them at all. A case in point is the issue of dioxin, the dangerous toxin used in Agent Orange during the Vietnam war. When news began breaking of delayed reactions among war veterans to Agent

Orange, some chemical companies, through their public relations departments, tried to cast doubt on the deadly seriousness of dioxin. They usually did this by employing a technique not common to many public relations departments (at least if the earlier Ryan study is correct). That technique is to tell *two sides* to the dioxin story, locating some scientific reports that say a solid link between dioxin and a higher mortality rate has yet to be established. Of course the reason may be that such studies are generally *longitudinal* studies done over time and focusing on many victims and that Agent Orange suffering is a relatively recent phenomenon. And, explain Jeff and Marie Blyskal in *PR: How the Public Relations Industry Writes the News*, this graying of the issue appears to be simply part of the normal, healthy debate in any democracy. They add:

After all, public relations' job is simply the noble task of "telling the other side." But there real intent of this "debate" is often to create a smoke screen of "facts" that obscures the truth. Crisis PR people will throw so much information at the press and the public that no one can be quite sure where the truth lies.[17]

The same situation exists to a larger degree in the tobacco industry. An industry whose life is dependent upon millions of people smoking regularly is certainly threatened by surgeon-general reports showing the dangers of smoking to a person's health. And it is even more endangered by having to place those warnings (albeit they are written in compromised fashion which is allowed because of the industry's successful lobbying efforts in Washington) right on their cigarette packs. So it is that the tobacco industry is trying a number of public relations tacks to counter these warning alarms. One is by designating industry PR people as tobacco issue sources to be used whenever reporters have questions regarding smoking. Advertisements touting these sources and encouraging the media to use them appear in the media professional publications such as *Editor & Publisher*. There is never a hint that these sources may be biased toward the industry that employs them, although any self-respecting journalist should know that. Another technique is found in the message appeal of cigarette ads (which now, of course, are allowed only in print media). One such message appeal begins "If you smoke . . . ," and another begins "If you are one of the millions of Americans who love smoking. . . . " In so doing, the ads are appealing to the heavy number of smokers still existing in the United States and the implication is that the industry recognizes that many do not smoke and is not necessarily trying to recruit them. The idea is that there is some sort of social conscience in this: that the smoking industry is only putting the smokers in harm's way (which, of course, the industry denies publicly), not the nonsmokers. That is unless you count secondary smoke as a threat as several government studies do, but which the tobacco industry disputes as one of those "gray" areas that is still "open to debate."

Another way in which public relations consultants attempt to use the media to tell their client's story is by coaching business executives on ways to wrest control of an interview away from a reporter and use it as a tool to tell the story the executive wants told. Television training for corporate executives is a fertile field for consultants, most of whom are former reporters, editors, or producers themselves. The rationale behind such coaching is that, since journalists have had years of training and experience in interviewing techniques, there is nothing wrong with the executive receiving some training as well. It evens up the odds and helps the executive resist the tricks of the reporting trade that work toward obtaining greater candor from someone who doesn't want to provide it.

Executives who want such training can get it, albeit for a fairly high price. In the 1980s, consulting groups like the Executive Television Workshop came on the scene. In addition, major public relations agencies, including Hill and Knowlton, Burson Marsteller, Ketchum Communications, and many others offer interview coaching to their clients. Also, in both the business and especially the political arena, media aides around such as Roger Ailes, consultant to George Bush, and Michael Sheehan, an adviser to four Democratic presidential aspirants in 1988.

Although techniques among these consultants may vary, the goal is the same: to allow the corporate executive to put the best possible face on his or her company, no matter what crisis that company or industry is involved in. For instance, in 1978 the Food and Drug Administration reported a link between sodium and the deaths of several laboratory animals who contracted cancer after eating sodium-laced foods. It wasn't long after the FDA report was released that the press picked up the story and wondered aloud, "Could this mean humans are in danger of contracting cancer by eating such high-sodium items as hot dogs and other preserved meats?"

Consumer fears began to rise, and at least one major manufacturer of preserved meats, Peter Eckrich and Sons, sent its consumer affairs director to Ketchum Communications for interview coaching. The Ketchum trainer described her coaching in the following manner:

We worked on content and manner of presentation, backed her up with technical information and helped develop comments that would be good for the media. For example, we found out a person would have to eat 200 hot dogs a day for 15 or 20 years to get the same amounts of sodium nitrates that had caused cancer in the laboratory animals. We also explained that sodium nitrates kept meat from spoiling and prevented botulism. Then we taught her to stress the positive things, that the company observed strict health and safety standards. We also drilled her in making ten-word answers to questions, so she could handle short and long interviews.[18]

Eliot Frankel, a former executive producer for "NBC News," says most coaching seminars stress three things:[19]

1. How to dress for the television camera.
2. How to present the story in the most positive way.
3. How to ingratiate oneself with the audience.

Trainers, Frankel says, also underscore the fact that television is a sound-bite medium that uses catch 20- to 30-second statements. Knowing this, an interviewee can prepare such zingers and almost predict exactly which of his or her statements will be picked up and aired.

Another interviewing coach, Jack Hilton, tells his clients that manner is more important than matter on TV and that audiences usually respond emotionally rather than intellectually. As a result, television watchers seldom remember what someone says. He also advises clients to put the most positive statements up front and work hard on making a good first impression on the audience, since being liked is so important.[20]

In describing his approach to coaching clients, Roger Ailes says a candidate must attract the media's attention by finding a different approach than what the other candidates are using. He or she must create some interest in their language, in the words and pictures they create. "If a candidate can't give a 10-minute speech and have reporters reaching for their pens in the first 90 seconds, he probably shouldn't be running," Ailes says.[21] He says some mistakes candidates make are in trying to befriend the reporter or seduce them or do something stupid. However, if a candidate can help them file a story that their editor will like and that may enhance their careers, they will give that candidate more ink or airtime. Ailes also takes credit for engineering George Bush's attack on Dan Rather during the interview Rather conducted with him in January 1988. He says that, while media bashing is not generally a good tactic, CBS was treating Bush unfairly in that interview and made the fatal error of trying to become the political opposition to Bush. When they did that, Ailes said, he coached Bush to counterattack on national television right during the interview.

Sheehan dispenses such advice as expressing a complex idea in 15 seconds, keeping gestures high and tight rather than low and fluid, maintaining eye contact, and smiling a lot. He also counsels that in a debate setting or a forum, a candidate must step forward as the one driving the debate and the one who delivers the most memorable line. The details of such coaching are evidenced by this Sheehan bit of advice:

The thing to do is answer the moderator for about two or three sentences. Then take it to the camera and talk to the people at home. At the end, you have the option of bringing it back and closing it with the moderator. But it's long stretches of uninterrupted eye contact that are critical on television. What you have to remember is everything about the television image—the face, the hair, the mouth, the eyes, the look, even the clothes—it's all like a mosaic. They all have to work together for you.[22]

These media consultants will be around for a long time, and the news media must realize that many of the corporate executives and politicians they interview have been coached on trying to take control of that interview for their own purposes. Journalists also must realize that they have a hard job in trying to puncture that manufactured image the candidate or corporate executive is trying to foist off on the public and instead get to the real person behind the mask. Actually, this media coaching process has been going on for decades. Media consultants simply have higher profiles these days and have become news in and of themselves. Amid the heat of the 1988 presidential campaign, several television and print stories focused as much on the media consultants for candidates and their strategies as on the candidates or issues themselves. There are even special-interest publications now produced on the subject of coaching political candidates through media campaigns. One such publication, sold by subscription for $48 per year or for $4.50 on the newsstands, is an 80-page slick magazine entitled *Campaigns and Elections*. One 1988 issue featured such articles as "Getting the Goods on Your Opponent," "Masters of the Media," and "Successful Media Strategies." Suffice it to say, the market is strong for media consultants who can train an executive or politician to deal successfully with the news media. In a sense, what most are selling is the training that enables their clients to pass shadows off as substance to a surprising unsuspecting public.

Is the Media's Consumer Slant Helpful?

Is one type of media focus—the consumer slant—helpful to portraying a realistic picture of events? If done correctly, it undoubtedly is. If a company is, in fact, dumping hazardous waste into a stream or sending dangerous pollutants into the air through its smokestacks, then it must be reported. If a toy has become popular with children despite the fact that, if handled incorrectly, it could cause them harm, it should be reported. If a company is guilty of false claims in their advertising, and consumers pay good money for bad results, then it should be reported. In all these instances and others, the media's consumer slant is a good one. It helps burst the shadow world of false claims, gets to the truth, and provides satisfaction for consumers who are being ripped off. It also addresses one of the needs the media meets for their readers and viewers. That is to help the public cope with a more confusing world on a day-in, day-out basis.

When, then, would this consumer slant not be beneficial to the public? Robert S. Goralski, director of information for Gulf Oil Corporation, has said the result of such consumer coverage is often oversimplified and distorted.[23] Consumer reporting does not often tell what has happened and why, he says. It only focuses on the results, and then in their most dramatic forms. For instance, when fuel costs or utility rates are increased, the media almost always fail to explain the reasons behind these increases, Goralski says. Instead, reporters generally focus on a family in dire financial straits who cannot afford to have their heating service continued during a cold winter. Similarly, layoffs in the auto industry feature the plight of the jobless without explaining the rationale for Chrysler's or Ford's cut in production. And in general, he says, television enjoys portraying itself as the compassionate counterpart to the uncaring corporation that allows rates to be hiked or workers to be laid off.

He notes that early in the 1980s, NBC News issued specific instructions to its journalists to look for emotional angles to stories and to tell those stories in human terms, hopefully showing individuals under stress as a result of whatever crisis they're facing.

Goralski suggests this type of consumer reporting should be replaced—or at least complemented by—stories which give a broader picture of the problem, focusing on the reasons for the problem in the first place. By focusing only on extreme results of these problems, he says, the media force Congress into acting precipitously and drastically in ways that usually are inappropriate, expensive, and detrimental to industry and the public alike.

Goralski's conclusions seem plausible, at least so far as complementing (but not replacing) result-oriented stories with stories dealing with causes of the crises. But he probably paints too narrow a picture of the coverage such crises actually get from the media. Few journalists would disagree that news coverage of a rate hike or auto industry layoff or gasoline price increase should include coverage of the reasons behind the crisis. In fact, it seems that most good stories do deal with the causes of these events. It is not uncommon to read a story about a layoff at the local Chrysler plant that says the layoff is caused by shrinking sales of domestic cars because the public is turning more to imports. And it is certainly appropriate for the press to produce other stories dealing with that domestic-versus-import car issue. And many newspapers do. But that doesn't mean the media can ignore or even de-emphasize coverage of how this crisis affects the average person who is caught up in it.

It is probably incorrect to say the media always look for the most drastic example of a problem's effect. Many news media go overboard trying to find out how a problem will affect the average family. When property or school taxes go up, for example, the media will usually translate that increase into what it would cost a family with a $70,000 or $100,000 home. They don't look at what it would cost someone at the poverty level who is just hanging on.

And, as far as causing precipitous action by Congress, it is not the responsibility of the media to set the agenda for Congress. Neither is it the media's fault if senators and representatives decide to take their cue from the media and overreact to stories or react inappropriately. Congress should be conducting its own investigations into the domestic auto situation vis-à-vis the Japanese imports. And their actions should be based on what they find, not what they read in the papers or see on television. Yet even if they do base their actions on media accounts instead of congressional probes and hearings, that still is not the media's fault. And it doesn't mean the news media should report solely to obtain congressional action on an issue. In large measure, the media should report for the average consumer who is wondering how he or she or their family will be affected by the crisis of the day, how they can get through the crisis with the least discomfort, and how such a future crisis might be prevented. Inevitably, these stories involve examination of *both* cause and effect.

When an International Focus Is Needed

As the U.S. economy is becoming more internationalized, so must reporters work hard to develop a world view of business. Part of that understanding is to learn how U.S. business operates overseas, because business reporting is no longer a strictly American affair. That is especially true when disasters occur on foreign soil involving U.S. or quasi-U.S. companies. If reporters covering such tragedies would develop more understanding of American business life overseas, they would be better able to explain why industrial accidents occur—and maybe even predict where the next ones are likely to occur. Often U.S. reporting of those incidents is better than the country's domestic reporting, but it still has a way to go.

Take the industrial accident in Bhopal, India, for example. Just before noon on December 3, 1984, the Press Trust of India, one of the country's two leading news agencies, issued a brief story about an industrial accident in Bhopal that had happened ten hours earlier. The story, which carried no special alert designation, said several hundred people had been killed or injured by a mysterious gas leak at the Union Carbide plant. The entire story comprised only a few paragraphs. The item caught the attention of the Reuters bureau chief in India. Sensing an even larger tragedy in the making, he dispatched correspondents to the central Indian city some 500 kilometers south of New Delhi. A short time later, Reuters bulletined a larger story with a much higher death count of what was an obvious disaster in this city of 900,000 people. The rest of the international press corps took note, India's major newspapers bore in, and soon both India and the world knew they were looking at history's largest industrial accident. As a result of the accident, the Indian government says, nearly 2,500 people died and 200,000 were injured—some permanently—by the deadly menthyl iscoyanate (MIC) chemical used in making pesticides.[24]

Over the next several days, numerous stories appeared in the media about the Bhopal tragedy. Few, if any however, examined the relationship of Union Carbide to the Indian government—or the extremely lax industrial safety standards in India—that some say helped set the stage for the deadly gas leak. It is also safe to say that most Americans were even unaware that Union Carbide *had* a chemical plant in India, or that hundreds of other U.S. companies have similar manufacturing facilities in this and other countries. That is due, in large measure, to the fact that few newspapers and almost no television networks or stations bother to do stories on international business or on U.S. businesses operating overseas. About the only obtuse mention the public ever hears of such plants is when Congress or the president decide to support— either monetarily or with armed troops—a foreign government "to protect American interests there." Those "American interests" are often plants that are at least partially owned by U.S. companies like Union Carbide. It's not that this is a bad reason for having the U.S. government support a foreign government; it's just that it would be nice to know exactly what those "American interests" are, so the American public can decide on its own if they are worth risking American lives or millions of American dollars to protect.

So in the case of the Bhopal tragedy, it took a massive gas leak of the chemical MIC to inform the American public that Union Carbide has a plant in India and that this plant might be operating under conditions dangerous to the public. The fact that it was not dangerous to the *American* public is probably what kept the plant out of the news prior to the tragedy. More often than not, news is only news to the U.S. media if it involves American lives. This plant employed mostly Indians and, frankly, much of the U.S. media couldn't have cared less.

But how many Americans know that life in these countries is, as AP's Victoria Graham says, "such a desperate business?" Indeed, how many residents of Bhopal itself knew the danger they were living under? How many stories were filed or cleared U.S. editors about the poor safety standards prevalent in India and other Third World countries? Even the Indian editors acknowledge the industrial safety standards are nonexistent in many cases. Simon Dubey, former editor of the 600,000-circulation *Indian Express*, said one of the major contributing factors to the high death count was that the plant was built in the middle of a huge population area.[25] Homes—and hovels passing for homes—were located right up next to the plant itself. That was a condition that should not have been allowed, he said, but it is an example of how slowly the Indian government responds to safety hazards at industrial sites.

It is ironic, and perhaps symptomatic, that an Indian journalist, Rajkumar Keswani, had worked for two years to warn the Indian public that the UCC plant was a time bomb, yet no U.S. journalists seemed to notice what he was saying.[26] Keswani's warnings appeared in his own weekly newspaper, *Rapat*, in Bhopal in the two years prior to the accident. Now a freelance writer for national newspapers, Keswani wrote a story in *Rapat* in 1982 warning the whole city could be wiped out if certain precautions were not taken. He entitled his article "Please Save This City." Two weeks later, he wrote a second article entitled "Bhopal: Sitting on Top of a Volcano." Four days after publication of the second article in 1982, there was a leak at the plant. No one died, but several were injured. That leak preceded the 1984 tragedy by two years but went largely unreported in India and almost totally unreported in the U.S. media. It is not so much that—in and of itself—it was a major story worthy of U.S. reporting. But to a U.S. media alert to indicators of danger, either the two articles from Keswani or the 1982 gas leak itself would have been worth looking at to see what they portended. Even a walk around a chemical plant anywhere in India would have produced adequate warning for most journalists who cared to make the trek.

That kind of story is not going to come by interviewing government officials in New Delhi. Indeed, one veteran U.S. correspondent in India said the Indian government is too closely linked with industry to enforce safety regulations. In a Third World country, the immediate goal is to succeed economically. If safety regulations are circumvented in the process, it is all in the name of progress. Government officials were being wined and dined in private guest houses in Bhopal right up until the disaster there, she said.

Another veteran correspondent in India assessed the situation this way:

In truth, India is full of Bhopals. I'm shocked we haven't seen another real big one. Here—there—plants making all kinds of lethal chemicals and petrochemicals. You just walk through a factory, and you see everything rotting, coming apart, rusting, nobody wearing goggles. But I just think they ought to do something about safety here, and I don't think anything's being done. When is the rest of this place going to go up?[27]

Alerting the public to dangerous conditions like this in India and elsewhere is one job of the U.S. news media. One gets the feeling, in talking with correspondents like Graham, that the reporters in the field know this already. Convincing their editors thousands of miles away that these stories should be advanced is something else again. Even if the wire service editors do advance them, however, they still must get through even tougher gatekeepers out in the hinterlands of America where the entire country of India conjures up only slight notions of newsworthiness among a newspaper editor or television producer.

In his 1987 book *Shared Vulnerability*, Lee Wilkins has this comment about U.S. reportage of the Bhopal tragedy:

Journalists . . . report such events according to very traditional standards. Much of what the public reads or sees therefore becomes episodic, disconnected from human historical and cultural context. The accident in Bhopal is, only tangentially, connected to the accident in Institute, West Virginia, or to the literally thousands of chemical spills reported in the developing as well as the developed world. What was happening "right now" became the most important element of the story; discussion of long-range issues was relegated to the bottom of the page, or to lengthy analysis and investigative pieces which only the determined reader or viewer would complete. Television did what it has always done well. The broadcast medium . . . omitted discussion of almost everything that was long-term and many-faceted about Bhopal. The event itself became the only story the medium believed was worth reporting.[28]

In fairness to the U.S. news media reporting from Third World countries, digging up and helping defuse potential time bombs is not an easy task. It is enormously more difficult than doing so in the United States, and even here it is not easy. Restrictions placed on foreign correspondents in most Third World countries put these reporters at an extreme disadvantage in getting candid information or access to potential trouble spots. Many of those risks are discussed in Chapter 3. Even in India, the world's largest democracy, access to information is not easy, and getting thrown into jail for your investigative troubles—or being asked to leave the country if you are a foreign journalist—is not that uncommon. Correspondents interviewed in New Delhi said they always feel the watchful eye of the Indian government when they go about their reporting and that, being outsiders and numbering only a few in the midst of the world's most heavily populated country, U.S. journalists are up against tremendous odds in getting at the reality of some important situations. The fact remains, however, that if you attach those problems to an unclear understanding of how global business operates and how a company in a specific country operates, then you are in real trouble. So the mandate is clear for economics reporters: Learn all you can about business on an international scale. Certainly that will be even truer after 1992 and the formation of the United States of Europe.

TV's Special Problem in Covering Business

During the peak of this country's oil crisis in 1979, *Los Angeles Times* reporter A. Kent MacDougall recalls the president of Mobil Oil Corporation was in Washington appearing before a congressional committee studying Mobil's unique oil proposals. William P. Tavoulareas tried to explain his company's position on price controls and the proposed windfall-profits tax, when he was confronted by a New Jersey congressman who was holding up a large placard reading, "No Decontrol." It was no coincidence that the poster went up when the television cameras appeared on the scene to cover the hearings. Holding the poster, Rep. Andrew Maguire asserted his staff had taken 13,000 such messages from constituents who were angry with Mobil and other oil companies. He then began attacking Mobil and the other oil producers for such crimes as price gouging, profiteering, and betraying the public trust.

In an attempted response, Tavoulareas spent a few minutes defending Mobil, but then gave up and walked out of the hearing chamber. That night, ABC's "World News Tonight" zeroed in on the confrontation between Tavoulareas and Maguire and almost totally ignored the hours of testimony preceding it. In so doing, television did what it always seems to do: put the spotlight on the clash of emotions, which is usually more visual and entertaining than digging into the issue as it was discussed in the hearing.

It is not surprising that Mobil and other large corporations feel a special contempt for television reporting of business news. Although they would probably place the reporting of most newspapers and newsmagazines somewhere between neutral and troublesome, they feel television stands alone in casting an unfriendly, inaccurate, and superficial eye toward business. In the process, it is at least partially responsible for turning public opinion against big business.

Writing in the *Times*, MacDougall noted all this and added that if television served only to supplement the business coverage the public gets from the print media, the resulting effect on public opinion would not be so harsh. However, public opinion polls show that the public gets the majority of its news—including business news—strictly from television. Many people get all their news from TV.[29] Indeed, three researchers—Herbert H. Howard, Edward Blick, and Jan P. Quarles—looked at media choices for specialized news in 1986. The purpose of their study was to discover which media source is preferred for medical, science, business, and consumer economics news. Surveying 310 people by telephone, the researchers found that local television news programs were the first choice in all four categories. Local newspapers finished second in most categories, and third for science news.[30]

"You can't tell the whole story in a minute and a quarter," explained

NBC business correspondent Michael C. Jensen. "Not only do you have to leave out nuances, you have to leave out major elements."[31]

MacDougall gives further evidence of what time compression and the lust for visual elements can do to the report of a business story:

The twin tyrannies of time and pictures condemn many important but non-visual business stories to TV oblivion. When the staff of the Federal Trade Commission released results of a 2 1/2-year investigation of whole-life insurance, concluding it was a poor investment for consumers, only one network, NBC, mentioned the FTC report, and its 30-second snippet left no time for the complexities involved, much less insurance industry rebuttal.[32]

To a great extent, the problems of television as it covers business are the same problems it has when it comes to covering other institutions like education or religion or even government. None of these institutions is especially visual, and they all involve a slew of seemingly endless debates over equally endless issues. Yet many of these issues are important to the public and should be aired. To its credit, network television has given birth to such analysis programs as "Nightline," and PBS has offered the "MacNeil-Lehrer News Hour" every weeknight for several years now. Both of these programs resist the urge to constantly focus on the dramatic and visual and have shown you can produce entertaining viewing with "talking heads," if those heads are queried intelligently and if they know what they are talking about. Other programs, like "60 Minutes," "20-20," and "PrimeTime Live," give in more to the dramatic, controversial, and visual. Still, their entry into prime-time television has certainly offered viewers more in-depth treatment of many issues. Even on these programs, however, the subject of business news gets short shrift. An exception, of course, is when the government issues unparalleled unemployment or inflation reports, or the stock market itself becomes big news because of a drastic rise or fall. On the day the stock market crashed in 1987, Ted Koppel devoted all of "Nightline" to the issue, but felt the public so incapable of understanding the event that he spent some 15 minutes providing an introductory course to basic economics. The fact that he did that, while commendable, is a sad commentary that most people who had grown educated via television needed to hear those basic definitions before they could understand what had happened that day at all. Most had never heard an in-depth discussion of stock market economics.

In this age of fragmented audiences, however, there is hope that more people can become better educated on economic issues by watching cable television. An industry that has arisen to take care of these audience fragments (some of which are quite large), cable television has given birth to numerous special-interest channels. One is the Financial News

Network and it, along with PBS programs focusing on economics issues, provides a wealth of information for those persons so inclined to tune in. The problem is, of course, similar to that of sticking important business news in the business section of a newspaper. Out of habit, many readers will toss the business section aside or flip past the business news channels, saying something like "Oh, business news isn't my thing." If business and economic news is not elevated in importance and given the same crack at the front page that general—and even sports—news had then a large segment of the population will go uneducated about basic economic concepts and about the impact business is having on the world and on their own lives.

The Hope and Challenge for Business Reporting

A national survey, reported in 1987, showed there is reason to take heart concerning the improving status of business reporting in the United States. The survey, done by J. T. W. Hubbard, showed a tripling of newspaper business staffs. Unfortunately, however, the same survey showed that coverage of business is becoming less aggressive.[33] Hubbard compared his survey of all newspaper business and financial editors listed in the *Editor & Publisher Yearbook* with similar surveys he did in 1965 and 1975. Among other things he found:

1. Editors perceive more popular interest in business news than before. Almost half of those editors feel that interest has "more than doubled."

2. Salary budgets for business editors and reporters at large dailies tripled between 1975 and 1985.

3. The increase in salary budgets, however, also has been accompanied by a parallel increase in the size of business reporting staffs, so the journalists have made little headway in actual salary increases.

4. Observations from several business editors suggest their publishers see business sections—and especially special business sections—as kind of clotheshangers for advertising. The only rule in doing business sections, said some responding editors, is that "we don't tread on any toes." It is hard to do aggressive reporting when that is the basic guideline.

5. In 1975, about a third of all editors felt they should not adopt a watchdog attitude toward business. Ten years later, that percentage had risen to 42 percent of all editors responding. In addition, in smaller-circulation dailies (below 100,000), 64 percent of all business editors said they "did not favor investigative reporting of local or regional business activity, or only favored coverage of corporate irregularities once they became the subject of formal hearings conducted by the courts or other regulatory agencies."[34]

So the hope is that more newspapers are beefing up their business reporting staffs, but the challenge is to do more hard-hitting, probing reporting on business conditions in the newspaper's market area.

THE STATUS OF SCIENCE AND MEDICAL REPORTING

There is no question that accuracy in science and medical reporting has improved over the past several decades and especially from the nineteenth century when the focus was more on pseudo-science and the bizarre. Only in the pages of the supermarket tabloids will one still find hyped front-page accounts of two-headed aliens visiting rural Indiana. The tendency for most mainstream media to shy away from the sensationalism of the past has created a more favorable environment in which science news can be reported.

Having said that, however, it should be noted there remain several problems in getting the full story across when it comes to scientific developments or disasters and near-disasters caused by scientific phenomena. While the sensationalism of the past has, to a large extent, been silenced, there is still the focus on the scientific event itself, the overgeneralization that often takes place about its impact, and little backgrounding or connecting of this event to related scientific events or discoveries. As in the case of business reporting, the blame must be shared between journalists and the scientific community. Nevertheless, the result is often a distorted version of reality when it comes to scientific successes or flops or disasters.

Results from a 1983 nationwide survey of science journalists conducted by Arizona State University drew 50 responses representing 45 newspapers. Results show science journalists working for major metro dailies tend to be highly educated, and several have advanced degrees, according to Conrad J. Storad, who was working at the time with the National Cancer Institute and who reported on the findings in *Editor & Publisher*. The problem is that their reporting in the specialty field of science is limited. Evaluating their field, some of the responding journalists had the following mixed feelings:[35]

- "There is emerging a new generation of science writers. This group is more enthusiastic, less didactic, and more in tune with the potentials of research."

- "Because this country is not in general well educated in science—many people are intimidated just by the thought of it—science reporting tends to reflect that in being somewhat superficial in approach. It is too often gee whiz reporting about a new discovery, too often single-source reporting."

- "Both the quality and quantity of newspaper science journalism are improving, but I still see hundreds of ill-conceived stories moving over the wire from major papers in Boston, Chicago, and even the San Francisco Bay areas."

- "Overall, the trend toward science writers with science backgrounds is helping story quality although readability sometimes suffers. At least fewer stories are dead wrong."

- "Quality has deteriorated as many reporters get caught up in trying to make every story sensational. I don't like 'controversial,' 'toxic,' or 'carcinogen' as key words in stories. I like them even less in headlines."

- One respondent to the ASU survey said newspaper science writing will not improve until "editors themselves realize they are among this country's science illiterates."

Three Mile Island and Mount St. Helens

We will move first to the most dramatic form of science reporting: the natural disaster which springs forth from the actual explosion of scientific elements. The twin examples of the eruption of Mount St. Helens and the radiation leak at the Three Mile Island nuclear power facility offer some insights into problems reporters face when covering science news.

On Wednesday, March 28, 1979, something went wrong at the Three Mile Island nuclear facility in Harrisburg, Pennsylvania. Radiation began leaking slowly from the plant, and by Friday, two more uncontrolled bursts of radiation went out into the atmosphere. By Saturday, more than 300 out-of-town journalists were on the scene and the incident was suddenly the major story of the year. By far, most of these reporters knew absolutely nothing about the subject of nuclear power. Yet here they were, dispatched from other beats by their editors, covering what was becoming the biggest nuclear power accident in history at that time. It was a story that could affect thousands of people in the surrounding communities, and were a meltdown to occur, an untold number of lives would be at stake. Most nearby residents would be basing their decision on whether to evacuate on the reports they received from television, newspapers, and radio. Yet most of those doing the reporting did not even understand what they were covering.

Yet given the makeup of most news media staffs where true specialists are almost nonexistent, it was the only way the event could be staffed. Once on-site, the reporters did the best they could and they, probably more than anyone else, knew what handicaps they were operating under by not understanding the subject at hand.

Jim Panyard, a longtime political reporter for the now-defunct *Philadelphia Bulletin*, said he was facing a story beyond his scope. Although his methodology was much the same as reporting on the legislature, his sources now were speaking words he did not understand. These words were about unknown objects such millirems, manrems, rads, and picocuries. He was also finding that even the scientists who did understand those terms did not always agree on the causes behind—or the potential danger of—the radiation leak. What were journalists like Panyard to do? Commenting on the quandary to the *Columbia Journalism Review*, Panyard said, "There is no doubt that the situation is dangerous, but how dangerous is the question. I'm concerned, and I think other reporters are, too."[36]

In short, what reporters were facing was a technical story that turned into a technical nightmare to cover. Studying the phenomenon, Peter M. Sandman and Mary Paden wrote:

At the beginning, at least, the vast majority of reporters had no idea what anybody was talking about. Anchorless on a sea of rads and rems and roentgens, of core vessels and containments and cooling systems, they built their stories about the discrepancies between sources, confident that the news, when they finally came to understand it, would center on the facts in dispute. What is surprising about the T.M.I. coverage that emerged is not that it was sometimes technically wrong, but that it was so often technically right.[37]

That the story *did* contain so many points of accuracy as well as inaccuracy is a tribute to the traditional resourcefulness that most good journalists possess. Stranded from personal knowledge about technical matters, they somehow manage to dig up enough to publish or air at least partially coherent stories. Sandman and Paden said the T.M.I. reporters were no exception, and they fell into one of four categories:[38]

1. *The Frankly Bewildered.* About one-third of the reporters on the scene were in this category. They could only breathe a sigh of relief when the interviewing of Nuclear Regulatory Commission scientists turned to nonscientific talk. They were unable to ask technical questions and relied instead on the only ones they really felt comfortable with such as "How dangerous is this leak?" and "Will the people have to be evacuated?" and "What are the chances of a meltdown?" Some even asked this last question without quite understanding just what a meltdown was. The only technical advice they received came from comparing notes with other equally bewildered journalists at the same press conference and checking the wire service copy before they filed their stories to be sure they weren't making any glaring mistakes.

2. *The Real Science Writers.* There were only a handful of these, characterized by their personal knowledge of nuclear power and its risks. They were the only ones who could ask highly technical questions boldly at press conferences, because they were the only ones who even understood their questions and who would be likely to understand the answers they got in return. They generally drew small crowds of other reporters who wanted to use them as their own sources or who wanted to know why they had asked what they had asked and what the answer meant.

3. *The Reporter cum Expert.* Maybe a fourth of the reporters arrived

with an expert in tow from back home or were dispatched one as quickly as possible or had one available at the other end of the phone line. These reporters could be seen actually reading their questions in press conferences, and from the hard time they were having even reading them, it was east to see they didn't understand what they were asking. Follow-up questions were difficult until they first checked the initial answers with their own personal expert to see if it *needed* to be followed up. CBS had a Long Island radiologist named Harry Astarita who arrived Friday night to monitor the radiation badges (all reporters were requested to wear them, signifying the amount of radiation in their personal space) for the CBS crew on the scene. He also was pressed into duty to edit the reporters' copy before it went out to millions of viewers.

4. *The Instant Experts.* Some reporters decided to do the seemingly impossible and study enough nuclear physics on the spot to make their own sense out of the answers buzzing around the press conferences. There weren't many of these, but a few traipsed off to places like nearby Penn State University to talk things over with professors of nuclear physics. In a few cases, this worked pretty well.

For most of the reporters covering Three Mile Island, getting information often meant relying on public relations sources for the NRC, the nuclear facility itself, for area utility companies, or for special-interest groups (both pro- and antinuclear power) that flocked to the site. Any journalist knows what kind of vested-interest and biased information any of these sources can slide into a story that reporters were trying desperately to make objective.

Similar problems arose thousands of miles to the west during the following year when Mount St. Helens decided to erupt, devastating forests and inundating small area towns with ash and mud, rendering all movement nearly impossible. Again reporters were encountering scientists and scientific data, and again they were unsure how to handle it all. For one thing, there was the philosophical difference between the two groups. Scientists at the scene, even before the eruptions, were worried about generalizing or overstating the data so as to cause undue panic among the surrounding population. Journalists, on the other hand, felt every bit of information was vital for residents and, if they were to err as reporters, it was better they erred on the side of sending residents packing instead of leaving them to face hot, molten lava at their doorsteps.

The problem was a multifaceted one. An area scientist for the United States Geological Service, Donald Peterson, noted, "If the scientists could have predicted an eruption that would create another Crater Lake, it would have caused panic, or it would not have been believed. Scientists were working with inadequate data."[39]

And, with only four information officers to work the entire country, the Federal Emergency Management Administration couldn't do much to translate things for the Montana reporters. Assessing the situation, Ron Lovell noted, "The effort was well-intended but out-of-sync with the daily news media. Scientists are not comfortable with saying, 'This is what is going to happen.' To get them to comment in any way that approached the speedy kind of dissemination the news media needs was hard."[40] Therein lies another conflict between the media and scientists: While the essence of the news media is speed, the essence of the scientific community is slow, systematic monitoring of data before making any conclusions. That may be why scientists often are reported as having reached conclusions or found cures when, in reality, all they have found are bits and pieces of information that might lead to cures or statements about causes.

Some Reasons for the Distortion

When looking for reasons behind distorted accounts of scientific phenomena, one certainly has to say the main one is the lack of scientific specialists who are writing for the news media. Only about one-fourth of the 1,000-plus members of the National Association of Science Writers (NASW) are staff writers for the news media.[41] And of the 300 reporters covering Three Mile Island, for instance, only about 40 of them were equipped to understand what was happening and to ask intelligent questions.[42] The other 85 percent of the reporting corps had to resort to the measures noted earlier to make some sense out of the scientific event. Most of the true specialists work on large metro dailies like the *New York Times* and *Washington Post*. Very few smaller papers, and almost no television stations, have scientific specialists. A few will have a medical doctor who gives a few minutes of advice each week, but that's about it. In large measure, it is the fault of media managers for not recruiting more specialists. Many editors actually fear the specialist, thinking he or she may actually produce material too technical and dull for the average reader or, worse yet, that they will become too sympathetic with the scientific community they are writing about and somehow have their objectivity distorted in the process. And many papers—medium and smaller dailies—and especially local television cannot even afford the luxury of specialists. Everyone in the newsroom must produce *daily* stories on a variety of subjects to fill the newshole or airtime.

Beyond the lack of qualified specialist reporters, however, there are some other reasons for distorted stories. Warren Burkett, in *News Reporting: Science, Medicine and High Technology*, sees some of them as the following:[43]

1. *Definitions of "Hypothesis."* One problem many untrained science

reporters have is in distinguishing the concept of a hypothesis from a conclusion. A hypothesis is nothing more than an educated hunch that gets the scientific experiment moving from one stage to the next. As a hunch, it is unconfirmed until the data are received and analyzed. Even then it may be rejected. And hypotheses are extremely narrow hunches. Even if one is confirmed that doesn't mean the larger theory is proven—just a portion of it. Also, the possibility exists that later tests will prove this initial hypothesis wrong. They are not carved in stone; they are tentative at best. Reporters, however, are looking for established fact that won't be disproven later on. The best facts, to a journalist are those that are unqualified and from which conclusive statements about a problem can be made. This is one reason why many scientists are leery of the media.

2. *Fragmented Reporting.* Science news is *not* spot news. There is little of an event-orientation to most science stories, since the scientific method moves in slow, minute steps. Maybe more than other types of stories, science stories require background that will lead to a proper perspective on the significance of the new finding. Even terminology may differ in meaning between journalist and scientist. For instance, Burkett points out that to a scientist the word "epidemic" can simply mean occurrences above the normal level. To a journalist, however, an epidemic is often construed as a kind of plague, out of control and taking on a widespread geographic significance.

The National Cancer Institute analyzed more than 2,100 cancer stories in one three-month period and found a lot of distortion emanating from the reporter's approach to the story. The Institute found few stories telling people how to prevent the disease or deal with its effect. Indeed, the study found, most stories emphasized the death effect much more than how a victim could cope with cancer and even beat it. In addition, stories about cancer-causing effects of chemicals seldom provided details about relative dangers from the substances or how people could cope with the hazard they presented.

Another common error of novice science reporters is to treat all types of cancers as the same, as well as the differing prognoses for survival among their victims.

The fact that reporters like unequivocal facts and hate qualifiers was evidenced by a 1983 decision of the now-defunct National News Council. In that decision, the council slapped the wrist of the *New York Times* for a story about the health risks from herbicides that were being used in the rice fields of Arkansas. Councilmembers felt a biochemist's statement was printed out of context to support a story lead that "doctors and scientists" supported claims to danger. The council's decision said the reporter left out facts showing that "some rice areas had low cancer rates while reporting death rates from a one-year report instead of using a lower, average figure over several years or even higher death-rate figures from an area that did not grow rice."

Dr. Arnold Relman, editor of the *New England Journal of Medicine*, noted recently that two scientific stories which were distorted in 1989 concerned the benefits of aspirin and oat bran. In a report on the benefits of aspirin in relation to heart disease, researchers noted that some doctors in a carefully controlled experiment took an aspirin a day and that led to lower heart risks for them. The media picked up the story and generalized it to the point where it said an aspirin a day leads to lower heart risk for everyone. Yet the study concerned only a carefully selected group of physicians who were in excellent condition and for whom there would likely be no harmful side effects from taking aspirin daily. Dr. Relman said the study did not generalize to a larger population, nor should the media have so generalized. In the studies on oat bran, an equal amount of distortion entered in, according to Relman. Oat bran was seen by the media as having positive effects for everyone when, in fact, two studies seemed to produce contradictory findings. One showed a benefit; the other didn't. "About the only thing we can say under those conditions," Dr. Relman said, "is we must wait for further study to be done to confirm one or the other finding."

Relman said he doesn't feel it is the scientist's job to interpret the findings for the general public. The researcher's only obligation is to accurately report the methodology used in the study and the conclusions reached. It is the news media's job, Relman said, to interpret those findings for the public, and the scientific community can only hope the journalists do an accurate job. "We don't put out press releases," he said. He added that when the media distort scientific findings, it makes scientists and doctors leery of further media contact.

3. *Conclusions and Policy Decisions.* Barbara Culliton, an editor at *Science* magazine and former president of the NASW, advised science reporters to ask scientists if their conclusions would support a government policy decision regulating or banning a certain chemical, product, or activity. If that question goes unasked, Culliton says, the impression may be left that the scientific data do support such a policy decision when, in fact, the data may not. Indeed, other considerations such as politics and intuition come into play in making policy decisions which, sometimes at best, are only guided by scientific data.

4. *Gee-Whiz Science.* Since the days of James Gordon Bennett and William Randolph Hearst, reporters have loved doing stories on bi-

zarre, often pseudo-scientific, claims, discoveries, and events. While most serious scientists would urge reporters not to publish such stories, competitive factors might suggest that they do—at least in some form. Often it is also impossible to tell, in fact, which discoveries are pseudo-scientific and which are legitimate scientific findings. Jeremy Bernstein, a physicist who writes for the *New York Times* and the *New Yorker*, suggests that reporters ask three questions when they come across an unconventional scientific discovery:[44]

- Does it explain anything? If so, what?
- Does it predict anything? Is the experiment subject to replication by other scientists to see if it proves true a second time? Prediction is really more the significance of most scientific discoveries than is the question "What use is this finding?"
- Is it connected to anything? Does this finding relate to any other great theories in science? If not, the finding should be considered dubious by the reporter.

5. *Hoaxes and Frauds.* It is not uncommon for someone to try and get a bogus scientific discovery past journalists. Sometimes it is done on purpose to prove that journalists are as gullible as they are. The example in Chapter 2 of the journalism professor disguised as a research scientist who found the cure for infertility is a classic case.

Obviously, some of the reporters had fallen into the trap of seeing Gee-Whiz Science as being the real thing and did not apply Jeremy Bernstein's suggested questions to that experiment and its alleged researcher.

More often, of course, the intent of a scientific hoax is to increase the reputation of the researcher who leaves hidden the fact that his findings are fraudulent. Science writers William J. Broad and Nicholas Wade of the *New York Times* say more than a dozen cases of scientific deception have occurred, and some of those bogus findings endured for decades before being exposed.[45]

Scientists and Journalists

How do scientists feel about journalists and how ready are they to talk to the media about their findings? A study reported in 1985 by Barbara Moore and Michael Singletary looked at scientists' perception of network television news. The researchers concluded, "Inadequate airtime and omission of detail are the most common objections by sources to science coverage on network news."[46] The researchers had identified a large sample of scientific stories and mailed them to the news sources identified in the copy. These sources were asked to comment on the accuracy of the stories and return the results. Among the findings were the following:

1. Fewer than half (48.5 percent) of the scientists said the stories were completely accurate.
2. Just over a third (34.3 percent) considered the stories to be generally accurate.
3. The most common source complaint was inadequate airtime devoted to explaining the story.
4. About 35 percent said essential details were deleted from the story.
5. Many of the scientists thought the coverage was too sensationalized by the reporter.

Two other studies done during the 1980s addressed the willingness or reluctance by scientists to be interviewed by the media. In one, Sharon Dunwoody and Byron T. Scott found:[47]

1. The notion that the average scientist has no experience with the media is not true.
2. Three-fourths of the surveyed scientists said they welcome media contact, while only 11 percent see it as a necessary evil.
3. Fifteen percent of the scientists initiated media contacts themselves.
4. Almost a third had written at least one story or publicity release about their own research.
5. Scientists feel magazines do a far better job than newspapers or television in covering science.

In a second study, Dunwoody and Ryan found part of the problem in distorted science stories lies in how journalists select their scientific sources. Among their findings, the researchers discovered that "in selecting scientists as sources, journalists do not always take into account the scientists areas of expertise."[48]

The researchers noted that—while reporters do feel a credible scientific source must be one who is communicative, accessible, and honest—the notion of credibility is too often left undefined. Is credibility more of an assumption on the reporter's part than an actual judgment based on the scientist's area of expertise? The research suggests that is the case. In their study, Dunwoody and Ryan discovered that:

1. Inexperienced researchers are more likely to discuss areas tangential or unrelated to their specialties.
2. The more a researcher discusses areas outside his or her specialty, the less productive in research is the scientist likely to be.
3. Forty-six percent of social/behavioral scientists discuss topics outside their specialty, while only 39 percent of physical/biological scientists do so.

4. There is no relationship found between a researcher's media contact and his or her belief in popular science.

5. The willingness of a scientist to go public may be related to a willingness to initiate contacts with the media.

Considering these findings, Dunwoody and Ryan suggested source-based criteria do not adequately predict the selection of scientific sources by the media. In fact, reporters ask one out of three scientists to discuss something outside her or his area of specialization. Therefore, journalists do not often consider the scientist's specialty as they choose sources for their science stories.

Still another study, done by Guido H. Stempel III and Hugh M. Culbertson, analyzed medical stories in Ohio's 11 largest dailies. To test several assumptions, the researchers analyzed more than 2,100 medical news articles, editorials, and signed columns from January to March of 1982. Among their findings were the following.[49]

1. Physicians are by far the most prominent, frequent sources of health-care news. They were quoted in 42 percent of all the medical news stories, giving them a 3–1 lead over other health-care professionals like therapists, psychologists, and nurses.

2. Only physicians are quoted or served as authors in substantially more items than they appeared in as objects of coverage.

3. Physicians are seen as more salient sources than medical administrative personnel. Overall, physicians were cited more than other sources in 72 percent of all stories.

4. Administrators, however, have reasonable levels of dominance in stories dealing with self-help, medical expenses, insurance, and miscellaneous topics.

5. Administrators focused more on system concerns, while physicians focused more on specific medical problems.

Finally, Dunwoody and Ryan found in another study that "scientists prefer direct contact with journalists and believe the public information office plays only a minor role in disseminating findings."[50] A large number of scientists see the public relations department as a hindrance in certain situations and prefer direct contact with the media.

Science and Medicine Are Big Business

It is worth noting before leaving this discussion of science and medical journalism that both fields represent big business interests for a lot of companies and private individuals. While popular television programs may portray the kindly Dr. Welby or the humanitarian and selfless hospital staff, the reality often is that researchers, doctors, pharmaceutical companies, pesticide manufacturers, aircraft makers, computer firms, utility companies, and even hospitals are locked in fierce competitive battles with each other. As such, most of them care very much about what is said—or not said—about their advances or their contributions to science, high-tech, or medicine. In a way, the scientific research field is like journalism. They are both in the business of discovering new information that will hopefully lead to a better world. But both scientists and journalists strive very hard to be the first to discover that information and apply it and to derive the publicity from that discovery, which may well result in a greater level of funding for their projects.

One of the things medical reporters, especially, must be aware of is that the hospital industry has become more competitive than ever before. Just because doctors don't place advertisements doesn't mean hospitals don't. With ever-increasing frequency they are not only placing ads in print and on television, but they are mounting massive and all-inclusive public relations campaigns to take patients away from competing hospitals. This results in the perplexing situation of having medical reporters finding themselves beset and confused by hospital public relations departments who insist that their hospital has the best cardiac care unit, or the best prenatal care, or the finest cancer detection program in the city. The reporter must know enough about recent advances and the state of the art in his or her specialty to sort out the truth from the hype in these requests for coverage.

Thus, as in all other forms of news coverage, the media run the daily risk of manipulation even by those professionals who would otherwise seem to be above the level of street fighting for clients, patients, funding, and survival.

NOTES

1. Jim Willis, comments made in a speech to business educators, Boston, June 14, 1986.

2. Stanley E. Cohen, "While S&Ls Were Robbed, the Press Watchdogs Slept," *Quill*, July/August 1989, pp. 21–22.

3. Ibid.

4. Ibid.

5. Ibid.

6. Ibid.

7. Lewis H. Young, "Business and the Media," speech delivered at the ITT Key Issue Lecture Series, University of Missouri, September 21, 1978.

8. Robert A. Peterson, Gerald Albaum, George Kozmetsky, and Isabella C. M. Cunningham, "Attitudes of Newspaper Business Editors and the General Public Toward Capitalism," *Journalism Quarterly* 61(1): p. 56 (1984).

9. Young.

10. Young.

11. "Business and the Media: Anatomy of a Libel Case," Columbia University Graduate School of Journalism Media and Society Seminar, Palo Alto, Calif., 1984.

12. Lester Thurow, "The Errors of Economic Reporting: A View from the Liberal Side," *Washington Journalism Review*, September 1982, p. 16.

13. Alan Reynolds, "The Errors of Economic Reporting: A View from the Supply Side," *Washington Journalism Review*, September 1982, p. 17.

14. Michael Ryan and David Martinson, "Journalists and PR Practitioners: Why the Antagonism?," *Journalism Quarterly* 65(1): p. 131 (1988).

15. Michael Ryan, "PR Practitioners' Views of Corporate Responsibility," *Journalism Quarterly* 63(4): p. 740 (1986).

16. Ibid.

17. Jeff Blyskal and Marie Blyskal, *PR: How the Public Relations Industry Writes the News* (New York: William Morrow, 1985), as quoted in "Making the Best of Bad News," *Washington Journalism Review*, December 1985, p. 51.

18. Eliot Frankel, "Learning to Conquer Mike Fright," *Washington Journalism Review*, July/August 1982, p. 32.

19. Ibid.

20. Ibid.

21. "The Power of the Tube," *Campaigns & Elections*, May/June 1988, p. 25.

22. "The Remaking of the Candidate," *Campaigns & Elections*, May/June 1988, p. 28.

23. Robert S. Goralski, "Television's Consumer Slant: Help or Hindrance?" *Business and the Media* (a quarterly newsletter of The Media Institute) Winter 1981–82, p. 1.

24. Jim Willis and Diane Willis, "India: A Case Study in International Reporting," *Nieman Reports*, Winter 1988, p. 25.

25. Willis and Willis, p. 29.

26. Ibid.

27. Willis and Willis, p. 51.

28. Lee Wilkins, *Shared Vulnerability: The Media and American Perceptions of the Bhopal Disaster* (Westport, Conn.: Greenwood Press, 1987), pp. 147–48.

29. A. Kent MacDougall, "TV Business Coverage is Struggle Against Superficiality," *Los Angeles Times*, February 5, 1980, p. 1.

30. Herbert H. Howard, Edward Blick, and Jan P. Quarles, "Media Choices for Specialized News," *Journalism Quarterly* 64(2): p. 620 (1987).

31. MacDougall, p. 1.

32. Ibid.

33. J. W. Hubbard, "Newspaper Business New Staffs Increase Markedly in Last Decade," *Journalism Quarterly*, Spring 1987, p. 171.

34. Ibid.

35. Conrad J. Storad, "Newspaper Science Writers Evaluate Their Field," *Editor & Publisher*, June 9, 1984, p. 100.

36. Peter M. Sandman and Mary Paden, "At Three Mile Island," *Columbia Journalism Review*, July/August 1979, p. 45.

37. Sandman and Paden, p. 54.

38. Ibid.

39. Ron Lovell, "Mount St. Helens: Reporting a Disaster," *Quill*, December 1980, p. 13.

40. Ibid.

41. Warren Burkett, *News Reporting: Science, Medicine, and High Technology* (Ames, Iowa: Iowa State University Press, 1986), p. 27.

42. Sandman and Paden, p. 54.

43. Burkett, pp. 61–70.

44. Jeremy Bernstein, "TV Science: D for Sagan, A for Miller for Obeying Bernstein's Second Law," *NASW Newsletter* 29(3): pp. 6–10 (1981).

45. William J. Broad and Nicholas Wade, *Betrayers of the Truth* (New York: Simon & Schuster, 1983).

46. Barbara Moore and Michael Singletary, "Scientific Sources' Perceptions of Network News Accuracy," *Journalism Quarterly* 62(4): p. 816 (1985).

47. Sharon Dunwoody and Byron T. Scott, "Scientists as Mass Media Sources," *Journalism Quarterly* 64(1): p. 21 (1982).

48. Sharon Dunwoody and Michael Ryan, "The Credible Scientific Source," *Journalism Quarterly* 64(1): p. 21 (1987).

49. Guido H. Stempel III and Hugh M. Culbertson, "The Prominence and Dominance of News Sources in Newspaper Medical Coverage," *Journalism Quarterly* 61(3): p. 671 (1984).

50. Sharon Dunwoody and Michael Ryan, "Public Information Persons as Mediators Between Scientists and Journalists," *Journalism Quarterly* 60(4): p. 647 (1983).

8

The Cult of Secrecy, the Breadth of Lies

Many of the causes of distorted reporting are beyond the easy control of journalists. One of the major causes is the widespread practice of lying and deceit among so many journalistic sources. Another is the mindset that mandates secrecy in so many U.S. and international institutions. Given the choice between keeping a document secret and divulging it readily and openly to the media, many executives in government and business would choose the former. The only exception would be if divulging the information would somehow help that source's personal star to rise. I was talking with a reporter for a metro daily following an especially frustrating time he had of trying to elicit information from a college public relations director. "Do you know what she told me?" he asked incredulously, referring to the PIO source. "She looked right at me and said, 'It's your job to get the facts; it's my job to keep them from you!' " If that was the attitude of a person who was being paid to pass information along to the public, he said, then the news media are in big trouble. And perhaps they are. Time and again, in the past two decades alone, U.S. institutions have shown how uncooperative they can be when it comes to disseminating non–self-serving information to the public. Yet when it comes to self-serving information, executives in and out of government will scream long and loud if the media don't pick it up and give it good play.

Part of the reason for this was discussed in Chapter 7. Many CEOs in business see a difference between corporate responsibility and social responsibility. With the possible exception of their stockholders, some business executives perceive it to be no one's business how their company operates. That is a difficult enough position to defend for businesses that do, in fact, have societal impact. Indeed, plant closings affect the welfare of hundreds and thousands of workers as well as the economic structure of towns and cities in which the plants are located. Also, manufacturing facilities that dump hazardous waste have a lot of public accounting to do. Pharmaceutical companies directly affect the health and welfare of millions of Americans, and yet on of the largest of these firms is especially reluctant to do interviews—especially on-camera interviews—regarding the drugs they manufacture, even when the company is being probed for quality control by the Federal Drug Administration.

SECRECY MOUNTS IN GOVERNMENT

The problem is that this cult of secrecy is not confined to many CEOs in business and industry. It also has become part and parcel of many governmental agencies up to and including the federal government itself. Political considerations and ramifications often are deemed more important by bureaucrats and officeholders than the public's right to know in a democracy. Perhaps that is inevitable in a governmental structure where officials go up for reelection every four to six years. Given the transitory nature of governments jobs, many officeholders seem swept up in a wave of insecurity that dictates they first predict how such and such news might affect their chances for reelection before divulging that news to the media. Still, the idea of the U.S. government is that its practitioners operate for the public good; not for personal gain. Although that may seem like a naive view, it is the law and ethics of American government.

Dr. Edward Teller, the nuclear physicist who directed the development of the hydrogen bomb, wrote almost 20 years ago that U.S. government should kick the secrecy habit.[1] As an example, Teller zeroed in on one fascinating aspect of the worldwide quest for harnessing energy from controlled nuclear fusion: focusing laser light on extremely small droplets of a liquid deuterium-tritium mixture. Although an important development, its work has been carried on in secrecy. Teller said he didn't understand that at all, and there was no reason for secrecy to cloak this development. Unfortunately, he wrote, secrecy becomes an addiction for governments and delivers a false sense of security. In reality, the impact often is that it just impedes scientific and technical progress and robs achievements available to all Americans and to the rest of the world.

In science, Teller asserts, there are very few real secrets in the first place. Interestingly, the U.S. government apparently feels some techniques are secret when they are actually found in publications available to the general public. This was pointed out when the *Progressive Magazine* decided to publish information in 1978 on how to construct a hydrogen bomb. The federal government protested, saying this is classified information. The editors of the *Progressive*, however, pointed out they had obtained this information out of reference works in libraries accessible to the public.

Of secrecy, Teller wrote:

The effect of secrecy on our defense is particularly questionable because openness is a deeply rooted academic tradition. Many of the best American scientists do not lend their talents to secret, defense-oriented research. This hurts us double. It weakens our defense potential and it slows down the peaceful applications that have accompanied almost every scientific military achievement. Ironically, secrecy even prevents us from working with our allies.[2]

Without a doubt, government secrecy continues to flourish in the name of national security and diplomacy. And undeniably it should in certain sensitive situations. But in a democracy, the government's need to protect information from disclosure ideally must be weighed against the public's need to know what its government is doing. In issuing his executive order on national security information, for example, Jimmy Carter said he was moving to effect a balance of those two interests by providing greater openness in government while protecting legitimate security information. Whether that happened or not is hard to tell, because in 1982 President Reagan issued a new executive order giving a kind of carte blanche to bureaucrats to classify more information than ever before. Even documents that were heretofore unclassified all of a sudden became classified.

Government secrecy is nothing new or unique to the United States. In fact, when comparing this nation's record to that of other "free world" countries—particularly Great Britain with its Official Secrets Act—it is argued that U.S. citizens enjoy one of the most open governments in the world. But official secrecy has long been a pervasive fact of U.S. government operation. This country's founding fathers drew up the Constitution behind closed doors. The authors of *The Federalist Papers* specified the need for secrecy in areas of diplomacy and intelligence gathering. In addition, leaders found another reason for secrecy in wartime, and information has been classified as secret or confidential as early as the War of 1812.

Federal agencies, until recent years, also took authority for secrecy from a 1789 law that simply required the establishment and maintenance of records. Then, a new category for secrecy—the "security classification"—was born, and government-held information became restricted in the name of "national security." The security classification was limited first to World War II military intelligence under orders of the War and Navy departments. A 1940 executive order from President Roosevelt gave the restriction broader standing, and a 1951 executive order from

President Truman extended the classification and authorized any executive branch department or agency to withhold information if considered "necessary in the interest of national security."[3] Then came President Eisenhower's 1953 executive order, an action that Arthur Schlesinger, Jr. believes unleashed the government's classification system and paved the way for subsequent abuses. Schlesinger has noted, "It was the result of this order that the system got completely out of hand, for it provides no effective control over the classification of documents and no feasible method for their declassification once the sacred stamp has been placed on them."[4]

While Eisenhower was taking action to protect national security, the legislative branch was having a say on secrecy through the Atomic Energy Act. This 1954 statute classifies all data concerning atomic weapons and the production and use of nuclear energy. The act also permits classification of such information from the time it is originated.

THE EVOLUTION OF OPEN-RECORDS LAWS

Some observers have felt over time that the United States should have access laws on the federal and state books. Others feel that the First Amendment should be enough ammunition for obtaining needed information. Those following this latter position feel that a key implication of the First Amendment is that it guarantees access to information. The reasoning is that if access is denied, then the story cannot be reported; if it cannot be reported, then prior restraint is at work. And almost every judge in the country will agree that prior restraint is what the First Amendment is all about and that it guarantees that there be none. Those observers opposing the access interpretation point out that the founding fathers conducted the Constitutional Convention itself behind closed doors. If access was what they had on their minds, why didn't they allow public access to that convention? To this observation, critics charge that access was not an issue in the late 1700s when the Constitution was drawn up, so why should it have been explicitly addressed? After all, they say, there is nothing about school prayer or abortion in the Constitution either, except by some peoples' interpretation. The point is that things change over time, new issues appear that were not problems in the past, and so the Constitution must be interpreted in light of these changing conditions. Access to information is very much an issue now, and it is not illogical to infer protection for it from the First Amendment.

As it has turned out, those favoring explicit access laws at the federal and state levels have emerged victorious. It all began when, in 1953, a freshman congressman from California was frustrated by his inability to get information from Sen. Joseph McCarthy about the Wisconsin senator's allegations of disloyalty by some government employees. Rep.

John Moss was infuriated partly because he was a member of the House of Representatives Post Office and Civil Service Committee. If that committee couldn't get any documentation from McCarthy, who was targeting people as Communists in civil service, then who could, Moss reasoned. His frustration led ultimately to the creation of the Freedom of Information Act (FOIA).

In 1955, with the help of two powerful Democratic colleagues in the House, Moss was named chairman of a new subcommittee to explore charges of executive branch practices that denied information to the public and the Congress. Some 11 years later, on July 4, 1966, the Freedom of Information Act became law. Moss said part of the reason for the 11-year delay is that he had to steer the legislation past three presidents, and there was a lot of presidential resistance to the idea. Every new president, Moss said, wants to tighten up the flow of information in America.[5] The law that emerged created greater opportunities for access to governmental information by not only reporters but also the public in general. It has not been without its drawbacks, however. Indeed, there are some nine exemptions to the law, and those exemptions allow certain information to be denied to the public. In some cases, such as national security, those exemptions have been abused and politicized. The most celebrated case of such abuse came when President Nixon tried to conceal the damaging Watergate tapes from public scrutiny, claiming executive privilege and danger to the national security. Both claims were found to be groundless.

Tales of FOIA abuses are numerous, and the following offer some glimpse into how widespread the abuses are:[6]

- The CIA granted a *Washington Post* reporter access to 3,200 pages of material under the FOIA. The problem was this came eight years, five months, and six days after the initial request was filed.

- The executive director of the National Security Archive received documents on the Afghan refugee problem four years after he requested them. The material had been declassified 16 months before it was finally released.

- In 1979, Angus Mackenzie, on assignment for the *Columbia Journalism Review*, sought information from the CIA on agency attempts to spy on the underground press. In 1982, the CIA agreed to grant him a fee waiver, two years after the agency had asked for a $30,000 deposit to find the information. Mackenzie was still trying to get the documents in 1989.

Jane E. Kirtley, executive director of The Reporters Committee for Freedom of the Press, said journalists often have trouble with the same agencies several times, but added that the source of the trouble is generally with the Justice Department. Kirtley said Justice officials are "usurping the editorial role of newspapers." If the department doesn't feel requested information is newsworthy, it won't grant a fee waiver. "For a small paper, that makes the difference in getting documents or not."[7]

But the fee waiver is only one of several problems associated with getting the government to grant access to documents via the FOIA. In some cases, an agency's FOIA official will respond to a request by saying the request for information isn't specific enough. In some cases, the official will say the document isn't in his or her office and won't tell where it can be located. In other cases, documents are shuttled from office to office so agency FOIA officials *can* say the document isn't there. And in some cases, the requests are ignored altogether with the implication to the journalist being, "If you want the information, sue us." Few news media can go to that expense and time, however. A final problem comes, of course, in the blacking out of entire portions of requested documents—in some cases entire pages are blacked out. In fact, it is not uncommon to request a 50-page document, only to get it with 40 pages blacked out for "national security" reasons. Although some— or even all—of these deletions may be valid, the journalist has no way of knowing that and must rely on the integrity of the government official doing the blacking out.

Moss noted recently that there is a need for a "rational system" to clearly identify when national security should not be used as a device to impede the free flow of information. He said Congress must be ever vigilant in overseeing the FOIA, and congressmen should insist on the right to know and the right of disclosure.[8] He feels Congress should go through a series of hearings to redefine the scope of the act and then move to expand it toward more disclosure.

The FOIA was strengthened in 1974 when Congress overrode President Ford's veto and passed amendments to it that reduced obstacles to access to government records. For instance, the wording of the national security exemption was tightened to allow withholding of documents that are "specifically authorized under criteria established by an Executive Order to be kept secret in the interest of national defense or foreign policy and are in fact properly classified pursuant to such Executive Order."[9] Overall, the FOIA amendments weakened the security exemption by requiring that agencies mark and segregate classified information so an entire document no longer could be withheld if only part of it required secrecy. As noted by one of the abuse cases listed earlier, this provision has been only partially helpful to journalists who may wind up with a document that has only a few unblackened lines remaining on it.

Under Ronald Reagan's presidency, journalists' access to information became even more limited. A 1983 Reagan executive order protecting classified materials said government employees suspected of leaking classified materials could be required to take lie-detector tests, and those refusing could be demoted or fired. The order also gave federal agencies the power to review and approve articles, books, and speeches by employees or former employees of government. Thousands of federal employees would be required to sign such secrecy agreements.[10]

Media historians Edwin and Michael Emery noted Reagan also launched attacks on the FOIA, increasing the authority of federal agencies to exclude materials from the FOIA provisions and encouraging agencies to charge fees for information sought. In its 1982 Freedom of Information report card, the Society of Professional Journalists gave the president an "F" on access issues.[11]

Despite its problems, the FOIA has proved to be a good law to have around. The following examples show how the act was used with positive effects by journalists in 1988 alone:[12]

- Two helicopter crashes were caused by pilot errors, according to reports filed by Marine Corps investigators. The *San Diego Union* obtained the reports under the FOIA. Five Marines were killed in the crashes, which occurred near Camp Pendleton. One of the reports concluded that safety procedures for pilots may need revisions.
- Former attorney general Edwin Meese took more trips at the expense of taxpayers than any of his predecessors, according to a story in the *New York Times*. Travel vouchers obtained through the FOIA showed that Meese took 22 foreign and 104 domestic trips during three years at the Justice Department. William French Smith, the second most-traveled attorney general, took nine foreign trips during his four-year tenure. The vouchers showed that California, Meese's home state, was the attorney general's most frequent destination.
- Hundreds of housing code violations were filed against the owner of a building in Washington, D.C., where three children were killed in a fire. In May 1988 the *Washington Post* obtained case records of the eight properties from the Department of Consumer and Regulatory Affairs (DCRA) through an FOIA lawsuit. The records showed at least 112 cases against the properties which cited the owner for hundreds of housing code violations since 1980. The *Post* story noted that the DCRA had no way of spotting repeated violations of housing codes at commercial buildings.
- A Washington, D.C., television station's investigation into ambulance delays may have prompted an inquiry by the D.C. fire department. WUSA-TV used FOIA requests to get copies of conversations between the ambulance dispatcher, caller, and emergency crew in a case where the victim died of a heart attack. The day after the station aired the story, the fire department began its own investigation.

In addition to the FOIA, all 50 states and the District of Columbia have passed open meetings and open records acts, and these acts also have proved useful despite abuses that occur which are similar to those occurring under the FOIA.

The result of all this access legislation is that more information is open, by law, to the public than ever before, although serious abuses still exist in following the spirit of both the FOIA and some state access laws.

SHOULD REPORTERS JOIN IN THE SECRECY?

At what point does it become unethical for reporters to divulge confidential information? Aren't there some secrets that should be kept and that, if disclosed, could endanger national security? These are two of the more difficult questions facing reporters, especially those plying their craft in the nation's capital. In 1986, for instance, journalists began digging into two intelligence areas that produced heated reaction from the administration. One of these areas was the status and kind of U.S. spying operations against Libyan's Col. Moammar Khaddafi. The Libyan military became the focus of attention when the media announced that U.S. intelligence said the Libyans were linked to the April terrorist bombing of a Berlin nightspot. A U.S. soldier and Turkish woman died in that blast. That press disclosure seemingly infuriated then–CIA director William Casey, as he said the press reports compromised U.S. intelligence activity and put lives in peril.

The second disclosure involved Ronald W. Pelton, an ex-National Security Agency cryptologist who sold U.S. intelligence reports to the Soviet Union early in the 1980s. The media faced warnings from Casey and other security heads that they should exercise caution and restraint in disclosing details of U.S. electronic spying against the Soviet Union.

Yet another warning came later from Casey and was directed toward *Washington Post* editor Bob Woodward and *New York Times* writer Seymour Hersh. The warning concerned their upcoming books dealing with the CIA and with the shootdown of KAL 007, and it stipulated there might be prosecution if too much classified data on U.S. communications intelligence activities were disclosed.[13]

The debate on reporters keeping state secrets often focuses on two opposing viewpoints:

1. Intelligence officials assert that journalists act as if they themselves should decide what information should be classified and what shouldn't. Never mind that they haven't had any training in intelligence-gathering operations nor do they know the larger intelligence picture that might be harmed by disclosures of certain information. The media want one thing and one thing only: to get the news out in the next edition or on the next newscast.

2. Under current federal law, journalists are given the right to make those decisions without government approval. The one sticking point that emerged under the Reagan administration is an obscure clause, Section 798, in the 1917 Espionage Act. That clause makes it illegal to

disclose "classified information" about codes and communications. That clause was installed during the height of the Cold War in the early 1950s but, until the Reagan administration came into power, it was not used as a club to keep reporters away from the news. It was the section that Casey used to threaten reporters with when they reported on the intercepted Libyan communications in 1986. The possible penalty for conviction under this clause: ten years in prison and a $10,000 fine.[14]

But the overriding issue is how much secrecy can and should exist in a democracy where people govern themselves and must know what is happening in order to make intelligent voting decisions?

Writer Michael Wines describes the dilemma Washington reporters face as follows:

Awash in hot information, writing in the self-proclaimed "year of the spy" [1986], Washington's national-security reporters and editors grouse about being bamboozled out of exclusives by administration brass who saw away at their sense of patriotism like the first chairs working over favorite fiddles. They fret about inadvertently getting bystanders killed in the Mideast, giving the Soviets a military edge, or—even worse—becoming an unwitting tool of disinformation battles between Russia and America, Defense and State, or Old Executive Office Building and White House West Wing.[15]

It's a tough job, and one national-security reporter noted that if he can get more than 51 percent of the facts straight, he feels he's doing a good job. "The minute you start to believe what your sources tell you, you're cooked. You never know if you're right or wrong. It's a terrible way to make a living," he said.[16]

So added to the reporter's list of duties and obligations is to somehow discern between information that is being kept confidential for true national-security reasons and that which is being kept secret for political reasons—or for no reason at all other than it is being maintained by members of the cult of secrecy.

That members of both the government and the journalistic community abuse security classifications in acknowledged by Richard D. DeLauer, former under secretary of defense for research and engineering.

One is left with the realization that the existence of so much classified data raises certain issues and creates an unusual environment in which the defense reporter must work. Unfortunately, this environment can be, and occasionally is, used as an excuse by both the government and the Pentagon press corps to hide incomplete and unprofessional work. . . . The facts to be reported must often be deduced or translated from bits and pieces of information that, in the aggregate, form a reasonable semblance of what is in reality a classified story.[17]

But DeLauer says opinion finds its way into those bits and pieces of stories and distorts the overall impression of the classification system.

In support of his argument he pointed to an April 19, 1983, story headlined "The Problem of Keeping So Many Secrets Secret." The story
described alleged abuses of the classification system by the Department
of Defense. To make the point, DeLauer said, the reporter quoted a
paragraph that, the article noted, was marked "Secret" in a DOD document. The problem, according to DeLauer, is that the reporter closed
his quotes too early. The obviously unclassified material quoted represented only about 20 percent of the original paragraph. The unquoted
part went on to outline more detailed objectives of air power that do,
indeed, warrant classification. DeLauer said most security reporters
should know the classification of a given paragraph depends on the
highest level of classification in that paragraph, which may contain both
highly secret and totally innocuous information. One has to wonder, he
said, when quotations are used so obviously incorrectly.[18]
   An obvious question arises, however, when thinking about DeLauer's
example. If the classification of a paragraph depends on some truly
classified information embedded somewhere in some portion of that
paragraph, what is to keep members of the government's secrecy cult
from simply writing longer paragraphs or joining shorter paragraphs
into longer ones so they can classify both security-endangering material
as well as politically embarrassing material into the same paragraph?

CONFLICTS BETWEEN THE MILITARY AND THE PRESS

   Skirmishes between the news media and the U.S. military over how
wars should be covered are nothing new. During the Civil War, for
instance, although correspondents were allowed to roam the front without restriction, President Lincoln ordered the suspension of some 20
northern newspapers for reporting which he considered dangerous to
the Union's cause. Lincoln was quoted more than once as saying that,
if he had to sever a limb to save the whole tree, he would not hesitate
to do it. In his metaphor, obviously the limb was the offending press
and the tree was the Union. Later, in the first and second world wars,
correspondents had a great deal of freedom to roam where they might—
indeed reporters stormed the Normandy beaches with the Allies, but
they still had to submit their dispatches to field censors for approval.
Sometimes this censorship was light; sometimes—as under Gen. Douglas MacArthur in the Korean War—it was heavier. In January 1951,
MacArthur imposed stringent restrictions on reporting. "His regulations
covered not only censorship of military information but also all statements that would injure the morale of UN forces or that would embarrass
the United States, its allies, or neutral countries. Correspondents con-
tended that MacArthur had imposed both political and psychological
censorship, as well as a military one."[19]

In probably the most controversial war involving the United States in history, the Vietnam war, only a minimum of actual censorship was imposed on correspondents in the field by the U.S. military command in Saigon. Instead, the main problems faced by U.S. correspondents came from the South Vietnamese government, critics back home in America, and a certain degree of deception and misrepresentation of casualities by some top U.S. military officials in order to make the U.S. effort look more successful. A cynical Morley Safer of CBS said recently he would advise a new reporter sent to cover a war that he should attend the military briefings daily for the first week—and then forget about them altogether. Safer said you will seldom get fresh, decipherable material from such briefings, and you will be lucky if you get a candid view of the war's status.

Despite these problems, however, the U.S. war correspondents in Vietnam had possibly the greatest freedom to report as any correspondents who have covered any other war. Certainly the U.S. correspondents in Europe could roam where they would during World War II, but their material was always contingent upon passing through at least one and sometimes several field censors.

In 1982, the British amended the rules for covering wars. Under the Thatcher government, the military imposed the following rules on the media in covering their war that year with Argentina in the Falkland Islands. The nature of this war, meaning the fact that it was some 8,000 miles from England and 400 miles from the nearest landmass, meant that correspondents needed Britain's Ministry of Defense to get them there. In return for access to the action, the correspondents decided to agree to the MOD ground rules, some of which, notes English journalist Philip Knightley, were crippling.[20] Among these rules were the following:

1. Only British correspondents were allowed to sail with the task force.

2. The 17 correspondents who were approved to go were required to sign forms agreeing to accept censorship at the source by the six MOD "public relations officers."

3. The defense ministry also controlled the means of communication, and reporters were issued a booklet telling them that they would be expected to "help in leading and steadying public opinion in times of national stress or crisis."

Cut out from the press pool, other correspondents—including U.S. journalists—had to rely on information coming from Argentina or the MOD briefings in London. Both turned out to be less than objective sources. Knightley cites the following example:

We have no reports of any major Argentine warships or auxiliaries having penetrated the maritime exclusion zone," [the MOD briefing officer] would say. And after a few seconds for closer, word-by-word study, the press corps would be on its feet trying to pin him down. What did he mean by "reports?" Why "major" warships? Did that exclude small ones and, if so, how small? Did "penetrated" mean from the mainland to the islands or from the islands to the mainland as well? And so on.[21]

The lessons of news management learned from the British were not lost on the U.S. military. When the U.S. version of the Falklands occurred in Grenada in 1983, the U.S. correspondents were not even permitted to go along for the ride. Indeed, they didn't even know the trip was in the works. The invasion—or rescue operation as the Reagan administration labeled it—was totally off limits to the media, and when some network television reporters chartered a boat and tried to get to the action themselves, they were warned off by naval vessels standing guard and watching for such zealous correspondents. In explaining this unprecedented denial of access, the Reagan administration said publicly, albeit vaguely, that it was related to considerations of safety for the journalists, logistics, and surprise. In discussing the safety aspect, administration officials could not answer reporters when they asked, "How was the danger of this invasion different from the dangers reporters faced when they accompanied U.S. troops onto the Normandy beaches?"

Regardless, the effect was a minor war in which information was totally in the hands of the administration who had authorized the military action in the first place. The government could portray it any way it wanted to, showing videotape shot by military photographers of secret "arms caches" showing how dangerous the island had become under unfriendly influences and how desperate was the plight of the U.S. medical students living there and how—as Reagan said on national television—"We got there just in time." This all may be, but if it was as obvious as the administration said, what was the harm in honoring a tradition of more than 150 years in letting U.S. correspondents go along and tell the story themselves? At the least, wouldn't the story have more credibility if told by neutral journalists than by the administration which waged the conflict in the first place? The answer would be yes, were it not for the specter of television bringing the battle scenes into the nation's living rooms as it had done so graphically in Vietnam. The U.S. administration seems to have learned from that experience as well as Britain's success in restricting its media. To the military, a big lesson of Vietnam was that the media might form "misconceptions" about the war and might even tend to criticize the way it was being fought. In any case, the nightly scenes of body bags do nothing for the morale back home and may even increase the rhetoric for retreating from the conflict entirely. Vice Adm. Joseph Metcalf, for instance, has noted that forcing the field commanders to think about public relations instead of military operations is a mistake.[22] And John E. Murray, retired Army major general, observed that "engaging the press while engaging the enemy is taking on one adversary too many. It's easier to straighten out an erratic [military maneuver] than straightening out the misconceptions of the media."[23]

When it was over, President Reagan emerged unscathed in the arena of public opinion when it came to the issue of denying media access to this conflict. Several public opinion polls which were carried out in the days and weeks following the Grenada operation showed a majority of people felt Reagan had made the right decision—both in sending troops to Grenada and keeping the media home.

The media protested loudly, however, and out of the Grenada action came a meeting of the minds between the Pentagon and the media regarding a pool arrangement for covering future military operations. The idea is to have a rotating media pool, with the military deciding when a pool will be put together and dissolved and also setting the operational rules. The arrangement allows the local military command to exercise almost total control over the comings and goings of pool members and act as a field censor for stories before they are filed.

The National Media Pool was tested—and found lacking—in the 1990 invasion of Panama by U.S. troops. In this case, the media were alerted to the operation, and a pool of correspondents went along with the troops sent to that country. The problem was that, while they were transported to the Panamanian airport and then to a briefing room away from the action, they were not given transport to the fighting itself—at least not for several hours. As a result, not a single journalist accompanied the first wave of U.S. fighting men. The pool did not get to the scene until four hours after the fighting began, and they were not allowed to file their stories for yet another six hours. In addition, there was extremely little coverage of the convoluted military situation and too much drivel about the U.S. chargé d'affaires in Panama, John Bushnell, being concerned about the "mischief" that Manual Noriega could generate. Steven Komarow of the Associated Press sighed, "We kind of missed the story."[24]

Nevertheless, even with these stringent restrictions, Panama was an improvement over Grenada when it came to media access to the war zone.

In a 1983 conference, "War, Peace, and the News Media," Brookings Institute Fellow Stephen Hess said reporters and government officials make strange bedfellows and that "leaks" figure prominently into their relationship.

While most Pentagon reporters and their sources almost seem to enjoy the fight over what should be a reasonable accommodation between secrecy and access—somewhat like an old married couple whose arguments only sound horrendous to outsiders—the Reagan administration suddenly turned up the decibel level of the controversy. At his news conference of January 19, 1982, President Reagan announced that leaks had "reached a new high" Leaks of any value rarely come from the bureaucracy. The policy-and-personality leaks that so disturb presidents come from their own appointees. Presidents have a right to try to conduct their internal business in an orderly manner and to try to time their moves to their advantage. Their views of what is the national interest may not be apolitical or correct, but they have been elected to receive greater consideration than the views of any other individual.[25]

In other words—and this is so well known it hardly bears stating—many Washington secrets get out not because of prying reporters, but because some staff member leaks the information either on his own initiative or because he has been ordered to leak it. The leak, in the latter instance, becomes a trial balloon or a dart at some political opponent or faction.

When it comes to future coverage of military operations, one would have to say that future is suspect. In all likelihood, it will depend on the popularity of the president in power at the time the military actions occur. Indeed, it probably was the popular mandate that both Reagan and Bush felt they had during their sanctioned invasions that bolstered them up to the bold—and ironic—position of denying U.S. war correspondents access to the war.

THE PROBLEM OF LIES

If secrecy makes it difficult for reporters to gain access to the truth, lies make it almost impossible. And yet lying has become so widespread and prevalent in American society that *U.S. News & World Report* recently produced a cover story on the subject entitled "A Nation of Liars," and PBS aired a Bill Moyers "Public Mind" episode in November 1989, entitled "The Truth About Lies." In addition, psychologist Paul Ekman produced a popular book in 1988 entitled simply *Telling Lies,* and another psychologist, Dr. Daniel Goleman, has published *The Vital Lie.* In many ways, say sources for these and similar works, lying and other forms of deception have become a way of life in the United States. Although Ekman makes a valiant effort at trying to show how a person can detect if someone is lying to them (i.e. dilated pupils and blinking, blushing, talking louder and faster, and raising the vocal pitch), these discernments seem pretty subjective and subject to misinterpretation by untrained observers. Of all observers, reporters should be among the most accomplished and yet even they cannot always tell when they are being lied to, especially if the person lying has been coached on ways to make the lie go down as truth. What's worse is that few professionals are more dependent upon getting the truth from people than are journalists. That's what is so troublesome about Ekman's observation that "there are few [human relationships] that do not involve deceit or at least the possibility of it. . . . Lying is such a central characteristic of life that better understanding of it is relevant to almost all human affairs."[26]

Reporters are dependent upon working relationships with sources every day of the week. How are they supposed to portray reality when their primary sources may well be shading the truth? That is one reason why the journalistic interview possibly should not be the linchpin of reporting technique. It is subject to so many problems and possibilities for distortion that it would make many journalists paranoid just to consider them in detail. Some of these distortive influences can be:

1. While the journalist's job is to get the truth, the source often feels compelled to shade that truth to make himself or herself or the cause the source is promoting look better. This practice does not belong exclusively to the public relations professional. At one time or another, we all engage in it.

2. The source may not be an expert about the issue under consideration. Yet he or she may be unwilling to let the reporter know that and opt instead to bluff through the subject, substituting guesses at appropriate times for actual knowledge.

3. Time and/or space may be too short to allow the subject to be explored in enough detail. Sweeping answers may be allowed to stand for more precise answers with the necessary qualifiers because of short time. This often happens in television interviews—especially live interviews—when both the reporter and the source are thinking in terms of ten-second soundbites. It also happens in the news pages, however, when a reporter has only a few inches to report a rather detailed interview. This is where the tight, short stories of USA Today and similarly oriented newspapers run into trouble. They may be better-read newspapers, but the content they are handing out is often too general and, as a result, distorted.

4. The reporter may not be as knowledgeable about the issue as he or she should be. The journalist may have been thrust into the interview on the spur of the moment without the necessary time to do homework on the topic and the interviewee, or the reporter may simply not be expert enough in the technical area to ask, or understand the answers to, the questions. This problem is discussed in more detail in Chapter 7.

5. The editor or producer may have a preconceived idea about the slant the interview and resulting story should take. That preconception may be so strong that the story is designed to fit it rather than let it run counter to the editor's premise.

6. The interviewee may have a particular axe to grind or an opponent to denigrate. In such cases, the information this source provides should be treated

with greater suspicion than if he or she were totally neutral. In fact, there are few cases in which an interviewee is totally neutral on an issue. If the source doesn't have a vested interest in the subject, then at least he or she probably has an opinion on it. It's not easy for a journalist to get fact— unadorned by opinion—out of a source.

7. The reporter may not ask all the right questions and leave a vital area or two unexplored because of lack of time, knowledge, etc. In such cases, interviewees often see no reason to help the reporter out by volunteering such needed information. In many cases, the source feels that he or she is not lying if they simply conceal or fail to volunteer answers to questions not asked.

This last distortive influence brings up an interesting topic. Is withholding information the same as lying? Psychologist Ekman says yes. "Concealing or withholding information is just as much a lie," he says. "It's just that the tactics are different."[27] One example that led to tragic results might explain this viewpoint. That example is the explosion of the space shuttle *Challenger*, discussed in Chapter 5. Although NASA and some other observers classify that disaster as an accident, several engineers close to the project say it could have been prevented if the engine's manufacturer, Morton-Thiokol, had disclosed doubts early on in the project.

"I can't characterize it [the shuttle explosion] as an accident at all," said Morton-Thiokol engineer Roger Boisjoly. "It's a horrible disaster, but it's not an accident. Because we [Morton-Thiokol] could have stopped it."[28] Boisjoly wrote a memo to his superiors in the company six months before the *Challenger* launch. In that memo, he pointed out certain dangers associated with the O-rings that could cause a catastrophe. Yet Morton-Thiokol never showed the memo to NASA.[29] There was still another chance to rectify the situation, however. The day before the launch, company engineers were concerned about predicted freezing overnight temperatures. They didn't feel the shuttle should be launched, and they advised third-level NASA officials to wait a day. Yet Boisjoly said the NASA officials were "beside themselves. They were appalled by the recommendation." He said they put pressure on the company to reverse its recommendation because NASA itself was under intense public and political pressure to launch on time. Morton-Thiokol representatives, also under pressure to keep NASA's lucrative contract, did reverse themselves and NASA accepted the revised recommendation immediately.

The problem was that, even at this critical stage, lower-level NASA officials decided not to inform higher-level officials of Morton-Thiokol's doubts. "For better or worse, I did not perceive any clear requirement for interaction with Level 2," testified NASA official Stan Reinartz to the presidential commission investigating *Challenger*.[30] It was Reinartz who had been contacted by Morton-Thiokol the day before the launch. Still, Morton-Thiokol engineers remained quiet. Recalling his and other engineers' thoughts on the morning of the launch, Boisjoly told PBS's Bill Moyers, "Now we all thought it was going to blow up on the pad, right when they ignited it."[31] And, following the explosion, he noted, "NASA tried to make it sound like an accident. We were told by our own attorneys to volunteer nothing."[32]

So is all this lying, or shall we call it business, political and/or legal expediency? In the end, it amounts to the same thing in the minds of many psychologists and laypeople. It may seem fantastic that it happens at all, but it did with regard to *Challenger*, and it has on several other occasions. In a somewhat stinging indictment of journalists, perhaps if they had bothered to explore the safety of the shuttle mission in more detail, they might have uncovered some clues leading them to air or print doubts surrounding the operation. But they didn't.

The reasons behind such subterfuge as Morton-Thiokol and NASA practiced are, in and of themselves, interesting. Part of the reason is found in what psychologist Goleman describes as the "shared lie" or the "vital lie." According to Goleman, a shared lie is one that a person or a group finds necessary to maintain in order to keep some sense of security or in order to avoid unpleasant anxieties.[33] For instance, if a mother and father know that their small child's grandfather is a convicted felon who was just released from prison, they may choose not only to keep that information from the child but to tell the child his grandfather has been on an overseas business assignment for the past two years. This sort of vital lie or shared lie lets the parents avoid the unpleasantries surrounding the grandfather and what they fear will be the child's reaction to that truth. In a closer sense, however, it also lets the mother and father put up a fantasy that says there is nothing wrong with this family. Everything is as it should be. It happens all the time with many families, and it also happens with larger groups like political parties and even nations, Goleman and Ekman say.

Goleman points to another historical event to make his point about shared lies and why they exist. Speaking on a 1989 episode of the PBS series "The Public Mind," he cited the 1962 Bay of Pigs fiasco. This was the planned invasion of Cuba by several hundred Latin American insurrectionists under the tutelage of the CIA. The intention was to raise the dissatisfied elements in Cuba to a level of insurrection themselves and eventually overthrow Castro. The plan failed and, what's worse according to Goleman, the Kennedy administration knew it would probably fail. For instance, he notes that Kennedy and his top aides who spent two to three months planning this invasion knew that the invading force would be outnumbered 140–1 and that a CIA clandestine survey of Cubans showed they would not rise up in defiance of Castro following such an invasion. Yet this information was never brought up in the planning meetings. "They suppressed all their doubts; they censored themselves," Goleman said. Why? "Because the collective mind—the public mind—has its own blind spots. The shared reality that we create is as susceptible to self-deception as we are individually. You don't want to be the one who brings up the unpopular truth. You want to be the one who can make it real; who can make this lie become truth. The pressure to go along, to shut up, not to notice and not to bring it up is incredibly strong even—and perhaps especially—at the highest levels."

Yet there are some high-level group members, like John Dean, special counsel to President Nixon during the Watergate era, that do blow the whistle. For whatever reason, Dean says he told Nixon that he would not lie for him.[34] When he viewed a 1972 press conference that the president held in which Nixon said his special counsel was leading a special White House investigation into Watergate, Dean said he had had enough. "I was the counsel and that was the first time I'd heard of my own report. He made it up out of whole cloth. Nixon was not alone in this regard. There's no doubt that presidents do lie. They are politically expedient animals, and they do it."[35]

Addressing Dean's exposing testimony, Goleman says, "People who blow the whistle do it because they see that living the lie is defeating the purpose of the group. So they speak the truth, but what they've done is violate the canon of the group that says to be a member of this group, you go along."[36]

A final case is worth noting, in that it was such a celebrated media event and was an important one for the whole country. When Marine Col. Oliver North went before the congressional panel investigating the Iran-Contra affair in 1987, he admitted boldly that he lied to Congress about using proceeds of arms sales to Iran to benefit the Contras in Nicaragua despite, he said, the fact that "lying does not come easy to me." It is not too extreme to say that, to much of the country, North became a hero following his testimony, and a large percentage of Americans felt he had just cause for his actions. Not so, says Ekman, who analyzed North's behavior before Congress a little more deeply. Although praising North for a bravura performance on television, Ekman says North hit on a popular theme: that it is okay to lie if you can save people from being killed. The issue, however, is whether Contra lives were really at stake and who North was lying to. He pointed out that, to a great extent, the issue of whether lives were at stake was a political judgment and not a personal one. Secondly, North was lying to the very people who are given the responsibility for forming that political judgment: Congress. Harkening back to North's premise for lying—to keep lives safe from murderers—Ekman concluded, "What he's really saying is *Congress* is the murderer. *They're* the ones who are murdering the Contras."

Further evidence of the nation's problem with lying is as follows:

Wall Street is still reeling from the Boesky scandals and corporate America is writing up codes of ethics to help keep employees honest. There has been a rash of revelations about hyped and falsified scientific research: A published study accused 47 scientists at the Harvard and Emory University medical schools of producing misleading papers. A House subcommittee estimated that 1 out of every 3 working Americans is hired with educational or career credentials that have been altered in some way. And just last week, a California coroner declared that Liberace's lawyer, manager, publicist and doctor all had lied about the cause of his death: In fact, the entertainer died of AIDS.[37]

A 1987 *U.S. News–CNN* poll indicated that more than half of Americans believe people are more dishonest than they were in 1977. Those polled seem to be particularly leery of public figures. Some 70 percent feel congressional leaders always or almost always lie, while 62 percent feel the president does as well.[38]

Some people, like philosopher Christina Hoff Sommers of Clark University, feel advertising is the chief culprit in teaching young people it's okay to lie. Even advertising executive Jerry Delle Femina admits, "We're conceived, born and deceived. By the time someone reaches age 10, he's pretty cynical." Others, like former presidential press secretary Jody Powell, believe the answer lies in the fact that truth has become a relative thing to most people and that nothing is absolutely right or wrong. And in the political arena, most people expect there to be a certain degree of truth shading and deception going on.[39]

Whether these people and the psychologists are right or not about the reasoning behind lying, it is obvious that deception is a big problem for journalists. Often it goes beyond simple lying to distorting images of issues and people, like political candidates for instance. In another edition of "The Public Mind" series, former Reagan aide Michael Deaver admitted, "We thought of ourselves, when we got into the '88 [presidential] campaign, as Hollywood producers."[40] Deaver painted a sad commentary of the American voter when he said he might enjoy directing a campaign that focuses on issues instead of imagery, but the public would tune it out. "If we lived in a society where people really cared about the issues, it would be different," Deaver said. "But we don't. People want warm fuzzies and they don't want to worry about the problems of the world."[41]

As a result, notes Bill Moyers, less than 10 percent of the coverage of the 1988 presidential campaign dealt with issues. The rest dealt with personalities and staged imagery like Michael Dukakis in blue jeans sitting atop bales of hay in Iowa or riding in an Army tank, or George Bush nearly wrapping himself in an American flag at a midwestern flag factory. In short, notes Moyers, the media were buying what Deaver and his colleagues were giving away. CBS White House correspondent Leslie Stahl acknowledges that is true. "I like to wallpaper my pieces with pretty pictures," she said. "I shouldn't like it, because I know it's deceptive. But I do."[42] And "NBC News" president Michael Gartner admits, "You basically have to use that [the staged imagery]. It may be a staged event, but it's still an event."[43] And former CBS producer Martin Koughan says, "It's much easier to be a good packager than a good reporter."[44]

Finally, concludes Moyers, "Reality is not enough. If the news isn't entertaining, it's not on the news."[45]

But deception and lying extend far beyond the halls of power in Washington, D.C. As Ekman and Goleman note, it begins in the home and leads out to all walks of life when the children grow up. And it has its effect on journalistic accuracy and, ultimately, on public perception of the world around them and on public reaction to this pseudo-world. The lack of truthfulness in the United States is one of the chief reasons for the existence of the shadow world.

NOTES

1. Edward Teller, "Kicking the Secrecy Habit," *New York Times*, May 27, 1973, op-ed page.

2. Ibid.

3. Roy Appleton III, "Official Secrecy: Rising or Demising?" *Freedom of Information Center Report No. 426* (Columbia: University of Missouri School of Journalism, September 1980), p. 2.

4. Appleton citing Arthur Schlesinger, Jr., "The Secrecy Dilemma," *New York Times Magazine*, February 6, 1972, p. 12.

5. Laird B. Anderson, "FOIA Founder Looks at Law Today," *1988–1989 Society of Professional Journalists FOI Report*, p. 13.

6. Stephanie Goodman, "FOI Obstacles Trip Up Users," *1988–1989 Society of Professional Journalists FOI Report*, p. 11.

7. Ibid.

8. Anderson, p. 13.

9. Ibid.

10. Ibid.

11. Edwin Emery and Michael Emery, *The Press and America*, 5th ed. (Englewood Cliffs, N.J.: Prentice-Hall, 1984), p. 624.

12. "Federal, State FOI Acts Help Break Major Stories," *1988–1989 Society of Professional Journalist FOI Report*, p. 10.

13. Michael Wines, "Tough Calls: Should Reporters Keep State Secrets?," *Washington Journalism Review*, November 1986, p. 33.

14. Michael Wines, "The Law That Can Put You in Jail," *Washington Journalism Review*, November 1986, p. 37.

15. Wines, "The Law That Can Put You in Jail" p. 33.

16. Ibid.

17. Richard D. DeLauer, "At Issue: Shape Up! A Pentagon View of the Press," *Columbia Journalism Review*, September/October 1983, p. 17.

18. Ibid.

19. Edwin Emery and Michael Emery, *The Press and America*, 5th ed. (Englewood Cliffs, N.J.: Prentice-Hall, 1984), p. 494.

20. Philip Knightley, "The Falklands: How Britannia Ruled the News," *Columbia Journalism Review*, September/October 1982, p. 51.

21. Knightley, p. 52.

22. Peter Braestrup, "Duty, Honor, Country," *Washington Journalism Review*, September 1985, p. 15.

23. Ibid.

24. Stanley W. Cloud, "How Reporters Missed the War," *Time*, January 8, 1990, p. 61.

25. Stephen Hess, speaking at the proceedings of a Gannett Foundation seminar "War, Peace & The News Media," New York University, New York, March 19, 1983.

26. Paul Ekman, *Telling Lies* (New York: Berkley, 1986), p. 23.

27. "The Public Mind: The Truth About Lies," PBS, November 17, 1989.

28. Ibid.

29. Ibid.

30. Ibid.

31. Ibid.

32. Ibid.

33. Ibid.

34. Ibid.

35. Ibid.

36. Ibid.

37. Ibid.

38. "A Nation of Liars?" *U.S. News & World Report*, February 23, 1987, p. 54.

39. Ibid.

40. "A Nation of Liars?" p. 39.

41. "The Public Mind: Illusions of News," PBS, November 10, 1989.

42. Ibid.

43. Ibid.

44. Ibid.

45. Ibid.

9

Public Reaction to the Shadow World

The previous chapters have shown examples of, and reasons behind, the wide gap that often exists between what Lippmann calls "the world outside and the pictures in our heads."[1] As has been seen, contrary to critical belief, only *some* of these reasons involve either sloppy reporting or consciously biased reporting. Many reasons involve factors beyond the easy control of journalists who are covering daily events, personalities, and issues. Whatever the reasons, however, the existence of the shadow world is not simply material for an academic discussion. If the media—and their portrayal of the world outside—had no effect on society and governmental actions, it *would* be just an academic debate, "full of sound and fury, signifying nothing." But the media do have an effect on society and government, possibly the strongest effect of any existing institutions. Decades ago Lippmann reminded us that the world responds not to the event itself, but to the media's portrayal of the event. In so doing, we respond to the insertion of this pseudo-world the media create. It is one that is created by necessity, because of the inability to replicate reality itself. This chapter will first explore some of the theories regarding media effects and will then look at how Americans have responded, sometimes inappropriately, to the media's images of reality—to the shadow world.

A THEORETICAL LOOK AT MEDIA EFFECTS

Even though the "Bullet Theory" or "Hypodermic Needle Theory" of media effects is no longer strongly held by media researchers, the realization does still exist that the media's influence *permeates* society, albeit in a more diffused way for most of us. That, say media researchers, allows it to shape our values, thinking, and even the way we think and what we think about. Other researchers place an important role on the influence that the *audience* has on media content, but they still find that audiences are influenced in their thinking and behavior by what they receive from the media. That is especially the case with value reinforcement.

Some researchers and theorists say it is the media content that does the shaping; others say it is the nature of the media itself that does it. Either way, there is little doubt that the news media and their portrayal of reality is one of the strongest effects on our lives today. And that effect is likely to grow only stronger as we become more media-attentive and become more a part of an information society.

Is the Medium the Message?

According to Marshall McLuhan and Harold Innis, the media affect us not so much by their content as their form. To McLuhan, the medium is the message and it massages our brain and psyche to learn and respond in ways different than we did with previous media.[2] McLuhan's theory has come to be called *media determinism*, in that it is the medium itself that determines the influence on society. Joshua Meyrowitz notes in his book *No Sense of Place*, that McLuhan "drew a surprisingly accurate picture of what would be happening in the streets of New York, San Francisco, Washington, and other American and European cities between 1967 and 1972."[3] Specifically, McLuhan prophesied, in 1961 and 1963, great social change, which he called "retribalization," of the decline of traditional feelings of nationalism, of the demand on youth and minorities and others for more hands-on participation in the system, and of the distrust of almost any authority figures. The media seer said such changes would emanate from the extensive use of the electronic media. Describing media as extensions of the senses, he asserted that the insertion of a new medium into a society will change the "sensory balance" of the people and also change their consciousness.[4]

For instance, he said television has destroyed most linear, logical thinking in the United States and has produced in its place an "all-at-onceness" kind of learning. We are no longer content to take time to read a newspaper story which proceeds from point to point and requires our thinking along the way. Instead, he says, we want to turn on the 6 o'clock news and get the news in its immediacy, or at least in its perceived immediacy. He also blames the electronic media for breaking down individual identity, which he says came from the phonetic alphabet and a reading society, and replacing it with group identity, a sort of tribalism that leads to a "global village" where everyone thinks similarly, draws their identity from the group norm, and is interested in everyone else's business.[5]

Like many of McLuhan's ideas, however, this one doesn't specify *how* the media do all this or offer clues as to why people with different sensory balances behave differently.[6] Yet despite what some media critics see as educated guesswork on his part, McLuhan has a solid place in the research of media effects. He seems on target in his logic, but he makes so many different assertions, it is difficult to test them all. Indeed, many of them, like the global village concept, defy testing at all, except on a localized level. Meyrowitz notes McLuhan sees the media "as extensions of the human senses or processes, and he suggests that the use of different technologies affects the organization of the human senses."[7] But, again, testing such propositions becomes difficult. Nevertheless, he and Innis probed an important area in looking not so much at content, which he described as a kind of decoy, but at the medium itself, which he described as the real culprit.

Research on Message Content

As mentioned before, most media research has moved away from a position of speculating a direct, immediate, and universal effect of the news media. That theory, known as the "Bullet Theory" or "Hypodermic Needle Theory," carries with it the problem of treating all audience members as having the same perception, based on similar backgrounds, of media content. It also treats the audience as relatively passive, as if it were a giant sponge, soaking up all the content that is poured onto it. Audience research studies, however, have shown that different individual needs and uses of the media, as well as different individual demographics, work against such direct, universal-effect theories. Indeed, the audience is now seen as a much more active agent in the mass communication process, demanding certain uses and gratifications from the media. Since these uses and gratifications change among different audience members and since the audience members will tune in or out programs that either do or don't satisfy those needs, the media are now— more than ever—trying to respond to those audience groups and the needs they represent. Television programming, in fact, has become part of the mass communication process where audience feedback is instantaneous (thanks to Nielsen's "People Meters," which monitor television viewing instantaneously, and break it down demographically and to the overnight ratings that many local markets receive).

More than ever, it is now difficult to find a starting point in the mass communication cycle—to find who is really the source and who is the receiver, to see who is really influencing whom. That seems to be one of the main themes in Paddy Chayevsky's *Network*, where a fictitious network's outrageous nightly newscast becomes a mirror image of what network managers perceive as America's taste. A chief component of that newscast, Howard Beale, has such a direct influence on viewer behavior that viewers are sent to their windows screaming into the night air, "I'm mad as hell, and I won't take it anymore!" This type of direct response then leads to more outlandish components to the newscast, including "Sybil the Soothsayer" and "Vox Populi."

In reality, television researchers with Nielsen and Arbitron are constantly feeling the pulse of U.S. viewers, with the result that some new series remain on the air only a couple of weeks before the networks are convinced—by this audience research—that viewers don't want them. Then they are pulled and others are tried, often with the same results again.

In newspapers the situation is similar, although the changes wrought by readership surveys are often less dramatic and are longer in coming. Also, there are a lot of newspapers that still rebel totally at doing readership surveys or paying attention to the results once compiled. Several of these papers have lost sight of their readers as a result, and some of these newspapers have died. Still, news marketing is a concept that is taking hold in most of the nation's daily newspapers as they try desperately to survive in an increasingly electronic age. Trying to find out who the readers are and what they want is an effort that is occupying much time and expense on the part of newspaper management these days. The best publishers will see how many of those reader desires they can satisfy while still maintaining editorial control of their paper and doing quality daily journalism.

Still, with the increased attention to audience desires on the part of media managers, we come to a position where some observers say it is more important to watch what the audience is doing to the news media than what the news media are doing to the audience.

Nevertheless, a large portion of American society still seems to believe in the Bullet Theory of media influence which, to many people, represents plain, common sense. It is at the basis of such widespread and popular criticism that television is warping America's sense of values and that televised violence causes more violence in the streets; to a large extent, it is also at the basis of McLuhan's theories.

Among mass communication theorists, however, more research has focused recently on the proposition that the media either affect the opinion leaders in society who then affect their followers or that the media's influence is diffused in society in conjunction with other influences such as family, friends, work and play groups, etc. The problem with the "Two-Step Flow Theory," which states the media only influence the opinion leaders, is that many studies indicate that major news stories are spread directly by the media themselves rather than by opinion leaders or personal contacts. Also, who is an opinion leader and who is a follower? Because of these difficulties, many researchers are now looking at *diffusion research*. News diffusion deals with how people draw their view of the world on the basis of the reports they get from the news media. This effect has "long-term and often systematic consequences," according to research Denis McQuail.[8] News diffusion, or the spreading of information and perceptions into society, is influenced by how much the people already know about a given event, the relative importance or salience of the event, the amount of information sent, and whether knowledge of the event came first from personal contact or the news media.[9] McQuail discusses one model, called the J-curved relationship which emanates from these four influences:

When an event is known about by virtually everyone (such as the assassination of John F. Kennedy in 1963), a very high proportion (over 50 percent) will have been told by a personal contact. When events are known by decreasing proportions of the population (which is the case with most events), the percentage of personal contact origination falls and that of media sources rises.[10]

One permeating effect that the media seem to have in society is creating a sense of national, and sometimes personal, *identity* in the minds of the audience. George Gerbner and his colleagues at the University of Pennsylvania have conducted several studies into this *cultivation* effect. Among their findings are that television has become the source of much instruction that is done in the United States. As Gerbner says, "The television set has become a key member of the family, the one who tells most of the stories, most of the time."[11] With the average viewer consuming four hours of television daily, the situation arises where much of the United States is learning a common view of the world, along with being presented common role models and a set of common values. This all sounds familiar to those devotees of McLuhan and his global village theory.

Responding to criticism that his cultivation theory treats all audience members as the same and as passive individuals, Gerbner modified his theory in 1980, adding the concepts of *mainstreaming* and *resonance*.[12] Mainstreaming, he said, comes about when *heavy* viewing (more than four hours a day) results in similar perceptions of the world across different socioeconomic groups. Mainstreaming does not work, however, across similar groups of *light* television viewers.

Resonance happens when the cultivation effect is increased for a particular group. Mass media researchers Werner J. Severin and James W. Tankard, Jr. cite the example where heavy viewers among both males and females are more likely than light viewers to agree that fear of crime is a serious problem. But the group that agrees most strongly with that notion is females who are heavy viewers, because of their special vulnerability to criminals. Thus that group is said to "resonate" with the media portrait of a high-crime world.[13]

It is important to note that the cultivation theory is at work not only in the United States, but also around the world. The concept of *media imperialism*, in fact, states that a Western view of the world, along with Western values, is being spread around the globe because of the intense amount of Western television programming exported to other countries. It was President Sukarno of Indonesia, in fact, who criticized American television for creating a revolution of rising expectations in his country in the 1960s. In one particular instance, he was highly critical of so many U.S. sitcoms showing life focusing on the home kitchen where a refrigerator was prominently displayed. Indonesians, by and large, had no refrigerators and began protesting in large numbers demanding that they be made available.

Mass media research also has investigated the media's effect on the collective behavior of panic and disorder arising from alarming and/or distorted accounts in the media. For instance, McQuail notes:

It has been suggested that the media, variously, can provoke a riot, create a culture of rioting, provide lessons on "how to riot," spread a disturbance from place to place. The evidence for or against these propositions is very fragmentary, although it seems to be acknowledged that personal contact plays a larger part than media in any ongoing riot situation. There is some evidence, even so, that the media can contribute simply by signalling the occurrence and location of a riot event (Singer, 1970), by publicizing incidents which are themselves causes of riot behavior, or by giving advance publicity to the likely occurrence of rioting.[14]

A great deal of anecdotal evidence existed in the 1960s that the news media, by virtue of their simple presence at a Vietnam war protest, caused the demonstrations to become more heated, more animated, and better attended. Over and over it was a real-life case of what the reader finds in Tom Wolfe's *Bonfire of the Vanities*, where street protests are designed and scripted for the television cameras that show up to report for the evening news. In such cases, the news media become participants in relaying these pseudo-events to the public. The same concept holds true in the media's coverage of terrorism, an issue which has caused many editors and producers to ponder how best to cover these events without giving rise to more of them. Indeed, the notion that the news media are held hostage itself by terrorists has now become widely held by those both within and outside of the media.

Other empirical evidence has surfaced for the belief that media reports can "trigger" individual, widespread, pathological behavior among certain types of people. Such data has shown that some suicides, automobile fatalities, and airline—both commercial and private—deaths have a tendency to increase following media publicity for suicides or murder-suicides.[15]

So media research, while providing little support for direct and universal effects of the media, still shows there is some direct effect among some people in our society. Largely those effects exist among children and members of socially or psychologically deviant adult groups. As far as indirect effects are concerned, however, the empirical support is much stronger. In addition to news diffusion, McQuail lists two such types of media influence in society: agenda-setting and the so-called "knowledge gap" effect.[16]

Agenda-setting, a term coined by McCombs and Shaw in 1972, looks at how much the news media tell the public what to think *about*. Although these two researchers studied agenda-setting in the context of political campaign coverage, theirs and other research suggests there is a definite similarity between the importance attached to certain events by the media and the importance attached to them by the public. Although anecdotal evidence indicates there is a strong possibility that the media actually set that agenda, there is a dearth of systematic, empirical research proving this cause-effect relationship.

Roy L. Behr and Shanto Iyengar found the television media do set the agenda for several issues such as energy, inflation, and unemployment.[17] On the basis of longitudinal data, they discovered also that the media's agenda-setting is *unidirectional*—that television news influences public concern about the issues of energy and inflation, and not the other way around. For the third area—unemployment—television was found to be following strongly the lead of real-world conditions in its placement of unemployment stories on its agenda. To a more limited degree, it also followed real-world conditions for energy and inflation. Nevertheless, the media's coverage of all three issues wound up influencing the public's agenda and increased concern for these issues, especially in the areas of inflation and energy problems. The study found real-world conditions to have more of an agenda-setting effect for the issue of unemployment. Possibly that is because unemployment—and the threat of it—is something that is felt so directly by certain segments of the public. Finally the study found that lead stories on newscasts were found to be significantly more powerful than other stories in the same newscasts in shaping the public's agenda about these issues.

Knowledge gap theory states that, although the media can perform a useful function in helping close gaps in knowledge that occur between people in different socioeconomic levels of society, they may not be performing that role at all. Common sense might suggest that prior to widespread attentiveness to the media, lower-level groups may have known much less than higher-level groups. Now, however, isn't that gap narrower because of the far-reaching impact of television and newspapers? While it sounds plausible, the research on knowledge gap theory is mixed. J. G. Blumler and McQuail showed in 1968 that, in some political campaigns, the gap may be closed in the short term. In other words, voters across socioeconomic levels may expose themselves to relatively even amounts of knowledge concerning some campaigns and candidates.[18] On the other hand, research by P. J. Tichenor and others, in 1970, has shown a reverse effect taking place—especially in the long run—where an attentive minority of the population obtains much more information than others simply by virtue of their heavy reliance on reading and watching the news.[19] So it seems true that there is a kind of class bias inherent in information attainment; the higher the status the person occupies, the more knowledge he or she will generally obtain, because he or she will generally be more attentive to events in the news. This is not necessarily because this person is more socially conscious than people at lower levels. It may simply be a function of how much of an investment that person has in the world and how much he or she wants to minimize risk by understanding the world better.

Severin and Tankard state it this way:

An old aphorism states that knowledge is power, and this means simply that knowledge gives people the capability to do things and to take advantage of opportunities. It is apparent, however, the knowledge, like other kinds of wealth, is not distributed equally throughout our society. People who are struggling with financial poverty are also often information-poor.[20]

Generally Accepted Ideas of Media Impact

While there is much debate about how the media goes about impacting society and how directly and universally that impact is felt, there are some generally accepted ideas about the kinds of media influence on the development of nations and cultures. Some of these ideas are the following:

1. A society depends largely on its mass media for a sense of historical and cultural identity.

2. Often people in a society also will depend on the media for a sense of personal identity and will use the media to show how they personally fit in to the larger surroundings.

3. A society often depends on its mass media to raise its level of consciousness about certain issues affecting the people.

4. A society often will use the mass media as a change agent and depend on them for its sense of how valuable concerted, group action is, as opposed to individual action.

5. A society's mass media will often be key transmitters of values and ideas and will often initiate new ideas and introduce new concepts to the people.

6. A society's mass media are often responsible for the level of expectations in that society. Sometimes the media increase those expectations beyond reality; other times—in more controlled societies—the media will be used by the authorities to diminish those expectations.
7. Not only can the media be used as national stimulants, but they also can be used as national sedatives, exerting a calming and stabilizing influence on society.

In terms of overall impact on the development of a society, media theorists generally hold one of four positions on the degree of that influence. Some adopt an *enthusiastic* position, feeling the media exert the strongest influence of any institution on national development; some adopt a more *cautious* position, agreeing the media exert an influence but feeling that influence is matched in impact by other societal institutions; others adopt a more *pragmatic* position, feeling it is impossible to generalize about the media's role in national development and each country must be looked at separately; and finally there are a few who adopt a *null* position, feeling the media have no real impact on a country's national development. Regarding this fourth position, it should be noted there is scant evidence for it, even taking into account countries which have no real mass media system. For, in those countries, a strong case can be made that the lack of mass media has strangled the growth and improvements that would have come had a media system been in place. In countries having media systems in place, however, it is impossible to avoid the conclusion that the media have a strong impact on those societies.

AMERICA IN RESPONSE TO JOURNALISTIC REPORTING

Setting aside the empirical research done on mass media effects, it is interesting to look into history and discover how America has responded to journalistic news reporting. Numerous examples can be found of Americans responding not to the event itself as it actually happened but to the reporting of that event which painted a picture in their heads of what happened. One of the earliest and most classic examples of this came late in the nineteenth century in the so-called Age of Yellow Journalism. Although some might think it unfair to look for examples in such a warped era of U.S. journalism, others believe the present age—at least as far as some newspapers and television programs are concerned—is not that much different. We still have a number of sensation-seeking tabloids—only a few of which are the supermarket variety—and we are witnessing a growing trend in television of syndicated news programs like "A Current Affair," "The Reporters," "Hard Copy," and "Inside Edition," all so popular and sensation seeking that William Randolph Hearst would have been proud to own them himself.

"Mr. Hearst's War"

One of the clearest examples in history of the country responding to what it *thought* was happening, thanks to distorted media coverage, was America's involvement in the Spanish-American War of 1898. Many historians have looked at that war in Cuba and concluded that, had it not been for the sensationalism of the age under the direction of William Randolph Hearst, the United States would have probably never become involved in what was essentially a Cuban civil war.[21] Marcus M. Wilkerson and Joseph E. Wisan early in the 1930s conducted systematic studies that provided incontrovertible evidence that Hearst's *New York Journal*, coupled with other similar papers of the day such as Joseph Pulitzer's *New York World*, provided such saturated, opinionated coverage of events in Cuba that a kind of war fever developed in the United States. Those same studies showed the coverage given to the sinking of the Battleship Maine in Havana Harbor on February 17, 1898, was the virtual straw that broke the camel's back.[22] Shortly after that incident, the United States was starting its four-month war with Spain.

Concerning the coverage of the New York papers of events leading up to U.S. involvement in the war, historians Edwin and Michael Emery wrote:

From March, 1895, when the Cuban insurrection began, until April 1898, when Spain and the United States went to war, there were fewer than a score of days in which a story about Cuba did not appear in one of the New York newspapers. This was due partly to the aggressive news policies of the big dailies, partly to the *manufactured stories* of the papers (notably the *Journal*), and partly to the increased reader interest in controversial stories.[23]

Typical of the coverage given the mysterious Maine explosion was the February 17 front page of the *New York Journal*. Not only was the entire front page devoted to the incident, but there were numerous headlines intimating Spain had committed the crime that killed "285" (later confirmed at 266) U.S. sailors. Indeed, the lead headline announced in capital letters "DESTRUCTION OF THE WAR SHIP *MAINE* WAS THE WORK OF AN ENEMY." Another headline on the same page speculated, "NAVAL OFFICERS THINK THE MAINE WAS DESTROYED BY A SPANISH MINE." Although that headline ran ahead of the officers' actual opinion, the *Journal* still carried an eight-column artist's rendering of how the Spanish sea mine probably caused the disaster. In the midst of it all were various headlines and stories announcing that the *Journal* was offering a $50,000 reward "for the detection of the perpetrator of the *Maine* Outrage!"

As Emery and Emery note in their compendium of journalism history, however, it should be remembered that the New York newspapers were aided in their influence on the American public by a general spirit of manifest destiny that was sweeping the country.[24] This was the spirit that inspired the push westward into America, and it was the same spirit that brought about the war with Mexico. Americans, led by the politicians and opportunists of the day, had the distinct feeling that it was perfectly all right for the country to expand where it might into the Western Hemisphere. But that spirit also was greatly aided by the newspapers of the day, and several newspapers like Hearst's did their part to keep the flame of manifest destiny alive and strong, even if a good fight was needed to do so. Indeed, a *Journal* headline on February 20, 1898, three days after the *Maine* went down screamed, "THE WHOLE COUNTRY THRILLS WITH WAR FEVER."

If there is any doubt as to the eventual belief that Hearst brought about America's involvement in the Cuban conflict, one should read the writings of a contemporary who should have been an expert on the subject. He was *Journal* correspondent James Creelman who wrote of Hearst in his retrospective *On the Great Highway*, published in 1901. Creelman, a correspondent for Hearst in the Spanish-American War who actually led a military charge at El Caney, wrote of Hearst visiting the scene of the battle and taking the account of the battle from Creelman who was lying wounded on July 1, 1898, the same day Teddy Roosevelt stormed San Juan Hill. Creelman wrote:

Someone knelt in the grass beside me and put his hand on my fevered head. Opening my eyes, I saw Mr. Hearst, the proprietor of the New York Journal, a straw hat with a bright ribbon on his head, a revolver at his belt, and a pencil and notebook in his hand. The man who had provoked the war had come to see the result with his own eyes, and, finding one of his correspondents prostrate, was doing the work himself. Slowly he took down my story of the fight. Again and again the tinging of Mauser bullets interrupted. But he seemed unmoved. The battle had to be reported somehow. "I'm sorry you're hurt, but"—and his face was radiant with enthusiasm—"wasn't it a splendid fight? We must beat every paper in the world!"[25]

Jazz Journalism

Other examples of conscious media distortion abound in history. The era known as "Jazz Journalism" in the 1920s produced a lot of fakery, much of it done by New York's tabloids who were battling with each other daily for more bizarre stories and pictures to pull in more readers. The most infamous of these tabloids was the *Graphic*, and its most outlandish effort at fakery came when it displayed a picture showing nothing less than Rudolph Valentino's triumphal passage into Heaven. Another faked photo showed Bartolomeo Vanzetti walking to the electric chair on August 23, 1927. These were two of only several faked photos that the *Graphic* ran, and they usually featured models who were posed to duplicate events a photographer had not been privileged to witness personally. These models' photos were then cut out and superimposed on the heads of actual participants. *Graphic* editors rationalized the process by calling it "composograph" and claiming that by so captioning the pictures, they honored their masthead slogan, "Nothing but the Truth."[26] When the last bell rang for the *Graphic*, however, it was a death knell, and the faked photos helped lead to the paper's bankruptcy in 1932. For although some 350,000 readers found the paper enticing on a daily basis, advertisers remained leery of it because of its spurious journalistic ethics and low credibility. Nevertheless, "composograph" is a technique that survived the *Graphic*, and in 1950 a faked photograph of Sen. Millard Tydings of Maryland that showed him listening to the Communist Earl Browder helped lead to Tydings' defeat.[27]

From Conscious to Unconscious Distortion

Although the Spanish-American War seems a vivid example of how America responded appropriately to a distorted picture of world events, but inappropriately to the events as they were really happening, it nevertheless represents an episode of *conscious* media distortion. The faked and distorted stories published in the pages of yellow journals like the *New York Journal* and *New York World* were malicious, in that the editors knew them to be exaggerated when they were published, and they were intended to produce the results they did. Looking forward through history, there are several other cases of such conscious media distortion among mainstream, traditional media, especially during the era known as Jazz Journalism in the 1920s and typified in the classic film *The Front Page*. And supermarket tabloids and pseudo-news programs on television, like those mentioned earlier, are keeping the tradition of Hearst alive even today. But when reality is distorted by the media, it is not always done so consciously.

McCarthyism and the Media

In the 1950s, the country responded to another type of media distortion: that trumpeting the wild accusations of Sen. Joseph McCarthy and discussed in more detail in Chapter 3. Although this was not a conscious distortion of reality by the media, at least not by most of the nation's media, it was the result of journalists feeling that they should be little more than public stenographers for newsmakers like McCarthy. This was especially so if the newsmakers were as volatile and popular as McCarthy. Despite the motive, however, the results were the same:

America wound up responding to a distorted picture of the world instead of the world as it really was.

The Vietnam Watershed

The Vietnam war provided a watershed period for U.S. journalism, as it spawned a clash of ideas regarding the nature of objectivity for reporters covering a war. History shows that those reporters who followed in the footsteps of previous war correspondents and reported mostly what they were told by military and government officials became victims of skilled media manipulators. Over the years, as a result, they passed on to the U.S. public a largely government-orchestrated view of how the war was going and of why the United States was involved in it in the first place. Still, media owners such as Henry Luce defended reporting the official truth. The other, he said, was propaganda aimed at overthrowing the Diem regime and compounding the confusion of Vietnam that Americans were trying to unravel. In response to that assertion, at least one *Time* correspondent on the scene in Vietnam is said to have resigned to protest.

Meanwhile, those correspondents who saw inconsistency between their own observations and the "official story" and who chose to become more skeptical of official sources often presented a more valid picture of the war but were roundly criticized at the time for doing so. Indeed, many Americans still believe it was reporters like David Halberstam, Neil Sheehan, and Malcolm Browne who helped the United States lose the war in Vietnam.[28] Yet they were only reporting what they saw, and Halbsertam and Browne shared the Pulitzer Prize in 1964 for international reporting.

Taking this latter group of the Saigon Press Corps first, many critics of the media's performance in Vietnam said, for example, it misrepresented the Tet Offensive in 1968. These critics say Tet was a clear victory for the U.S.–South Vietnamese forces, and yet the media portrayed the offensive as a gigantic loss. In so doing, the argument goes, the media eroded morale among Americans back home and caused a general collapse of support for the war effort at a time it was needed most.[29]

Responding to that criticism, former Vietnam correspondent Charles Mohr noted:

The revisionists ascribe the erosion to hysterical reporting from Vietnam; my own belief is that it was the result of strong public shock following the highly optimistic public claims of progress by American officials in the fall of 1967. A few journalists lost their composure, but most Vietnam correspondents did not.[30]

So which portion of the Saigon Press Corps was presenting shadows in place of substance in its reporting of Vietnam? In a sense, both were.

Some correspondents who became jaded after a series of distorted statements and briefings (that came to be known as the "5 o'clock follies") may have, as Mohr suggests, become carried away to the extreme of unjustly characterizing U.S.–South Vietnamese efforts as failing miserably. But the portion of the press corps that fed virtually undiluted official reports to the people back home was maybe even more guilty of shadowy reporting. For instance, Pulitzer Prize–winner William Tuohy said lies told by government officials during Vietnam "fed the growing mistrust between American public servants and the press corps." He also noted that the government's lying wreaked havoc among journalists accustomed to believing official sources. "Officials should realize that you deceive journalists at your own risk," he observed. "Our system is based on a certain amount of good faith, and if the press doesn't believe what it's being told—and thus their audience—the government and the nation can get into real trouble."[31]

Still, the criticism persists from several quarters in America that the news media played a decisive role in the outcome of the war and of the foreign policy from Washington that led to that outcome. Media researcher Oscar Patterson III notes, for instance, that of four major events between 1968 and 1980 (the moon landing, Watergate, Iranian hostage crisis, and the Vietnam war), media critics and historians seem to agree that it was only with the Vietnam experience that the media played a decisive role. "For the first time in American history, it is reported that a sitting President decided not to run for reelection . . . because he had lost the support of a television news anchorman."[32] That anchorman was Walter Cronkite, who became severely disillusioned about the course of the war after returning from a trip to Vietnam. And one other critic concluded that for "the first time in modern history, the outcome of a war was determined not on the battlefield, but on the printed page."[33]

That may be true, but it should be noted that the United States may have become so heavily involved in Vietnam in the first place because of warped reporting. That reporting, for the most part, presented the more optimistic, government version of how the struggle was going. It also failed to present the broad spectrum of reasons for U.S. involvement in Vietnam that the controversial Pentagon Papers did later when published by the *New York Times*. A more alternative style of reporting didn't really begin surfacing until the mid–1960s, and the United States had been involved in the war for several years prior to that point.

Regardless of whether one buys the argument that the media caused the United States to bail out of Vietnam too early, there is the undeniable conclusion that they did influence the course of history in the Vietnam era. America was more vocal than ever during the 1960s and early 1970s, and most of the shouting was about the Vietnam war—or at least the picture of the war the country received from the media and from government officials. There is no doubt that a good deal of that picture was distorted in both optimistic and pessimistic ways.

Attitude Extremity and Trust in the Media

An interesting study published by Albert Gunther in 1988 found a curvilinear relationship existing between extremity of attitude toward an issue and trust in the media's coverage of the issue.[34] He had hypothesized that trust in news media coverage of an issue would be highest when attitude extremity on that issue is moderate. On the other hand, trust would be lower both when attitudes are highly polarized and when they are neutral. Secondly, he theorized that trust in the media would be highest for those of medium extremity of political ideology; trust in the media would be lower both for those who are low and for those who are high in extremity of political ideology. His results confirmed such a curvilinear pattern for both newspaper and television coverage of each issue. Media trust ratings went up as extremity of attitude increased from low to moderate and then turned down again as attitude extremity increased from moderate to high. In other words, the study provided evidence for the position that highly opinionated people seem to trust the media's version of reality less than do people who have low to moderate degrees of opinion.

The Stuart Murder Case

If there is one incident in recent memory that shows how the public, its law enforcement agencies, and even city hall itself can be aroused to take inappropriate action as a result of distorted media coverage, it is 1989's bizarre Boston murder of Carol Stuart. In that well-publicized case, husband Charles Stuart was first cast as a grieving widower who saw his pregnant wife gunned down in their parked car by a black assailant who then shot Stuart himself in the stomach. According to the first reports, Stuart then used his mobile phone to help Boston police locate his position and, in the ensuing weeks, gained the sympathy of millions of Americans.

The Boston media painted the young couple as having their dream world shattered. Several politicians attended Carol's funeral, while others called for the death penalty for the fugitive assailant Stuart described to police. One Boston city councilman longed publicly to meet the assailant alone in the street so he could kill him with his own hands. Mayor Raymond Flynn ordered all available detectives to work on the case. As a result of all the hysteria, hundreds of men in Boston's predominantly black Mission Hill area were detained and frisked only because they were black, and one, Willie Bennett, was actually arrested for the crime.

About the phenomenon, reporter Margaret Carlson wrote: "Stuart tapped into assumptions about race and crime so powerful that they overwhelmed skepticism about his tale."[35]

The problem with the media coverage, as it turned out, was that it was totally off-base. Reporters had been victims of an apparent hoax pulled by Stuart who jumped off the Mystic River Bridge several weeks later, leaving behind a note that most observers feel indicate he killed his wife himself. That episode threw the whole case into a sea of doubt and police and media are still trying to unscramble it.

More to the point of this discussion, however, the media's manipulation at the hands of Stuart resulted in a massive manhunt in all the wrong places that tied up Boston police for weeks on end. Instead of looking for gaps in the smooth, tragic story that Charles Stuart had told, they spent endless hours searching Boston for a black man with a raspy voice. Like many reporters involved in cases such as those discussed in Chapter 8, the media were victimized here by a big lie. In so doing, the media made a bad situation even worse for the black residents of Boston. Undoubtedly the media pressure—and anticipation of it—forced city hall into ordering the dragnet that wound up denying a lot of blacks some basic civil liberties in the ensuing days and weeks. As ABC "Nightline" reporter Jeff Greenfield said, it resulted in a scenario where, "To be black is to be guilty."[36] Whatever the reason, city authorities and public temperament responded to another slice of life from the media's shadow world.

Former Chicago reporter Ellis Cose said the media made the case much more believable by portraying an ordinary couple as extraordinary who were victims of scum.[37] Cose said this scenario is played out in the media every few weeks. Such was the case with the Central Park rape and beating of a white woman jogger.[38] So, to a great extent, Carol and Charles Stuart become symbols—stereotypes—victims caught up in a wave of racial hatred, drug crimes, and general inhumanity.[39]

In the face of such far-ranging critical onslaught, the media and politicians tried to focus more on exactly what caused this particular case of distorted coverage. Phil Balboni, former news director of WCVB-TV in Boston said, "Why would anyone doubt the word of a man suffering from such a horrible gunshot wound himself?"[40] And, as Mayor Flynn pointed out, there was only one witness to the crime; that was Charles Stuart, and this was his story. It was only natural to believe him. Gregory Moore, assistant managing editor of the Boston Globe, said, "We were dealing with a con artist . . . who played on our perceptions of social reality and the fact that it was possible that a crime like this could have happened."[41]

Still, Louis Elisa, president of the Boston NAACP, expressed outrage at the police and media handling of the incident and of the false alarms they spread throughout the city. Yet even he admitted, "We were a nation that was primed to be duped," because of saturation coverage of the Willie Horton case (the black who committed heinous crimes while on furlough from a Massachusetts prison) and the Central Park case. Nevertheless, Elisa criticized the media for failing to sound an alarm similar to the Stuart alarm when 104 blacks were being shot in Boston during the 52 days prior to the Stuart case. "The newspapers created the atmosphere," Elisa said.[42]

Whether the media's fault or not, this portrayal differed widely from reality. And what effect did all this have on the journalists themselves who covered the incident? "This has really shattered people in the profession," Balboni said. "We need to always test and retest our assumptions."[43]

The Saga of "Jimmy's World"

The Stuart murder case was not the first time the news media have been victimized by a hoax. On September 28, 1980, one of the best newspapers in the country, the *Washington Post*, ran a story entitled, "Jimmy's World: 8-Year-Old Heroin Addict Lives for a Fix." The story, by Janet Cooke, resulted in one of the most embarrassing incidents for a U.S. newspaper and certainly the most embarrassing for the *Post*. For the story, purporting to be about a real-life boy who had been addicted to heroin by his mother's boyfriend, turned out to be a fake. In this case, it was the reporter herself pulling the hoax. There was no real-life Jimmy, and reporter Cooke conveniently forgot to mention that fact to anyone at the *Post*. Making matters worse was the fact the story received a Pulitzer Prize which, upon discovery of the hoax, the *Post* returned.

Responding to the incident later, then metro editor Bob Woodward said he had no reason to distrust Cooke's reporting, although other reporters mentioned the possibility to him that the story might at least be distorted. Woodward said he chalked those comments up to newsroom rivalry and professional jealousy. City editor Milton Coleman also had dismissed the suspicions of others on the *Post* staff for similar reasons. Even when a reporter described to Coleman Cooke's obvious unfamiliarity with Jimmy's neighborhood and the fact she couldn't point out his home, the story was still nominated for the Pulitzer. Coleman even discarded another editor's warning that she had experienced trouble with Cooke's truthfulness prior to Cooke's reassignment to the city desk.

The thing about the Janet Cooke story was that, like the Stuart murder story, it sent a city into shock and sent a lot of public servants out into the neighborhoods to try and track down this unidentified Jimmy. Cooke had refused to divulge his name, pleading reporter-source confidentiality and physical harm to herself. She said the mother's boyfriend, Ron, had threatened her should the police ever identify him through her story. Before long, her truer reason surfaced for keeping the boy's identity secret. There was no boy. But in the meantime, the Washington, D.C., government reacted by launching an intensive search for Jimmy. The search involved volunteers from schools, social-welfare services, and police.

Washington mayor Marion Barry bluffed at first that he knew the whereabouts of Jimmy, but later had to admit the story was probably a fake. Starting to smell trouble and apparently pressured by public opinion to get the boy some help, the *Post* even sent 11 of its own reporters into the ghettos to try to locate Jimmy. In addition to causing a manhunt for the fictitious youth, the story caused angry parents to accuse school board members of sloppy work in not holding teachers and principals accountable for seeking danger signs among the city's drug-threatened children and for not cracking down on truants. Even *U.S. News & World Report* reprinted Cooke's story in its October 13 issue and headed it "The Story That Shocked The Nation's Capital." Trusting the credibility of Cooke and the *Post* entirely, the magazine's editors noted in the story's preface:

A Washington, D.C. boy is a heroin addict at the age of 8. He lives with his unmarried mother, who is also an addict, and her live-in lover who has turned the home into a drug center and a gathering place for junkies.... Citizens, suddenly aroused, demanded that officials do something. Police, social workers, school authorities, the mayor—even members of Congress—sprang into action.[44]

The Janet Cooke hoax was largely believed because, like the Charles Stuart hoax, it fed upon white readers' uninformed perception of how horrible and immoral life must be in the city's black ghettos. As such, it was an example of racial stereotyping, made even more believable because it was a black reporter who was doing the stereotyping. Ironically, some of the newsroom doubters were other black reporters who wondered aloud how a drug pusher would "shoot up" either himself or a child in the presence of a reporter in designer jeans from the *Washington Post*.[45] So it seems, even though white perceptions of black ghetto life fed the believability factor of the story, that was not the case with some blacks who knew the realities of that life. And it there was journalistic arrogance present at the *Post*, it came from white editors who felt they knew black neighborhoods better than black reporters.

The real tragedy of the Janet Cooke story is that because of the fabrication, it is harder now for editors to buy stories about that ghetto world. The story also put the use of confidential sources—necessary in some situations—into peril, as more editors now insist on knowing who the reporter's sources are, despite the fact that confidentiality has already been agreed to by the reporter. That puts the reporter—and his or her story—into a very difficult position.

Was this infamous journalistic hoax the only one of its kind? It was certainly the highest-profile hoax in recent memory, but it was not the only one. Timothy Noah reminds us that in 1964, the *New York Times* carried a four-part series on an alleged Harlem youth gang called the "Blood Brothers," said to be "roaming the streets of Harlem with the avowed intention of attacking white people." The Blood Brothers, Junius Griffin reported, were "trained to maim and kill."[46] Unlike the Cooke story, however, the series done by Griffin apparently was based on a police tip. From that point on, however, exaggeration and rumor took hold and the alleged "gang" was reputed to number as many as 400 when, as it turned out, it probably numbered no more than a dozen tough-talking blacks. The blunt implication of the series, Noah recalls, is that "Harlem thugs would soon overrun all of Manhattan."[47] Like the Stuart hoax and the Cooke hoax, this exaggeration fed upon white fears in New York City of Harlem blacks.

Also like the Stuart and Cooke story, public reaction to this shadow series was swift and predictable. New York police commissioner Michael J. Murphy said, "We are aware of this. We are keeping abreast of the ramifications and taking certain measures. We are prepared." Certainly police reaction to street blacks took on a more somber tone in the weeks during that series which ran from May 3 to May 29.

Other deliberate reporter hoaxes also have plagued some of the largest newspapers in the United States as recently as the past two decades. About the same time of the Cooke incident, reporter Michael Daly of the *New York Daily News* invented an eyewitness to describe to him events in Northern Ireland. The story was published and believed all around until Daly admitted the faked source.

Concerning such fakery, *New York Daily News* media critic Jane Perlez wrote, "other fabrications, on a less spectacular scale, go by every day in news stores. Every day, reporters 'embellish' quotes from an individual to make them 'sound better' or to fit the point of the story."[48] And writer Ronald Turovsky talked about the practice of making up direct quotes. "In some cases the quotes are pure inventions. In others the reporter tries to come close to what was said, but rewrites, approximates, corrects, eliminates. In either case he is, of course, violating the rules."[49]

Hoaxes that are caused deliberately by journalists not only work toward tearing down the carefully constructed credibility newspapers strive for, they also ignite the public and its institutions to take action which is time- and money-wasting and totally inappropriate to what is really occurring. The journalistic community is right in condemning such action and firing the perpetrators of such hoaxes. But the responsibility remains with the editors to constantly monitor their own stereotypes and misconceptions which may add to the advancement and publishing of such faked stories. They must also try to analyze the situations (like intense intramural competition) that lead reporters to develop such faked stories and quotes in the first place and, when possible, work to tone down those situations.

The Hidden Face of Foreign Rulers

In earlier chapters, the problems with international coverage were assessed. It seems appropriate to bring the subject up again here because of several stories which may have caused inappropriate public reactions. One such set of stories involved the American image of the late Egyptian president Anwar Sadat. Doreen Kays, ABC News bureau chief in Cairo from 1977 to 1981, said Sadat's heroic image in the United States was largely manufactured by television and that Sadat had a much different image in Egypt with the people he served.[50] The American image, which came about as a result of Sadat's peace mission to Israel in November 1977, the Camp David peace accords in September 1978, and the signing of the peace treaty in March 1979, was not altogether accurate of a man who was seen as a villain by many Egyptians. However, Kays says the Sadat story fell victim to "the paradox of TV news: media overkill on the one hand; one-dimensional images on the other."

In the version that ran for four years on American TV, the protagonist was Anwar Sadat, Egypt's magnanimous president for eleven years; a leader who did what no other Arab dared; a brave, courageous, charismatic, hero who won the Nobel Peace Prize and the attention of much of the world. . . . In the version never shown on American TV, the story's protagonist was also Anwar Sadat, Egypt's autocratic president for eleven years; an opportunist who signed a peace treaty with Israel in return for his beloved Sinai; a megalomaniac who, in his desire to forge a favorable imprint on history, silenced his opponents and critics at home . . . and neglected the economic and social welfare of his poverty-stricken people. . . . Few Egyptians and fewer Arabs wept at his death, for Sadat did not inspire the same love at home that he did abroad.[51]

Not unlike the imagery surrounding other foreign leaders like the deposed Shah of Iran, Sadat's portrait here was only partly accurate. In the case of the Shah, despite an abundance of signs that he, too, was a different man to his countrymen than to those in the West, the U.S. media still treated his image gently and tried to show how like our image of a prince he was. Barbara Walters poked fun at the Shah in a televised interview for his chauvinistic attitude toward women, but both ended the interview smiling and laughing. Just another close-up look at a sort of storybook prince in the Middle East who had become a friend to the United States. Scant treatment was paid to the fact that barbed wire had to be strung around grounds where the Shah would throw lavish parties or that his troops were armed with submachine guns to protect him from his own people. Often the Shah was portrayed as a rather charismatic leader who was only trying to bring his backwards country into the twentieth century. Who could be against that?

A lot of Muslims were. By 1978, Iranian resentment against the Shah's imperial arrogance started a revolution that spread across all of Iran and ended with the Shah's exile and the ascension of the Ayatollah Khomeini.

And it was only after his death that incontrovertible evidence began mounting that, under the reign of the Shah, thousands of Iranian political prisoners had been grossly mistreated and many tortured for their sins of rebellion against his dictatorial rule.[52]

A similar misleading image was portrayed of Sadat—not that he should be compared to the Shah in every respect, but it was not the image that many of his countrymen saw and feared. In that respect, his image was distorted and the public accolades in the United States (*Time* cast him as its "Man of the Year" in 1977) were only partially deserved. Reflecting on Sadat's American image, Kays called it "a theatrically sublime image of a modern-day pharaoh played to perfection by Anwar Sadat. But this was not an actor playing the role of Pharaoh. It was a pharaoh playing the role of actor."[53] The Egyptian image of conditions, she said, was that Egypt was dying economically and politically, hope and euphoria of peace had been replaced by despair, and Sadat had turned from benign dictator to dangerous despot. Kays proposed doing a multidimensional story on Sadat for ABC, but the network news executives rejected the idea. Sadat's popularity was growing in the United States, and network executives thought there were too many domestic stories in need of coverage to devote a documentary time slot to Egypt.

So Sadat continued to beguile U.S. news media despite dissolving the parliament where opposition to the Israeli treaty was surfacing; rigging a national referendum treaty; banning all public debate on the treaty during the campaign to elect a new parliament, whose elections were also rigged in his favor; and clamping down on the media's coverage.[54]

Sadat's American imagery—much like Shah Reza Pahlavi's—resulted from the hard-sell job foreign bureaus have of convincing viewers back home to stay tuned for news from abroad. Since international news seems too far removed from the average viewer—and dull on top of that—it is often "sold in drag—dressed up in show-biz razzmatazz, sometimes beyond recognition or meaning."[55] The Sadat story fell victim to this phenomenon.

It may be that former *Harper's* editor and novelist William Dean Howells is calling journalists home again in his instruction to do their homework on people before characterizing them in print. A leader in the Realist Movement, Howells believed it was unwise to judge a person on the basis of one or two acts. Instead, he said it is most important to look at how that person has conducted his or her affairs over time and to "see life steadily and see it wholly" before reaching conclusions about a person. Obviously, Howells's wisdom takes too much time for modern-day television news to follow, and it may also water down the clear, unambiguous image they want to portray to their audiences, even when that monolithic image leads us into the shadow world.

KAL 007: Ethnocentrism and Ideology

It is not unrealistic to think that the favorable and unfavorable images which the U.S. news media sketch of foreign powers have an influence on U.S. public opinion and government foreign policy toward those countries. It is unfair to say it is the media which are always responsible for originating false or misleading images. Often the media simply publish or air the image of leaders being handed out by the State Department or the White House, since few journalists actually get the chance to interview a Daniel Ortega or spend enough time in the country to get a first-hand feel of a more proper image. That luxury is often reserved only for those who staff foreign bureaus for large news organizations. So if the U.S. government wants to help justify an incursion into foreign territory or a bombing strike into a Libya or even its name-calling or policy toward the Soviet Union, the popularity of that mission is helped immensely if the media will only pass on the official image of the foreign powers in question. When that happens, the media's only crime is their gullibility, not their intentional presentation of a false image.

Often, however, it also seems that what sociologist Herbert J. Gans calls the enduring value of *ethnocentrism* creeps into the media's reportage of incidents involving foreign governments—especially hostile governments. This ethnocentrism, coupled with a curious naiveté and the penchant for believing administration sources, leaves the media wide open for some lopsided reporting which results in lopsided public opinion toward other countries.

The U.S. media's handling of the 1983 shootdown of Korean Air Lines Flight 007 is a classic case in point. In that coverage, much of the nation's media not only helped expedite government policy toward the Soviet Union, they also contributed to the instantly felt and long-lasting rage of the American people regarding the Soviet government.

Conversely, other publications espousing liberal orientations seized upon the shootdown of the Korean airliner to show how, once again, a conservative presidential administration was trying to cover up its own ineptness by rattling the sabres and casting total blame on the Soviet Union for another unthinkable act.

It is interesting to look at how an international incident involving the United States and the Soviet Union is covered by a magazine many feel to represent a conservative editorial viewpoint—*Time*—and a publication many feel to represent a liberal viewpoint—the *Nation*. As was found in their coverage of the shootdown of the Korean airliner, these publications featured extensive reports that seemed to support polarized opinions and assumptions about the United States under the administration of Ronald Reagan and of the magazines' perceptions of the Soviet Union.

A brief recap of the tragic incident shows that on the last day of August 1983, KAL Flight 007, a 747–200B Superjet commercial airliner, was shot down by a Soviet SU–15 fighter over Sakhalin Island in the eastern Soviet Union. All 269 people aboard were killed as the aircraft dropped more than 30,000 feet into the Sea of Japan. As Yale researcher David Pearson noted in the *Nation* a year later:

The U.S. government took the high ground, suggesting that the airliner had accidentally strayed into Soviet territory unbeknown to U.S. agencies and had been shot down without warning. In that view, which prevailed in the U.S. press and the minds of most citizens, responsibility rested squarely with the Russians and could be attributed to their indifference to human life.[56]

The problem is that too few media bothered to try to secure answers to the basic questions of why the KAL flight was so far over supersensitive Soviet territory for so long, how it could happen with the abundance of on-board and ground-based navigational and tracking systems available, and how long—if at all—before the shootdown U.S. and Japanese officials knew that the airliner was over Soviet territory. The answers to these questions were admittedly very hard to get. U.S. officials were reluctant to address them, and the cloak of defense secrecy in which the State Department shrouded the incident made matters worse. Causing even more problems was the alleged American erasure of some important radar tapes later which could have helped provide answers. When U.S. officials did address the questions, they handed out summary answers that often seemed to beg the question. Also they painted the attack as unprovoked and depicted the Soviet Union as an evil empire of liars who were trying to save their image by offering a preposterous tale of the flight being part of some kind of spy mission. According to U.S. sources (who were usually not named), it was a classic, unequivocal confrontation between the good guys and the bad guys. The Soviet Union was portrayed as clearly in the wrong while the United States was—once again—just an innocent victim. The ironic thing is this was not primarily a U.S.–Soviet incident, but a Korean-Soviet incident if we go on the nationalities of those killed and the fact it was a Korean airliner. Also considering the fact that answers to the tragedy's cause were slow in coming, why were the media so quick to quote these same officials in laying conclusive blame on the Soviet Union? In hindsight, it seems the Reagan administration took a defensive stance right away, trying to deflect any hint of U.S. culpability in setting the stage for the shootdown before that hint even surfaced.

An analysis of how a usually more skeptical publication covered the incident can be had by looking at the September 12 and September 19 issues of *Time* magazine in 1983. Happily, the *Time* of 1990 seems to have matured from the nationalistic perspective it took in covering the KAL shootdown in 1983. Indeed, the magazine has emerged as a leader in solid reporting and writing with 1989 stories like "Hail to the Ex-Chief," about the popularity of Jimmy Carter since he left the White House; "Free to Fly Inside a Cage," about modern-day China; and "Trail of Shame," about the shameful slaughtering of elephants in Africa. But in its coverage of the KAL tragedy, its reporting seems less than objective. From the covers inward, the two issues evidenced a lack of caution in interpreting the event and devoting almost no space in the first issue to the unanswered questions. Moreover, in place of comment on those questions, *Time*'s writer seemed to make several undocumented assumptions and value statements about how unprovoked the incident was and how premeditated and criminal was the act of the Soviet Union.

The cover of the September 12 issue depicted an artist's dramatic rendering of a Soviet fighter blasting the KAL flight out of the sky under the headline "Shooting to Kill." Inside, the cover story was headed "Atrocity in the Skies."[57] Thus even before the text began, the implications were that the attack was totally unprovoked, that the KAL flight had been on an innocent mission, somehow straying over Soviet territory, and that the Russians simply decided to shoot it down without warning and purposely kill all on board.

Once into the massive piece, the implication and assumptions—and ethnocentrism—become even more evident. For instance, of the 143 column inches of text devoted to the story and sidebars, only *three* inches even suggest the existence of the many unanswered questions. Then, having posed the issue, the reporters never got any government officials to respond to these questions. It never even said any government officials were asked about these questions. But the article does contain numerous characterizations of the Soviets by U.S. officials.

For instance, the article cites graphic excerpts from Charles Lichenstein, the U.S. representative to the U.N. Security Council, who delivered the U.S. version of the attack in a meeting of the council. In it, the article notes graphically he attacked the Soviets as lying. It then proceeds to give the entire U.S. version of the event. Yet, from the same U.N. session, the article summarily states the Soviet representative "proceeded to read the TASS account of the episode to the delegates."

Among excerpted phrases that seem to rest more on undocumented assumptions than facts are (italics added):

- "Korean Air Lines Flight 007 had been *cold-bloodedly* blasted out of the skies . . ."
- "The incident, moreover, seemed to be a *crime against all humanity,* a violation of the most fundamental rules of the air . . ."
- "it was *clear* that the Soviets had committed a *brutally provocative* act, one that demanded an *unambiguous* U.S. response."
- "*Common sense* suggests . . ."

The reporting encounters similar problems in the September 19 issue.[58] Although *Time* seldom devotes its cover to the same subject two weeks in a row, it did so this time. There was President Reagan and a photo of a U.N. Security Council meeting hearing the words, "The target is destroyed." The phrase was the last one heard on a voice transcript of the Soviet fighter pilot who downed KAL 007. The tape was recorded by the Japanese Defense Agency and passed on to U.S. officials. Inside, a five-page main article on the shootdown featured several other undocumented assumptions.

Following the main piece, *Time* ran a full-page interview with President Reagan which reiterated his accusations against the Soviet Union. Then, to its credit, it published a three-page Q&A dealing with some of the unanswered questions the incident posed. The ever-present problem with anonymous sources was shown here, however, as *Time* did not identify U.S. officials (whom it simply called "experts") as they provided some reinforcement for the U.S. version of what happened. Why were these people so afraid of going on the record with the administration's own version of what happened? It is interesting that when it referred to the Soviet version of the incident, *Time* was able to identify their sources. Why were the Soviets willing to go on record, yet the U.S. sources weren't?

Just as troubling in this Q&A is that the article carried 13 unattributed statements of conjecture and opinion. They all supported President Reagan's version of the incident, and they were all riddled with familiar phrases like "apparently" (used three times), "presumably," and "probably." Again, answers to the questions posed here were tough to nail down, especially from administration sources. But how many Watergate stories would have slipped passed editors at the *Washington Post* with phrases like this to support their theses?

At one point, the reporting reaches the point of citing an "unidentified U.S. source who was all but positive" the Soviets knew they were shooting down a commercial airliner and not an RC–135. That would not pass most editors as being documentation.

The Q&A piece "answers" the mystery of why Flight 007 was off course with conjecture that (1) the flight's electronic navigational systems all went awry despite admitted astronomical odds or (2) that the crew ignored at least three standard rules of procedure in setting or not attending to the navigational computers and notifying ground checkpoints—despite the fact the article paints the KAL pilot as a cautious and skilled retired Korean Air Force pilot who had been chosen to fly for President Chun Doo Hwan in 1981. Nowhere does it speculate that the pilot actually knew he was off course or that the flight may have been part of a U.S. spy mission, possibly in concert with the nearby RC–135 spy plane. As far-fetched as this sounds, it seems no more unrealistic than the first two conjectures.

Five years later, in July of 1988, the U.S. Navy shot down an unarmed Iran Air airbus with 290 civilians aboard over the Persian Gulf. The similarities between this tragedy and the shootdown of KAL 007 are uncanny, yet *Time* devoted no covers to this incident and only one story in the few weeks following the incident.[59] There were no damning accusations permeating that July 18 story or its headline and no assumption of U.S. "crimes against humanity." Now the whole focus of the story was on how the tragedy happened, and the article's headline provides *Time*'s answer. It read "High-Tech Horror," and the five-page article that followed concluded:

The U.S. and, by extension, other countries using high-tech weapons, may have become prisoners of a technology so speedy and complex that it forces the fallible humans who run it into snap decisions that can turn into disaster. . . . The tragedy seems to have resulted from a collision of random events.[60]

All this, despite the same lack of detailed answers that the media were supplied by U.S. officials following the KAL shootdown five years earlier, and despite the facts needed to support this article's conclusions.

It is reporting like this that best exemplifies the existence of the shadow world, and, when it fuels Americans' emotions and opinions regarding foreign powers, it is when the shadow world becomes most troublesome.

But it wasn't only the generally reliable *Time* which treated these events in this fashion. In fact, much of the nation's media did likewise, echoing the U.S. government's version about how innocent it was in causing the disasters and how utterly and solely responsible the Soviets were in the first and high technology was in the second.

Another publication opting for a similar thematic treatment as *Time* was the *New York Times*. The difference between the two publications is that, while *Time* may be perceived by many to take conservative editorial stances, the *New York Times* is not so perceived. Thus, ethnocentrism seems to be a value that permeates many conservative as well as more liberal news media. That value seems to have found its way into the first several stories which the *Times* carried on the tragedy on September 2, 1983. Researching that coverage, Jack Lule concluded that, despite its being an international incident only tangentially involving the United States, the *Times* nevertheless made it into a U.S.–Soviet incident and covered it with American nationalism. He writes:

In the world of the *Times* report, the international incident can first be understood in the narrow context of U.S. affairs. Firmly grounded in U.S. culture, the report gives heavy emphasis to U.S. officials, U.S. reactions and possible U.S. reprisals, and affirms a dominant U.S. role in world affairs. The report is *U.S. news*.... Another perspective on the text world then emerges, one tied to representations of the Soviet Union in U.S. culture.... As violator of the world order, the Soviet Union "deserves the censure of the entire world."... The report creates and then castigates an enemy shared by a group. [It] offers integration, identification and social cohesion through the degradation of another.[61]

If the media were press agents for the U.S. government, okay. But they aren't. Reporters went into shooting wars in Vietnam trying hard to remain objective, so why shouldn't they have done the same when it came to this terrible tragedy—at least until the answers to *Time*'s "unanswered questions" were in hand? Even at the time of the incident, reporters had good reason to ask the difficult questions of possible U.S. culpability and to try to get answers elsewhere if not from government officials. The most charitable explanation of why much of the media reacted this way is that the nation's journalists, like everyone else in the United States, were caught up in the wave of sorrow and frustration that legitimately followed these tragedies. But if journalists can find a way to remove themselves emotionally from other tragedies they cover, why can't they do the same for international tragedies like these?

It is curious that it was a nonjournalist who seemed to work hardest at finding answers for *Time*'s "unanswered questions" regarding the

KAL shootdown. David Pearson, a Ph.D. candidate in sociology at Yale University, spent a year researching the incident, and a report of his study appeared in the *Nation* a year after the shootdown (and was published as a book by Summit in 1987). The *Nation* gave lead-story play to Pearson's discoveries, which provided strong support for the magazine's ideological position of Ronald Reagan's misreading of the Soviets. Ironically, however, Pearson's study made little dent in major media retrospectives of the shootdown a year later. Possibly it was because the bulk of Pearson's evidence was circumstantial and some of it was conjecture built upon the process of elimination. As at *Time*, however, editors at the *Nation* let some speculation slip by under the guise of harder documentation. For instance, Pearson labels as "virtual certainties" the following (italics added):

- Several intelligence agencies, including the Air Force, National Security Agency, CIA, North American Aerospace Defense Command and the National Military Command Center at the Pentagon, *must have known* that the KAL flight was over Soviet territory well prior to the attack over Sakhalin.
- These same agencies *must have known* the danger the flight faced in flying over territory where a major Soviet missile test was under way.
- These same agencies had the time and means to warn KAL 007 to correct its course, but none of them did so.
- *It seems likely* that Soviet radar systems were jammed at least on Kamchatka Peninsula and perhaps on Sakhalin Island as well.
- *It seems probable* that the Secretary of Defense and the White House knew of the danger facing KAL 007 well before it was shot down.

Pearson concludes:

The most charitable interpretation is that U.S. military and intelligence agencies suffered an extraordinary series of human and technical failures which allowed the airliner to proceed on its deviant course. If that was the case, it would mean that the most serious failure in the history of the U.S. early warning and communications, command control and intelligence (C^3I) systems occurred that night. However, a much more likely and frightening possibility is that a conscious policy decision was made by the U.S. government . . . to risk the lives of 269 innocent people on the assumptions that an extraordinary opportunity for gleaning intelligence information should not be missed and that the Soviets would not dare shoot down a civilian airliner.[62]

As evidence to support his thesis, Pearson offers the following:

- The Soviet Union and its allies, since 1950, have downed several (some sources cite 27) other U.S. aircraft flying illegally over Soviet airspace. Therefore, purposeful intrusions into Soviet territory by U.S. airplanes have not been an uncommon experience.

- Many of these incursions have happened at potentially constructive moments in the process of arms control negotiations between the United States and the Soviet Union. The same was true for the timing of the KAL disaster.
- There were several irregularities surrounding the KAL 007 flight:

1. An unexplained 40-minute delayed takeoff from Anchorage.

2. The addition of 9,800 pounds of fuel at Anchorage which was neither needed for this scheduled flight nor accounted for in the pilot's subsequent position reports to air-traffic controllers.

3. The fact that, 50 minutes after takeoff, when the airliner was passing its Bethel checkpoint, Air Force radar in King Salmon, Alaska, showed it was already some 12 nautical miles off course, although the KAL pilot reported to air-traffic control that his airliner had passed Bethel on course. And this despite the on-board presence of three state-of-the art, independently programmed and operating navigational systems.

4. Military air-traffic radar along the route has a range of in excess of 250 nautical miles and all but certainly spotted the flight's deviation then and later.

5. KAL 007 continued to deviate ever more from its "Red 20" route, and the pilot did not comply with air regulations that he notify checkpoint air-traffic controllers if he is going to be more than three minutes late.

6. That the pilot changed speeds several times without notifying air-traffic controllers, despite air regulations requiring him to do so.

7. That an RC–135 Air Force reconnaissance plane, which crossed the jetliner's path at least twice, must have known that the airliner was intruding into Soviet territory.

8. A close examination of official accounts of the incident and maps of the area reveal that the RC–135 was likely much closer to KAL 007 than U.S. explanations implied, and that the two aircraft may actually have flown in close proximity to each other for several minutes.

9. That U.S. radar and other data that could have settled this last issue were denied to the public by the government.

10. That there was, in fact, a U.S. spy plane operating in such close proximity to a jetliner that was obviously intruding into Soviet airspace.

Obviously, most of what Pearson found was circumstantial evidence, and he links a lot of possibilities—if not probabilities—together to support his conclusion of U.S. culpability in the tragedy. Still, there is more merit in its abundance and his interpretation of events than there was in reporting such as *Time*'s a year earlier. But then, Pearson did have a year to reach his conclusions. *Time* writers, a week after the incident, did not.

It would certainly have helped both sets of reports if appropriate government officials would have discussed the possible U.S. culpability more openly, but they didn't. In fact, for three days following the shoot-down, neither Secretary of State George Shultz, President Reagan or any administration spokesperson made any mention at all of the RC–135 spy plane.

Pearson's report is not unparalleled. At least one other book (*Shootdown: Flight 007 and the American Connection* by R. W. Johnson) was written on the subject expressing many of the same conclusions and even accusing the Reagan administration of a cover-up. Naturally, the book was turned into a television movie of the week, with some of its more damning accusations toward the White House deleted for no apparent reason other than NBC's owner—General Electric—is a major defense contractor.

And *Science News* noted the astronomical improbability of all three onboard navigational systems failing on Flight 007. The magazine cites 1,000 cases of navigational abnormalities over the previous five years, and says most were attributable to human error either in reading them or programming them. It also quotes a PanAm pilot who has often flown north Pacific routes as saying that, "by using its on-board weather radar system, the Korean airliner should have been able to delineate landmasses and to know easily where it should not have been."[63] Like most other publications, *Science News* was forced to conclude, "Whether the intrusion was caused by a string of instrument failures, however implausible, or because of pilot carelessness or a deliberate violation of Soviet airspace may never be known."[64]

The News Media and Domestic Policy

But journalistic reporting not only affects U.S. foreign policy; it also affects domestic policy. In a series of empirical studies done for *Public Opinion Quarterly*, researchers found media disclosures on a series of domestic issues were influential in changing the attitudes of government policymakers.[65] The first of these studies, done in 1983, concluded that a nationally televised investigative news report on fraud and abuse in the federally funded home health care program had significant effects on the agenda of both the public and policymakers. Actual policy changes also resulted, albeit more from direct pressure for change by the journalists themselves.

A second study the group did in 1985 looked at the impact of a *Chicago Sun-Times* investigative series revealing government irregularities in the way city rape cases were reported and handled. In response to the series, legislators held hearings and Chicago city officials looked inward to see how they could clean up these improprieties. An interesting effect of this series was that many more and longer stories about rape began appearing in the pages of the *Sun-Times*. It seems that, not only did the series increase the salience of rape cases for city and state officials, it did the same for editors at the *Sun-Times*.

The third investigative report was a five-part local television series entitled "Beating Justice" about brutality by some Chicago police officers.

The reportage had a strong effect on viewer attitudes about police brutality and brought about some major revisions within the Chicago Police Department.

The fourth study analyzed the public opinion and policymaking impact of a Chicago television series about the toxic waste disposal habits of the University of Chicago. One of the primary targets of the series was the Chicago Fire Department and its regulatory safety practices regarding hazardous waste disposal. Like the other series, policymaking changes resulted in the fire department making changes, although—like the home health care series—some of these changes resulted from outright journalistic lobbying through city officials.

Summing up the results of the four studies, the researchers noted that three of the four investigative reports caused general public impact, two caused impact among the city's elite, and all four resulted in some type of policymaking response and/or changes. It is interesting to note that the one investigative series that did not result in either general public or elite impact was done by a newspaper, while the three others were television series. That probably underscores the fact that television has become such a prominent influence with the public and, therefore, with the government policymakers.

In conclusion, the researchers note:

For public attitudes to change, two factors seem to be important—the nature of the media portrayal and the frequency of attention by the media to the issue in the past. When the media portray an issue in an unambiguous way with dramatic, convincing, and clear evidence, public attitudes are more likely to change. In sum, the actual importance or seriousness of a problem may be less significant for influencing public attitudes than its "mediated reality."

The second factor . . . is the nature of the issue that the media are addressing. Certain issues receive fairly consistent treatment by journalists. Investigative stories about recurring issues have lower impact potential. We would suggest that news media investigative reports with the maximum ability to produce attitude change are those that involve unambiguous presentations of nonrecurring issues.[66]

The Effects of Media Polls

According to a 1980 study by John N. Rippey, "more than one-third of newspapers report they have used polls to gather information for news stories [and] most did so for the first time in the last decade."[67] So with 37 percent of newspapers alone using polls—and all three television networks plus CNN—there are plenty of them around for readers and viewers to see, especially during election years. More germane to this chapter's topic, however, is that about 20 percent of those same newspaper editors considered their polling stories to have had a "substantial effect" or "great effect" on community decision making.

In 1986, researcher Michael B. Salwen looked at the credibility of newspaper opinion polls. His results showed that: (1) trustworthiness and expertise are the underlying dimensions of source credibility, as are objectivity and clarity, and (2) all these dimensions can be enhanced in the reader's mind by the use of probability sampling procedures (scientific random sampling). This last predictor of credibility argues against using the "man-on-the-street" survey, as readers feel it is much less credible than a more formally structured random sampling procedure.

Most of the studies focusing on polling effects have centered on pre-election polling and exit polling practices of the media. Philip Meyer, author of *Precision Journalism* and a strong advocate of the survey technique, nevertheless warns of one of the problems with election polling:

Pre-election polls provide newsworthy checks on the validity of the polling process itself. Pollsters and media often prefer to avoid such checks, and so they offer ambiguous results capable of a variety of post-election interpretations. The most popular ambiguity-preserving device is to do nothing about the undecided who can then be blamed for whatever deviations occur between the poll and the outcome.[68]

Meyer suggests two ways of factoring in this undecided group. First, pollsters can look at how the distribution of opinion shifts when the "leaners" are added to it. The pollster can then assume this movement will continue in the same direction and speed until the election when those leaners cast their votes. A second way is by using the computer analysis technique of discriminant analysis, comparing voters with a preference to their demographics and issue preferences. From this cross-tabbing an equation can be constructed to predict which demographic cum issue preference will vote for a particular candidate. Since the demographics and issue preferences of most undecideds are also known, the equation can also rope them in and predict how they may vote.

Obviously, some polls have this and other distortive effects. Analysts Karen S. Johnson and Dan Nimmo wrote in 1986, "As reported, . . . news media polls do less to provide public knowledge about issues, events and personalities than superficial acquaintance with public perceptions. The result is gross oversimplification of the political opinion process, leading to public misinformation."[69] They further contend that polls too often are too broad in the range of questions they ask, and do not get deeply enough into any one particular issue. Instead, they offer a large number of specific questions about different issues asked at a specific time in the long election campaign. They should not be construed as anything larger than that. One reason many media don't have their pollsters ask more questions is because of the expense involved. It costs about $20 an average call for telephone surveys,[70] and the more questions asked, the longer, and more expensive, the call becomes. In fact, given the expense involved in nationwide polling, it is sometimes difficult for pollsters to dump out questionable respondents and pay for other phone calls to take their place.

Sometimes people will even offer responses to *faked issues*. One study, conducted in 1975 to test for this phenomenon, asked voters for their opinion of the Public Affairs Act of 1975. Despite the fact this was a nonexistent act, about a third of the respondents still offered an opinion on it. "To the degree news media polling taps such pseudo-opinions, published results are misleading," the researchers said.[71]

Still another criticism of media polling practices is that, while they often measure accurately the *direction* of public opinion on a given issue or candidate, they rarely try to measure the *intensity of feeling* toward the same object.

One type of media poll that has become popular over the past decade is *exit polling*. These are face-to-face polls done on voters as they exit the voting booth. They have come under criticism because often television has announced results of exit polls in the East, while the polling places were still open in the West. Looking at the question of whether exit polls influence voter behavior, Seymour Sudman wrote in 1986 that "an important issue is the perceived closeness of the election before the election occurred and the perceived closeness of the election based on exit poll results. This was the case in 1980, when a close race was expected based on preelection polls, but the exit poll showed a Reagan sweep. This was not the case in the 1984 elections, where the exit polls simply confirmed what the preelection polls had already forecasted: a wide Reagan victory."[72] So, as analyst John Jackson discovered, exit polling could have the reverse effect of getting more people out to vote if those polls indicate the race is running closer than previously expected.[73]

Former NBC News correspondent Marvin Kalb joins the chorus of those who feel the news media, through their saturation polling practices, distorted the outcome of the 1988 presidential race. For the first time, he notes, newspapers like the *New York Times* regularly ran poll stories on its front page, sometimes as the lead story. Was this manufactured news? Some think so, and ultimately, it depends of the validity of the polling process used and, therefore, the validity of the results. Nineteen eighty-eight gave the country a wave of jointly sponsored polls as well, with the *New York Times* joining hands with "CBS News," the *Washington Post* hooking up with "ABC News," and the *Wall Street Journal* and "NBC News" producing their poll. Not to be left out was CNN, which joined with *USA Today* in producing their own polls. Assessing the results, Kalb wrote:

The American people are left bedazzled, one moment polled and the next moment informed of their sentiments before being polled again. Network officials find a degree of comfort in the assertion that "there is no evidence that the polls influence elections." Nonsense. If more than 70 percent of the American people get most of what they know about the world, and the campaign from television, and if most of television news is pegged to polls, then it is inescapable that the polls are having an influence. The influence . . . is magnified by their effect on television and print journalists covering the campaign, whose stories in turn shape voters' perception of the race.[74]

NOTES

1. Clinton Rossiter and James Lare, eds., *The Essential Lippmann* (Cambridge, Mass.: Harvard University Press, 1982), pp. 94–95.

2. Marshall McLuhan, *Understanding Media: The Extensions of Man* (New York: McGraw-Hill, 1964).

3. Joshua Meyrowitz, *No Sense of Place: The Impact of Electronic Media on Social Behavior* (New York: Oxford University Press, 1985), pp. 19–20.

4. Ibid.

5. McLuhan.

6. Meyrowitz, pp. 22–23.

7. Meyrowitz, p. 17.

8. Denis McQuail, *Mass Communication Theory: An Introduction* (London: Sage, 1983), p. 195.

9. McQuail, pp. 195–96.

10. McQuail, p. 196.

11. George Gerbner, L. P. Gross, M. Morgan, and N. Signorielli, "The "Mainstreaming" of America: Violence Profile No. 11," *Journal of Communication* 30 (3): p. 14 (1980).

12. Werner J. Severin with James W. Tankard, Jr., *Communication Theories: Origins, Methods, Uses*, 2d ed. (New York: Longman, 1988), p. 314.

13. Ibid.

14. McQuail, p. 188–89.

15. McQuail, p. 189.

16. McQuail, pp. 196–99.

17. Roy L. Behr and Shanto Iyengar, "Television News, Real-World Cues, and Changes in the Public Agenda," *Public Opinion Quarterly* 49; pp. 47–51 (1985).

18. McQuail, p. 197.

19. McQuail, pp. 197–98.

20. Severin with Tankard, p. 285.

21. Edwin Emery and Michael Emery, *The Press and America*, 5th ed. (Englewood Cliffs, N.J.: Prentice-Hall, 1984), p. 290.

22. Marcus M. Wilkerson, *Public Opinion and the Spanish-American War* (Baton

Rouge: Louisiana State University Press, 1932); Joseph E. Wisan, *The Cuban Crisis as Reflected in the New York Press* (New York: Columbia University Press, 1934).

23. Emery and Emery, p. 289.

24. Emery and Emery, pp. 288–89.

25. Louis L. Snyder and Richard B. Morris, ed., *A Treasury of Great Reporting* (New York: Simon & Schuster, 1962), pp. 246–47.

26. Douglas Steinbauer, "Faking It With Pictures," *American Heritage,* October/November 1982, pp. 52–55.

27. Ibid.

28. Charles Mohr, "Once Again—Did the Press Lose Vietnam?," *Columbia Journalism Review,* November/December 1983, p. 51.

29. Ibid.

30. Mohr, p. 53.

31. M. L. Stein, "What Vietnam War Taught the Press," *Editor & Publisher,* February 19, 1983, p. 9.

32. Oscar Patterson III, "Television's Living Room War in Print: Vietnam in the News Magazines," *Journalism Quarterly* 61, p. 35 (1985).

33. Ibid.

34. Albert Gunther, "Attitude Extremity and Trust in Media," *Journalism Quarterly* 65, p. 279 (1988).

35. Margaret Carlson, "Presumed Innocent," *Time,* January 22, 1990, p. 10.

36. "Nightline," ABC, January 22, 1990.

37. Ellis Cose, "Turning Victims into Saints," *Time,* January 22, 1990, p. 19.

38. Ibid.

39. Ibid.

40. "Nightline."

41. Ibid.

42. Ibid.

43. Ibid.

44. Janet Cooke, "A Story That Shocked the Nation's Capital," *U.S. News and World Report,* October 13, 1980, pp. 56–57.

45. Thomas Griffith, "The Pulitzer Hoax—Who Can Be Believed?" *Time,* May 4, 1981, p. 50.

46. Timothy Noah, "Jimmy's Big Brothers," *New Republic,* May 16, 1981, p. 14.

47. Noah, p. 15.

48. Griffith, p. 51.

49. Ronald Turovsky, "Did He Really Say That?," *Columbia Journalism Review,* July/August 1980, p. 38.

50. Doreen Kays, "The Television Pharaoh," *Quill,* May 1985, p. 12.

51. Ibid.

52. "The Emperor Who Died an Exile," *Time,* August 4, 1980.

53. Kays, p. 41.

54. Ibid.

55. Kays, p. 12.

56. David Pearson, "K.A.L. 007: What the U.S. Knew and When We Knew It," *Nation,* August 18–25, 1984, p. 105.

57. "Atrocity in the Skies," *Time,* September 12, 1983, pp. 10–14.

58. "The U.S. Has Moscow on the Defensive over the Downed Korean Airliner," *Time*, September 19, 1983, pp. 12–14.

59. "High-Tech Horror," *Time*, July 18, 1988, pp. 14–16.

60. "High-Tech Horror," p. 16.

61. Jack Lule, "Victimage in *Times* Coverage of the KAL Shooting," *Journalism Quarterly* 66:3, p. 620 (1989).

62. Pearson, pp. 105–15.

63. I. Peterson, "Stray Jets: The Human Factor," *Science News* 124, p. 196 (1983).

64. Ibid.

65. David L. Protess, Fay Lomax Cook, Thomas R. Curtin, Margaret T. Gordon, Donna R. Leff, Maxwell E. McCombs, and Peter Miller, "The Impact of Investigative Reporting on Public Opinion and Policymaking," *Public Opinion Quarterly* 51, pp. 166–85.

66. Protess, et al. pp. 180–81.

67. John N. Rippey (1980). "Use of Polls as a Reporting Tool," *Journalism Quarterly* 57:4, p. 642.

68. Michael B. Salwen, "Credibility of Newspaper Opinion Polls: Source, Source Intent, and Precision," *Journalism Quarterly* 64(4): p. 813 (1987).

69. Karen S. Johnson and Dan Nimmo, "Commentary: Reporting Political Polling: Avoiding Public Misinformation," *Newspaper Research Journal* 7(3): p. 69 (1986).

70. Ibid.

71. Ibid.

72. Seymour Sudman, "Do Exit Polls Influence Voting Behavior?," *Public Opinion Quarterly* 50, p. 332 (1986).

73. Sudman, pp. 332–33.

74. Marvin Kalb, "How the Media Distorted the Presidential Race," *Editor & Publisher*, November 19, 1988, pp. 56–57.

10

From Shadows to Substance

We noted at the outset that any one of three results could occur from a journalist's looking inward to the difficulties he or she faces in reporting:

1. The journalist could become so paranoid about these obstacles, he or she decides to call it quits as a reporter and go into some other line of work.

2. The journalist could wrap all these obstacles up in what Daniel Goleman would call a "vital lie" and try desperately to believe these problems don't really amount to much, that they're good for academic discussions, but not much more.

3. The journalist could see these obstacles as challenges to be met with improved, innovative reporting orientations and methods and push on until he or she can honestly state, "I've done the best I can, and it's not bad."

The best journalists will take the third option, and it is for them that this book is written. It is understood in researching and writing this book that, as Ron Javers said, "Reporters are ordinary people who have an extraordinary mission."[1] Most extraordinary missions are fraught with dangers, and miscalculations can cause all kinds of trouble. Reporting and editing are no different. It's just that reporters' and editors' mistakes result in trouble for readers and viewers who pick up a false signal of what is actually going on in the world or in their little corner of it. They then react to what they see and not to what really *is*. So the quest goes on for better journalism that can somehow leap all the hurdles—or at least some of them—presented in the previous chapters and result in that truthful portrayal of reality. If they are not already obvious from the challenges discussed heretofore, the following guides should help the reporter in that quest for quality journalism.

GUIDE NO. 1: BE YOUR OWN PERSON

Previously cited examples have shown that Javers is right when he suggests that newspapers have abandoned their credibility in favor of respectability. He notes:

Too often *our* assumptions are the assumptions of the government and business elites. Too often we tend to be like and think like the people we cover. Police reporters begin to act like cops. . . . Those assigned to cover government bureaucracies begin to think in terms of the bureaucracy, where the guiding ethic is "Protect your ass," and "Don't take risks." Too often, we speak in the hushed tones of authority, from the ubiquitous "police said" . . . to the more insidious "according to authorities." We seldom stop to ask *who* these authorities are and what biases they entertain. The media are, in fact, structured to deal with authorities and not with people.[2]

Perhaps that is a starting point then on the road from shadows to substance. Perhaps it is time to really take the stance of an objective, detached chronicler of events instead of just hiding behind that stance as a way of deflecting every little criticism that comes our way. Perhaps we worry too much today about remaining detached from the reader or viewer (because we don't want to be accused of pandering to their low tastes!), and we worry too little about remaining detached from the people we report *about*. Perhaps the whole thing should be reversed: that we try to get closer to the reader or viewer and further removed from our cozy relationships with sources. As mentioned in Chapter 5, there was a police reporter for a metro daily who got so close to the police that they actually made him an honorary sergeant and gave him a badge. In response, the reporter helped pat suspects down on occasion and helped police in their arrest procedures. In return for all of that he got a lot of exclusive crime stories, but he seldom—if ever—reported on the *internal* problems in the department.

We hear a fair amount these days about the symbiotic relationship between the media and politicians, about how reporters need the politicians for the stories and ten-second soundbites, and how the politicians need the media to increase their own exposure. But we don't hear too much about how much individual reporters might rely on their sources to further their own journalistic careers. An obvious example is the case of the network television reporter assigned to cover a presidential candidate who wins the election. The next thing we see is that political reporter now becoming the network's White House correspondent because he or she knows so much—or at least so we assume—about the man who now resides inside the White House.

But this phenomenon happens at lower levels and on other beats as well. A quotable police chief who is always involving the press in his drug busts makes great copy and certainly doesn't hurt the career of the lucky reporter assigned to go along on the nightly raids. Sometimes it is an issue that elevates a reporter to fame and fortune as was the case with Dan Rather who appeared so regularly on national television in reporting the civil rights disturbances in the South in the 1960s. Having been seen on television so much, Rather became a celebrity himself, just as countless other television correspondents do. Their career feeds off the personalities, issues, and events they cover, and most of them dream of tying into the big story—partly because it challenges them as report-ers, partly because it represents a path to the top of their profession. The best of these reporters will focus on the task at hand and do a credible job of reporting reality, letting the personal rewards come as a result of a job well done. The worst will simply use these events, issues, and personalities as a stepping stone to the upper echelons of journalism, caring little about deviating from the safe, standard story and less about doing an innovative job of reporting.

So, in summary, the first mandate for moving from shadow to sub-stance is to remain psychologically detached from your sources and tell the story that should be told. If you become a hero in the process, like Woodward or Bernstein, great. You deserve it.

GUIDE NO. 2: PLAN THE WORK, WORK THE PLAN

A second suggestion for achieving more substantive reporting would be to add more structure to your reporting method. Journalists don't have to rely on "firehouse research," as McCombs, Shaw, and Grey call it.[3] Nor do they have to implement the exhaustive, tedious methodology of the research scientist as they set about looking for truth. Happily, there is a middle ground. It consists of thinking out your reporting procedure before barging into it. It also consists of bringing more than one fact-finding method to bear on the story. Few stories should be based soley on a single interview; most shouldn't even be based only on multiple interviews. Given the potential distorting factors inherent in interviews, all of them should be supplemented with other forms of research, and this research should be done *before* the interview. Sadly, for many journalists, conducting that research is one of the dullest as-pects of reporting, and so it often is a stage that is bypassed. The result is reporters are left not knowing what to believe during the course of their interviews, and they are much more vulnerable to being led exactly where interviewees want to take them.

It is no accident that, of the ten steps to the "Anatomy of an Interview" that Ken Metzler describes in his book *The Creative Interview,* four of those steps come before actually meeting the respondent and starting the interview. In order, those initial steps are defining the purpose of the interview, conducting background research, requesting the interview appointment (armed with your research data at hand), and designing the path you expect the interview to follow.[4]

Elise Keoleian Parsigian provided journalists with a kind of road map through the reporting task and, in the process, showed how similar to scientific research reporting can actually be if done correctly. In her model, she cites the behavioral scientist's steps, followed by the journalist's steps. In the Winter 1987 edition of *Journalism Quarterly* she laid out these similar methods:[5]

1. *Draw a clear statement of the problem.* The editor or producer presents a statement of the problem upon assigning a reporter to cover the story—a bank robbery for instance.

2. *Conduct preliminary research on the problem.* The reporter examines police records of the incident.

3. *Design the data-collection strategy.* The reporter determines what to ask of whom, and what to ask about. He or she also determines if other forms of research are needed, such as analyzing previous incident reports about similar crimes.

4. *Collect the data.* The reporter observes, interviews people, reviews references and documents obtained from as many pertinent sources as possible.

5. *Code the data.* The reporter reviews the collected information and organizes it, eliminating items irrelevant to the problem and setting up who said what to whom at what time.

6. *Analyze the data.* The reporter reviews the organized data for confirmations, contradictions, discrepencies, relationships, evidence of source reliability; checks on source statements, documents; and obtains checks from supervisors on his or her analysis of the data.

7. *Draw conclusions.* The reporter draws conclusions and, on some stories, may need to get clearance or confirmation or conclusions from the editor.

8. *Write the research report.* The reporter now writes the story.

In discussing the journalist's methodology, Parsigian writes:

There is little reason to believe journalists are less orderly than the rest of the population. The notion that journalists operate intuitively has been challenged again and again, yet the notion prevails. One reason for this may be that journalists themselves like the idea that they are viewed as craftspeople, artists whose creative source is a mystery beyond human understanding.[6]

The problem, of course, is that many journalists don't follow all of the above steps and quite often jump past the research phases into the interview, which is often a lone interview, and then leap to the last stage of writing the story. Although time considerations and the ubiquitous deadline will, at times, require such corner cutting, the reporter and editor should be prepared for the consequences of a story either full of naiveté or a story that is flat-out wrong. They must also understand that the follow-up story containing the previously missing responses and/or clarifications will seldom be as widely seen as the initial story unless its content is as dramatic.

GUIDE NO. 3: TAP INTO DATABASES

One of the innovations that in recent years has helped speed up story research and widen the base of that research considerably is the introduction of databases and database services. A database is a collection of text or numbers that is stored in a computer and which can be accessed by a reporter with a terminal, phone modem, phone number of the host computer, and a password or number. There are hundreds—maybe thousands—of databases existing in computers at all levels of government, from the local police department to the State Department. Many of these databases contain public records and are available to reporters or anyone who wants to search them. To help the process run smoother, several database services have come into existence over the past decade to serve the specialized needs of reporters and business and government officials. Probably the best known of these services is Nexis, which stores the contents of—at last count—20 newspapers, 54 magazines, 15 wire services, and 50 newsletters. Also available are such things as every 10-K report filed with the SEC, every patent issued since 1975, every volume of the *Federal Register* and every issue of *Congressional Quarterly*. Other large database services marketed primarily to news media include VuText, Data Times, and Dialog.

In 1986, some 80 of 155 daily newspapers surveyed were using databases, compared with just 20 in 1982.[7] Although their use has been chiefly among large metropolitan dailies because of the high cost of subscribing and searching out information, recently more medium-size dailies have begun subscribing as well as several television stations.

In addition to the database services, some reporters are tapping directly into government databases. Elliot Jaspin, a former Pulitzer Prize–winning reporter for the *Providence Journal-Bulletin* and *Philadelphia Daily News*, suggests that the following should be in every newspaper's library of computer tapes:[8]

• *Criminal and Civil Court Records.* In the 1970s the now-defunct Law Enforcement Assistance Administration developed a computer program that allowed the courts to keep track of the cases flowing through the criminal and civil courts. The tracked information can be purchased and, with basic software, can be used to determine if someone has ever been involved in a criminal or civil case.

- *Campaign Contributions.* Maintained by the Federal Election Commission, a tracking of campaign contributions to federal candidates is available to anyone who requests them. Also, some states also keep computerized lists of donations to state and local candidates.
- *Voter Registration Lists.* Several states maintain computerized voter registrations that can yield an abundance of information about who is voting and who is not.
- *Driver's License Records.* Since most women are not listed by their own names in the phone book it is hard to get in touch with them to interview them. It is also hard to know just how they spell their name. But, since most women have a driver's license, the chance of locating that woman in the state's computerized driver's license record tapes is excellent. It may only take a few seconds.
- *Corporation Records.* When a corporation registers itself, many states place information about that corporation on the computer, including the names of its officers and directors. If a journalist needs to know the business in which a person is involved, a search of this file can quickly reveal a number of leads.

The systematic use of these databases has helped reporters uncover a number of stories they might have otherwise missed. For instance:

- "The Color of Money," a four-part series done by reporters for the *Atlanta Journal and Constitution*, was largely based on the results of database searches. In those searched, records of 109,000 mortgage loans were added up by a computer which then matched them, district by district, with 64 census tracts. The results showed that white borrowers who received bank mortgages outnumbered black borrowers, 5–1.[9]
- When police arrested Mehmet Ali Agca for shooting Pope John Paul II, a CBS researcher keyed Agca's name into Nexis and found 13 previous mentions of the suspect. That information included stories of a prior arrest and death threat that Agca had made. Tom McNichol notes that CBS went on the air with the information five minutes after the shooting, scooping its competitors.[10]
- After several Rhode Island children were run over by buses in separate incidents in 1985, reporters turned to computer tapes to see if any pattern existed. It did. Analyzing tapes that listed every area traffic ticket over a three-year period and every criminal court case over nine years, the *Providence Journal-Bulletin* reporters discovered bus drivers who were dealing drugs and others who were hired despite having terrible driving records.

Like any tool, however, databases are only as good as the thought that reporters put into using them. Since database services and the additional computer tapes that the news media can buy from individual databases are so expensive to use, reporters must have a plan of attack for searching out information instead of aimlessly meandering through the nooks and crannies of these computer tapes. Even if the cost were not a factor, the regular press of the deadline insists that reporters use these databases efficiently and effectively.

A couple words of warning about relying on databases, however: remember if you are quoting another newspaper or magazine account of a story you are relying on *that* reporter's credibility and the accuracy of his or her story. Therefore, if you have any reason to doubt the accuracy of a report, verify the statements just as you would verify your own sources' statements. One problem with extensive database reporting is that it could lead to magnifying an innaccuracy many times as other reporters continually tap into an inaccurate story.

Second, don't let database searches lead you into laziness as a reporter. The information you find in databases is meant to add background and context to your *own* interviews and original research. Sometimes reporters are guilty of ending the research process when they turn off their personal computer. That is one reason why NBC president Michael Gartner recently characterized database reporting as potentially dangerous to innovative journalism. Like an editor who uses too much wire copy to fill his or her newspaper, a reporter can use too much database copy to fill his or her story.

GUIDE NO. 4: TREAT RUMORS AS RUMORS

Journalists are rightly appreciative of any kind of news tip they might receive. Tips serve the same purpose for a journalist as hypotheses serve for a behavioral scientist. They point each fact finder in a particular direction; they provide a focus for the study at hand. Where the worst journalists and scientists jump the track, however, is in treating tips, rumors, or hypotheses as conclusions instead of possibilities to be researched and that may or may not lead to the truth. To a scientist, sometimes a hypothesis is simply a hunch. It works that way for journalists, too, although journalists also use rumors as news tips. In large measure, news tips are even more dubious than a scientist's hypothesis, which may arise out of someone else's previous research. But that's okay, because the journalistic method of fact finding is not identical to the scientist's, although they are similar. A journalist, as William Rivers notes, "pursues facts for their own sake, many of them amounting to information that may have neither value nor significance. A reporter can seldom know as he sets out to cover an event whether it will be banal or significant, nor can he always judge its value in the hot moment of occurrence."[11] The problem comes when the research of that rumor takes too many shortcuts, possibly in interviewing only one source or relying too heavily on only one piece of documentation.

An example of a rumor that became a conclusion is the story that CBS broke in the 1980 GOP convention in Detroit that Ronald Reagan had picked Gerald Ford to be his running mate. Discussed in more detail in Chapter 6, the Ford story was even announced publicly by that pillar of journalistic respect and credibility, Walter Cronkite, who told viewers watching the 1980 Republican convention, "Gerald Ford will be his [Reagan's] selection as his vice-presidential running mate.

Obviously, that never happened and it started becoming apparent within minutes after that announcement that it would not happen. Yet, in the mad rush to beat opposing networks by even a few minutes, CBS fell into the trap that too many reporters fall into: reporting rumors as fact without bothering to get clear verification of the rumor. This is one case where truth and speed mix about as well as oil and water. Too often, under the press of deadline, speed takes precedence over truth. After all, some journalists rationalize, there is always the next news bulletin to correct or clarify ourselves or there is always tomorrow's newspaper to run the other side—or sides—to the story.

Sometimes the fact that a rumor is floating around becomes a story in and of itself. Despite the fact there is no reason to believe it is true. Columnist Mike Royko recalls the rumormongering that surrounded the story in Chicago about Oprah Winfrey's alleged rift with her boyfriend. Royko wrote that what he found "most interesting" about the whole reporting incident is the reason the *Chicago Sun-Times* columnist gave for printing it. She said, "It is a vicious rumor, but I wanted to run the item even though there was no way I could verify the rumor."[13] Royko countered, "That is one of the most embarrassing admissions I've ever heard from someone in the news business. If she could write that Oprah's 'staid neighbors' were shocked, couldn't any of those staid neighbors *verify* that they were shocked? Or staid?"[14]

A *Psychology Today* article once noted about rumors:

Even frivolous-seeming rumors do not take root simply because they make titillating gossip. They persist because they touch on the real uncertainties and anxieties of the times. . . . Since rumors explain confusing events and thus relieve the tension of ambiguity, they flourish in an atmosphere of secrecy and competition.[15]

This is probably why Washington is a city so full of rumors, since there are so many secrets and so much ambiguity existing there. It is also why, unfortunately, so much of the reporting emanating from Washington is based on rumors, many of them unverified.

As newspaper readers, we come to expect that the bread and butter of the gossip column and the supermarket tabloids will be rumors. Most news consumers are intelligent enough to recognize them as such, even though that sill is not excuse for printing or airing unverified rumors. The larger problem comes when rumormongering becomes a part of mainstream reporting. There are hundreds of reasons that sources start rumors, and only a few of them are because those rumors are true and they want the truth to be exposed for the public good.

In a working paper for the Gannett Center for Media Studies, W. Phillips Davison examined mass media, civic organizations, and street gossip. Among other things he found that person-to-person communications, much of it the rumor variety, is one of the main channels of information for a community. From his research on one town in particular, Kingsbridge, New York, Davison offered these suggestions to help portray a more valid picture of life in any city:[16]

• Any news medium should tap into as many sources of community information as possible for every story. Especially important is the need to go to the "less formal interpersonal networks that provide the basis for much of a community's activity."

• Coverage of the community's official spokespeople and groups will rarely reveal why things are as they are in the city. To find the answer to that important question, journalists must look to the people and groups affected by those official actions, because they probably had an influence in those actions in the first place and they are the ones who must live with the consequences.

• Journalists should also pay attention to activists within the community realizing, as always, their vested interest in the subject at hand. These activists are generally interested in the quality of life in the community and their comments and insight can help to round out the official-source comments as well as those affected by the policies for good or for bad.

• Neighborhood organizations should pay more heed to the news requirements of their area media. Identifying with other groups in the city which have similar goals and developing joint programs or demonstrations with them will help further them toward their goal of improvement and make them more newsworthy in the process.

• Contrary to some critical belief, the city's media should strive for a level of cooperation with those pushing for community improvement. Overriding the fear that media reports will be slanted as a result of such cooperation is the knowledge that the existence other channels of communication in the city (of the interpersonal and organizational types) will limit the media's ability to slant the news and retain credibility among townspeople.

GUIDE NO. 5: SPECIALIZE

Chapter 7 discussed the problems with generalist reporters who are called upon to cover issues and events which require special knowledge and background. The areas in which too much reporting come up as either naive or flat-out wrong are the fields of business, foreign affairs, and science. Of just one of these areas, Robert Anderson notes in his review of Dorothy Nelkin's *Selling Science*:

From AIDS to nuclear winter, Bhopal to Chernobyl, a cat's cradle of improbable, outsized, and often terrifying issues has landed in the science writer's lap. Of baffling complexity and often global consequence, these issues impose severe, perhaps impossible, demands on science reporters. Writing to deadline on a breaking story is one thing; writing to deadline while interpreting an alien "social reality" is quite another. Too often the harried—and snowed—reporter resorts to shortcuts, stock framing, facile imagery, and pumped-up controversy.[17]

J. Edward Murray, past president of both the American Society of Newspaper Editors and the Associated Press Managing Editors, is on target with his recommendation that the news media add more staff specialists to upgrade the quality of their news content.[18] Murray points out that, in the area of foreign affairs, there is a Third World perception that Western editors are interested only in coups and earthquakes. "They wanted process-oriented news of their slow progress in education, agricultural productivity, health and sanitation; stories on reducing child mortality, increasing longevity, liberating women. And less event-oriented news of famines, earthquakes, military coups and communal violence. Such violence, incidentally, is usually triggered by religious prejudice. It is almost always caused by economic desperation."[19]

To get that kind of coverage takes at least two things: a reporter who has background knowledge of the country and the problem at hand, and the courage of editors to experiment with different forms of international coverage so that Americans can obtain a more accurate picture of life in other countries

There has been a fear among many journalism students that developing a reporting specialty will limit their employment possibilities, thinking that most news media want reporter generalists. In the present age of splintered audiences and readers, however, that is becoming less the case, especially with large newspapers and specialized magazines which try to present insightful material to satisfy the needs of each of those subgroups of readers.

Achieving this goal of staffing the newsroom with more specialists will also entail the willingness on the part of media managers to reward that second college major or graduate degree with an increased stipend. In only a minority of cases is that happening today among the nation's media.

GUIDE NO. 6: DON'T FORGET THE LARGER TRUTH

There is something of a debate going on in academia and some journalistic circles about whether journalists should focus on the event at hand or show it as a link in chain that sometimes runs very long. What we're talking about goes beyond context; it goes to the level of antici-patory reporting, trend reporting, and even—to some extent—predicting the future. McCombs, Shaw, and Grey refer to the antithesis of this reporting as "iceberg" reporting, where reporters are like a ship's re-volving beacon, scanning the horizon for evidence of icebergs or other obstructions. The problem with iceberg reporting is that, like the beacon, you can see only the tips of those icebergs. You have no way of knowing how large the obstruction is beneath the surface of the water unless you turn to other fact-finding techniques. The ship's captain might use sonar; the journalist can borrow from social scientists' techniques like random sample surveys, content analysis, field experiments, and participant ob-servation. These are all techniques that, used properly, can help present the "larger truth" of the situation, show a trend, and maybe with some accuracy can even predict the future (as sophisticated political polling is coming closer to doing).

The journalist also can borrow from the historian's techniques of ana-lyzing the past. For the journalist, that means looking mostly at traces of the past left by its documents and surviving members. This analysis checks one trace against another in an effort to validate the statements and opinions of those who observed the past. As with current-day sources, these observations may be skewed, so such contrast and com-parison often is necessary. The purpose of these techniques, for a jour-nalist, is to show how abnormal and/or important a current-day event or development—or even idea—is. Without examining the past, a story can be misleading or, at best, naive.

Yet there are some who feel the journalist's job is not to present the "larger truth," but to focus on more specific points of coverage and leave the larger truth to others. Roger Rosenblatt wrote in 1984, for instance:

The business of journalism is to present facts accurately. . . . Those seeking some-thing larger are advised to look elsewhere. . . . journalism rarely sees the larger truth of a story because reporters are usually chasing quite small elements of information. . . . Journalism tends to focus on the poor when the poor make news, usually dramatic news. . . . But the poor are poor all the time. It is not journalism's ordinary business to deal with the unstartling normalities of life. . . . People may have come to expect too much of journalism.[20]

I've used that essay in some of my graduate classes to spur discussion on the role and scope of journalism, and it always produced mixed reactions from my students. Perhaps that is what it was intended to do when it was published in *Time*. My own feeling is that it begs the question and provides justification for iceberg reporting which has so many ob-vious flaws they are hardly worth delineating. Some of the problems with Rosenblatt's theory are:

1. It is a reaction to an equally dubious position expressed by the *New Yorker's* Alastair Reid who wrote in 1984, "A reporter might take liberties with the factual circumstances to make the larger truth clear." If I were responding to Reid's statement, I might make some of the observations that Rosenblatt did himself. Reid's theory is at the basis of much of the new journalism being practiced today, and it also provides the producers' rationalization for television docudramas. But to make a sweeping statement that seeking the larger truth is not the job of the journalist at all is gross overreaction and leads reporting back to pre-interpretive journalism days of Curtis MacDougall. It takes us back to the "straitjacket journalism" days of the McCarthy era where journalists did as Rosenblatt suggests: focus on the event or accusation at hand and leave it at that.

2. It's true that reporters spend a lot of time chasing bits and pieces of information. That is because each must be examined and verified so it can be used as a building block to the larger truth. This is what Bob Woodward and Carl Bernstein did when they went beyond covering the simple arraignment of seven burglary suspects to link it, ultimately, to a plot by top presidential aides and possibly the president himself to help the GOP win reelection to the White House in 1972.

3. Rosenblatt's theory seems to equate *what is* with *what should be* and, because something is happening, it's okay. For instance, he notes that reporters reduce most of the stories they cover to political considerations and ignore the larger story. No doubt that is exactly right. But is it right to say that, because of this, journalists should not seek the larger truth? Is this reporting good enough to let stand without efforts to improve it by seeking the larger truth? Obviously not.

4. The structured order, which he says that the media impose on stories, does exist. Without question. Rosenblatt notes that this structure ignores the larger truth of a "chaotic universe." Again, true. But, again, can we not experiment with no structures that will allow more truthful reporting to come through? J. Edward Murray thinks we can, and he calls for the need of a "basic transformation in newspapers . . . a deep structure change in their news-handling."[21] Murray says such an overhaul would increase the space for hard news and upgrade the editor's ideas and formulae on what news is and what it isn't.

5. Rosenblatt says journalism must guard against numbing the sensibilities of readers and viewers by presenting too much depressing news because solutions to these problems seem too distant. This may be the most ridiculous point of his whole thesis, and I can't imagine many journalists buying into this idea. Think of the reverse: What if the media did not present problems plaguing society? What kind of attention would these problems receive from responsible parties? Very little. It is not

inappropriate either, as the *Christian Science Monitor* has tried to do over the years, to look for solutions to these problems and report on them.

6. The essay seems to muddy the definitions of "accuracy" and "truth." Rosenblatt seems to say that the journalist's job is pursuing accuracy, leaving truth to others. One of the theses of this book is that the journalist's job *must* be the pursuit of truth. Accuracy can simply result in reporting accurately a set of false conclusions. As it did earlier in this book, the image of reporter Megan Carter in the film *Absence of Malice* comes to mind. Yes, she reported accurately the contents of a file left on the special prosecutor's desk that the office was investigating Paul Gallagher. But no, that wasn't really true. The prosecutor was simply trying to smoke Gallagher out to use him as a government witness against crime figures, knowing he himself was not involved in the crime activity. So the prosecutor used a reporter who failed to verify the truthfulness of the file's contents. Accuracy and truth are not always the same thing, and both should be the province of the journalist.

7. As to whether we expect too much of journalism, I believe most journalists would say no. We can't expect too much of journalism, because it has such a pervasive influence on our daily lives at every level, from our personal lives to our nation's development. We may expect too much of journalism as it is being practiced today, when it is operating under the organizational and marketing restrictions which it does. But that doesn't mean that its structure and its rules can't be changed for the better, as Murray suggests doing.

Rosenblatt is right when he places part of the responsibility for an informed society on the people themselves. Certainly news consumers must look to other forms of information such as books, history, nature, education, and—especially—personal conversation. But they also must be able to look to daily journalism. And quality journalism doesn't take away from a person's ability to access other forms of news. If anything, it may whet the appetite for that additional information.

GUIDE NO. 7: LOOK FOR GOOD ROLE MODELS

Journalism is a cynical business at times, and journalists are so skeptical and independent that they often refuse to look for—and try to emulate the work of—some solid role models. That's a shame, because there are some excellent ones out there. Knowing how much some journalists disdain reporting contests, what follows is nevertheless my picks for best reporting and editing in special fields.

1. *Small-Town Journalism.* The winner is the *Columbia Daily Tribune*, which does business in the university town of Columbia, Missouri (population 60,000). This small daily (circulation 18,000) is shining proof that being small is not synonymous with being inferior. Every year the *Trib-*

une finds itself looking for quality reporters because of veterans who leave and wind up on papers like the *Philadelphia Inquirer, New York Times, Miami Herald, Hartford Courant,* and papers of similar reputation. This is partly due to the fact that the *Tribune* operates in the shadow of one of the best journalism schools in the country, over at the University of Missouri. Several Missouri students begin their journalistic career reporting part time, and then full time, at the *Tribune* and then go on to greater heights. But part of the reason is also because of the owner-publisher of the *Tribune,* Henry J. Waters III. Waters is a strong believer in local ownership of newspapers and of quality journalism. It was noted in 1985 that he spends about $135,000 a year more on his news operation than the average comparable daily, according to the Inland Daily Press Association. That year, the *Tribune* employed 34 full-time and 11 part-time newsroom employees, while the average for similar-size dailies was 22 full-time and 6 part-time.[22] Waters and his editors puts those reporters and editors to work doing quality daily journalism as well as something even larger dailies are shying away from—hard-hitting, time-consuming, local investigative reporting.

2. *Big-City Journalism.* If you're looking for a role model here, you will find it in the *Dallas Morning News.* While few critics would judge this to be the best newspaper in the country, it has to rank first in the comeback category. In many ways, working for a paper that is trying harder is better than working for a newspaper that is on top and runs the risk of growing complacent about its lofty position. Complacency was the battle the *News* fought in the 1970s when, as discussed in Chapter 6, the Times Mirror Co. came to town and bought the crosstown rival, the *Dallas Times Herald.* Up until 1970 neither paper had distinguished itself as even being the best newspaper in Texas, let alone the country. But throughout the 1970s and most of the 1980s the story changed, and Dallas newspaper readers were the winners. What makes the comeback of the *Dallas Morning News* especially appealing is that it has been a home-owned newspaper, the flagship paper of the Dallas-based A. H. Belo Corp., yet there is nothing overly provincial about this newspaper which has the look of an East-Coast metro daily. With direction from Robert Decherd and Burl Osborne at the top and strong newsroom leadership from managing editor Bill Evans and news editor John Davenport, this paper not only came back to answer the *Times Herald* challenge, but outlasted the larger Times Mirror Co. in the process. A couple of years ago the Times Mirror company decided to leave the battlefield in Dallas, realizing it had met its match and deciding it wiser to try its hand in other cities.

3. *Story Researching.* And the winner is . . . *National Geographic.* Some people who work for *National Geographic* feel that research is, in fact, its main business. In addition, of course, the magazine is one of the best-

written publications in existence and certainly has set the standard for photojournalism. Every writer for the *Geographic* knows that, when he or she comes back from an assignment, the arduous business of reporting has only just begun. Now they must confront the steely-eyed research department which will probably run them through the wringer before releasing the story for publication. By the mid–1980s, the *Geographic* employed 23 people whose only job is to research stories done by staff writers. Said writer Peter White of the researchers, "I consider them very important and reassuring. . . . When they ask for some backup, well, it's like defending a Ph.D. thesis."[23]

It is noteworthy that the *Geographic's* insistence on truthful reality portrayals is a concept not confined to getting simple facts straight. Joseph Judge, associate editor of the magazine, noted in 1984, "Reality is approachable from all kinds of perspectives. If you rely on facts [alone], you may miss the damn truth of the thing. . . . Facts ought to be straight, but so should your insights."[24]

4. *Print Reporting.* In many ways, this honor should go to a man who decided several years ago to leave the daily grind of newspapering behind and do some intensive reporting by actually going out and living with the people he wrote about. That man is Richard Critchfield, and he has a unique perspective on reporting. Critchfield reports mostly on the Third World, and he feels the best way of portraying truthfully the changes occurring in these countries is to avoid the traditional power centers and move out into the countryside with the people. So, armed with stacks of notebooks and an interpreter, that is what he has done for several years. He moves into villages, works with the inhabitants, reduces the intimidation that a reporter normally brings to interviews by staying with these people for months at a time. Through it all, he is talking, exchanging comments, asking a lot of questions. He tries, as much as he can, to record actual dialogue in his notebooks, although that often must wait until the end of the day. Critchfield feels that since most cultural revolutions begin (and end, in the case of Iran) with the people, what better way to discover what is really happening in a country than by spending time with its people? In the process, he has produced several insightful stories for publications like the *Economist* of London and the *Christian Science Monitor* and has written four books on changes in Third World countries. While most reporters cannot avail themselves of the kind of luxury that Critchfield does in spending so much time on his stories, they can learn valuable lessons from his perspective and apply many to their daily researching techniques.

5. *Broadcast Reporting.* Although he died 25 years ago, you still can do no better than following the model of Edward R. Murrow. Dubbed the conscience of broadcast journalism by many of his peers and followers, Murrow left tracks that are hard to fill. Murrow made a name for

himself as chief of the European staff of CBS Radio during the years when Adolf Hitler was starting his march across that continent. He delivered daily broadcasts on that march and supplemented them with nightly broadcasts from London, even while German bombers were pelting the ground on which he stood. He helped pull together probably the best team of broadcast war correspondents ever with men like William Shirer, Eric Sevareid, Howard K. Smith, Charles Collingwood, Richard C. Hottelet, and David Schoenbrun, to name a few. He also was a key figure in the birth of television news, not as a nightly news anchor—as television broadcasters today make their fame—but as a sort of early-day Ted Koppel doing in-depth news shows like "See It Now." In fact, it was on a 1954 "See It Now" that he achieved one of his greatest coups in destroying Sen. Joseph McCarthy on live television. An early-day prophet of things to come, he saw in 1961 that television news was headed into an entertainment/personality emphasis, and he decided he did not want to be a part of it. He resigned to direct the United States Information Agency and died in 1965. Yet his legacy is there for modern-day journalists to emulate.

In closing, it seems appropriate to look at a few qualities that go together to make a great reporter. Three points were laid down in 1985 by Eugene Roberts, then–executive editor of the *Philadelphia Inquirer*, one of the best dailies in the business. In brief, Roberts feels the best reporters are those who are good at "sourcing." He notes that:

Some reporters have an almost magical ability to win confidence. They project a level of assurance and integrity so constant that it's like a placard saying: "I keep my word." There are other reporters who are so shy it hurts . . . yet they have a persistence and drive to get the story, so they show up again and again until they do. There is no perfect way, no wallet-size guide to reporting.[25]

Roberts also feels the best reporters are those who have gotten experience performing as many jobs in daily journalism as possible. Usually, he says, this means starting out on a small daily—or even weekly—where you can report on every conceivable type of story, write, edit, compose headlines, shoot pictures, design pages, and even fill in for missing carriers on occasion, getting to know what the subscribers think of your day's work.

Third, the best reporters are those who have what Roberts calls "a consummate drive to get to the center of the story and then to put the reader on the scene."[26] He calls upon journalists to read the work of reporters like Richard Harding Davis, whose account of the German entry into Brussels 75 years ago still stands as a legend of "you-are-there" descriptive journalism. To do that kind of reporting—and writing—obviously takes a gripping command of the English language and the understanding that precision is vital if you want to show rather than tell.

If I were to add to this list, which stands fairly complete in itself, I would suggest that the best reporters are those who know themselves, and who know the business they are in. Knowing yourself becomes important when you encounter all those ethical dilemmas you will face at any level of reporting. As Ralph Potter of the Harvard Divinity School reminded us years ago, we ultimately must test our ethical decisions against our own values, principles, and loyalties before we can come up with a solution we can live with. We can certainly receive help from the several codes of ethics lying around the newsroom or hanging on the bulletin boards but, in the end, most of those codes prove too general for the specific dilemma we face, and we will have to understand ourselves before we can understand how we can deal with the problem.

Knowing the business of reporting is important so that we don't take it too lightly or fall into the trap of believing we know how to master the art. Few—if any—journalists are masters of this craft because of the myriad of challenges it presents. One way of understanding the contemporary arena of reporting better is to read as much as you can get your hands on about reporting. That means reading some of the best critiques in the business like *Columbia Journalism Review, Washington Journalism Review, Quill,* and *Editor & Publisher.* It also means keeping up-to-date on useful media research published in journals like the *Newspaper Research Journal* and *Journalism Quarterly.* The first of these two journals is making a valiant effort to produce readable research for the practioners in the field. And *JQ,* while directed at media academicians, nevertheless has useful findings for the working journalist in every issue.

In closing, a word or two about the reformist nature of the press seems in order. The news media have been called liberal by so many people, the description has almost become trite. Yet Gans and other analysts have shown that, contrary to being liberal, much of the media is simply seeking to bring us back to some mainstream values that people and institutions often violate for personal gain or because of plain stupidity. Whether liberal or reformist, the media certainly can—and often do— spark revolutionary ideas in the minds and hearts of men and women. There is an old saying that the newspaper's job is to "print the news and raise hell." While that isn't its only job, it remains as one of the most important. I. F. Stone recalls a story about a delegation which went to Washington to talk to Franklin D. Roosevelt about some reform they were pushing. When they had completed their presentation the president said, "Okay, you've convinced me. Now go on out and bring pressure on me." Roosevelt had the good sense to know that believing in something isn't always enough, especially when it comes to getting politicians to take action. Pressure is needed. The news media can apply this pressure by keeping unpopular issues before the American people. They did this with Vietnam and with Watergate and, more recently, with Irangate. Commenting on this, Stone noted during the 1960s, "It is a painful business extricating ourselves from the stupidity of the Vietnamese war; we will do so only if it becomes more painful not to."[27]

I agree with Stone that we ought to "welcome revolt as the one way to prod us into a better America."[28] This is not a call to embrace E. W. Scripps old crusading slogan, "Whatever is, is wrong!" That carries too much of a presupposition into the reporting situation and, to a large extent, is more a reflection of a personal outlook than a professional response to reality. Yet reporting does often foment revolutions—sometimes mild, sometimes major. The fury in this country in the 1960s to do something about racial inequities resulted in the Voting Rights Act and other civil rights legislation. Much of that fury came about because of the media's heavy coverage of how those rights were being denied blacks in the South. Television was especially effective in getting this message across, as its cameras caught the violence directed at blacks. It was unpopular news for most of America, but then revolt is always disturbing, as was the Revolutionary War in America. But it was necessary then, and in some areas of life, it is needed now. The news media have a job to do in awakening America to the fact that, in so many areas of life, people in power and the institutions they control have deviated from values like responsible capitalism and altruistic democracy. We certainly need to see stories about role models who have upheld these principles, but we also need to see stories about people and institutions who violate them so we can get ourselves back on course.

Following the guides in this chapter and understanding the challenges presented throughout this book will help arm journalists for the battle of reporting and increase their chances of winning.

NOTES

1. Ron Javers, "Journalism: The Necessary Craft," *Nieman Reports*, Autumn 1979, p. 16.
2. Javers, p. 17.
3. Maxwell McCombs, Donald Shaw, and David Grey, *Handbook of Reporting Methods* (Boston: Houghton Mifflin, 1976).
4. Ken Metzler, *Creative Interviewing* (Englewood Cliffs, N.J.: Prentice-Hall, 1977), pp. 9–22.
5. Elise Keoleian Parsigian, "News Reporting in the Midst of Chaos," *Journalism Quarterly*, Winter 1987, p. 721.
6. Ibid.
7. Tim Miller, "The Data-base Revolution," *Columbia Journalism Review*, September/October 1988, p. 36.

8. Elliot Jaspin, "Out With the Paper Chase, In With the Data Base," speech delivered to the Gannett Center for Media Studies, March 20, 1989.

9. Miller, p. 35.

10. Tom McNichol, "Databases: Reeling in Scoops with High Tech," *Washington Journalism Review*, July/August 1987, p. 27.

11. William Rivers, *Finding Facts* (Englewood Cliffs, N.J.: Prentice-Hall, 1975), pp. 14–15.

12. "A Convention Hall of Mirrors," *Time*, July 28, 1980, pp. 54–55.

13. Mike Royko, "Heard the Latest? Check It First," *Indianapolis Star*, May 23, 1989, p. A3.

14 Ibid.

15. Ralph L. Rosnow and Allan J. Kimmel, "Lives of a Rumor," *Psychology Today*, June 1979, pp. 88–89.

16. W. Phillips Davison, "Mass Media, Civic Organizations, and Street Gossip," Working Paper for the Gannett Center for Media Studies, New York, 1989.

17. Dorothy Nelkin, *Selling Science: How the Press Covers Science and Technology* (New York: W. J. Freeman, 1987).

18. J. Edward Murray, "Quality News Versus Junk News," *Nieman Reports*, Summer 1984, p. 19.

19. Ibid.

20. Roger Rosenblatt, "Journalism and the Larger Truth," *Time*, July 2, 1984, p. 88.

21. Murray, p. 19.

22. Steve Weinberg, "*The Columbia Daily Tribune*: What's Right with Small-Time Journalism," *Washington Journalism Review*, May 1985, p. 40.

23. Thomas J. Colin, "The Facts Checked Round the World," *Washington Journalism Review*, November 1984, p. 32.

24. Ibid.

25. Eugene Roberts, "What Makes a Great Reporter," *Washington Journalism Review*, February 1985, p. 11.

26. Ibid.

27. Neil Middleton, ed. *The I. F. Stone's Weekly Reader* (New York: Random House, 1971), p. 306.

28. Ibid.

Selected Bibliography

Adams, Valerie. *The Media and the Falklands Campaign*. London: Macmillan, 1986.

Agee, Warren K., Phillip H. Ault, and Edwin Emery. *Introduction to Mass Communications*. New York: Harper & Row, 1985.

Argyris, Chris. *Behind the Front Page: Organizational Self-Renewal in the Metropolitan Newspaper*. San Francisco: Jossey Bass, 1974.

Bagdikian, Ben H. *The Media Monopoly*. Boston: Beacon Press, 1983.

Boorstin, Daniel J. *The Image: A Guide to Pseudo-Events in America*. New York: Atheneum, 1985.

Brendon, Piers. *The Life and Death of the Press Barons*. New York: Atheneum, 1983.

Broder, David S. *Behind the Front Page: A Candid Look at How the News Is Made*. New York: Touchstone, 1987.

Burkett, Warren. *News Reporting: Science, Medicine, and High Technology*. Ames, Iowa: Iowa State University Press, 1986.

Chafets, Ze'ev. *Double Vision: How the Press Distorts America's View of the Middle East*. New York: William Morrow, 1984.

Christians, Clifford G., Kim B. Rotzoll, and Mark Fackler. *Media Ethics: Cases and Moral Reasoning*. New York: Longman, 1983.

Cirino, Robert. *Don't Blame the People*. New York: Vintage Books, 1971.

Clurman, Richard M. *Beyond Malice: The Media's Years of Reckoning*. New York: New American Press, 1988.

Cooke, Alistair, ed. *The Vintage Mencken*. New York: Vintage Books, 1954.

DeFleur, Melfin L., and Everette E. Dennis. *Understanding Mass Communication*. 3d ed. Boston: Houghton Mifflin, 1988.

Ekman, Paul. *Telling Lies*. New York: Berkley Books, 1986.

Emery, Edwin, and Michael Emery. *The Press and America: An Interpretive History of the Mass Media*. 5th ed. Englewood Cliffs, N.J.: Prentice-Hall, 1984.

Epstein, Edward Jay. *News from Nowhere: Television and the News*. New York: Vintage Books, 1974.

Gans, Herbert J. *Deciding What's News*. New York: Vintage Books, 1980.

Goldstein, Tom. *The News at any Cost*. New York: Simon & Schuster, 1985.

Gurevitch, Tony Bennett, James Curran, and Janet Woollacott, eds. *Culture, Society and the Media*. London: Metheuen, 1982.

Halberstam, David. *The Powers That Be*. New York: Alfred A. Knopf, 1979.

Hayakawa, S. I. *Language in Thought and Action*. 4th ed. New York: Harcourt, Brace, Jovanovich, 1978.

Hulteng, John L. *The News Media: What Makes Them Tick?* Englewood Cliffs, N.J.: Prentice-Hall, 1980.

———. *The Fourth Estate*. Englewood Cliffs, N.J.: Prentice-Hall, 1984.

Isaacs, Norman. *Untended Gates: The Mismanaged Press*. New York: Columbia University Press, 1986.

Johnstone, John W. C., Edward J. Slawski, and William W. Bowman. *The News People*. Urbana, Ill.: University of Illinois Press, 1976.

Kaplan, Justin. *Lincoln Steffens: A Biography*. New York: Simon & Schuster, 1981.

Keir, Gerry, Maxwell McCombs, and Donald L. Shaw. *Advanced Reporting Beyond News Events*. New York: Longman, 1986.

Kessler, Lauren. *The Dissident Press: Alternative Journalism in American History*. Beverly Hills: Sage, 1984.

Lichter, S. Robert, Stanley Rothman, and Linda S. Lichter. *The Media Elite: America's New Powerbrokers*. Bethesda: Adler & Adler, 1986.

Liebling, A. J. *The Press*. New York: Ballantine, 1961.

Lippmann, Walter. *Public Opinion*. New York: Free Press, 1922.

Lipstadt, Deborah E. *Beyond Belief: The American Press and the Coming of the Holocaust*. New York: Free Press, 1986.

MacDougall, Curtis D. *Interpret:ve Reporting*. 8th ed. New York: Macmillan, 1982.

McCombs, Maxwell, Donald L. Shaw, and David Grey. *Handbook of Reporting Methods*. Boston: Houghton Mifflin, 1976.

McLuhan, Marshall. *The Gutenberg Galaxy*. Toronto: University of Toronto Press, 1962.

———. *Understanding Media: the Extension of Man*. New York: McGraw-Hill, 1964.

McQuail, Denis. *Mass Communication Theory: An Introduction*. London: Sage, 1983.

Martin, L. John, and Anju Grover Chaudhary. *Comparative Mass Media Systems*. New York: Longman, 1983.

Merrill, John C. *The Imperative of Freedom: A Philosophy of Journalistic Autonomy*. New York: Hastings House, 1974.

Merrill, John C., and Harold A. Fisher. *The World's Great Dailies: Profiles of 50 Newspapers*. New York: Hastings House, 1980.

Meyer, Philip. *Precision Journalism: A Reporter's Introduction to Social Science Methods*. Bloomington, Ind.: Indiana University Press, 1973.

Meyrowitz, Joshua. *No Sense of Place: The Impact of Electronic Media on Social Behavior*. New York: Oxford University Press, 1985.

Milton, John. *Areopagitica and Of Education*, edited by George H. Sabine. New York: Appleton-Century-Crofts, 1951.

Powell, Jody. *The Other Side of the Story*. New York: William Morrow, 1984.

Riess, Curt. *Joseph Goebbels*. New York: Ballantine, 1960.

Rivers, William L. *Finding Facts: Interviewing, Observing, Using Reference Sources*. Englewood Cliffs, N.J.: Prentice-Hall, 1975.

———. *The Other Government: Power and the Washington Media*. New York: Universe Books, 1982.

Rossiter, Clinton, and James Lare, eds. *The Essential Lippmann: A Political Philosophy for Liberal Democracy.* Cambridge, Mass.: Harvard University Press, 1982.

Rubin, Bernard. *Media, Politics and Democracy.* New York: Oxford University Press, 1977.

Salisbury, Harrison. *Without Fear or Favor.* New York: Ballantine, 1980.

Schmidt, Benno C., Jr. *Freedom of the Press vs. Public Access.* New York: Praeger, 1976.

Schudson, Michael. *Discovering the News: A Social History of American Newspapers.* New York: Basic Books, 1978.

Sellers, Leonard L., and William L. Rivers, eds. *Mass Media Issues: Articles and Commentaries.* Englewood Cliffs, N.J.: Prentice-Hall, 1977.

Severin, Werner J., with James W. Tankard, Jr. *Communication Theories: Origins, Methods and Uses.* 2d ed. New York: Longman, 1988.

Snyder, Louis L., and Richard B. Morris, eds. *A Treasury of Great Reporting.* New York: Simon & Schuster, 1962.

Stempel III, Guido H., and Bruce H. Westley, eds. *Research Methods in Mass Communications.* Englewood Cliffs, N.J.: Prentice-Hall, 1981.

Tuccille, Jerome. *Rupert Murdoch.* New York: Donald F. Fine, 1989.

Weaver, David H., and G. Cleveland Wilhoit. *The American Journalist: A Portrait of U.S. News People and Their Work.* Bloomington, Ind.: Indiana University Press, 1986.

Westin, Av. *Newswatch: How TV Decides The News.* New York: Simon & Schuster, 1982.

Wilkins, Lee. *Shared Vulnerability: The Media and American Perceptions of the Bhopal Disaster.* Westport, Conn.: Greenwood Press, 1987.

Willis, Jim. *Surviving in the Newspaper Business: Newspaper Management in Turbulent Times.* New York: Praeger, 1988.

———. *Journalism: State of the Art.* New York: Praeger, 1989.

Index

ABOUT THE AUTHOR

JIM WILLIS, a veteran of the news business, has spent the past twelve years teaching and writing about the news media. His first book, *Surviving in the Newspaper Business*, was published by Praeger in 1988. His second, *Journalism: State of the Art*, was published in 1989. Willis cofounded the graduate program in journalism at Northeastern University in Boston and directed that program for four years. In 1988 he joined the journalism faculty at Ball State University, where he coordinates the News-Editorial Sequence in the Journalism Department. His articles on the media have appeared in a wide range of publications including *Nieman Reports, Editor & Publisher, Journalism Educator, The Oklahoma Publisher,* and *Grassroots Editor.* Willis, a speaker at state press association seminars, holds the Ph.D. from the University of Missouri School of Journalism and a B.A. in journalism from the University of Oklahoma. He lives in Indianapolis with his wife, Diane, and son, David Min.